Table of Contents

Introduction: Hollowing Out America's Middle Class With Corporate Globalism.	11
Chapter 1. New World Order Corporate Globalism.	25
Chapter 2. The Political Ideology of U. S. One World Authoritarian Corporatism.	53
Chapter 3. The Destructive Economic Power of the New World Order Western Globalist Trading Alliance On American Middle and Working Class Citizens.	78
Chapter 4. The Vulnerability of Rules-Based Corporate Globalism to Regional Radical Technology Innovation.	154
Chapter 5. The New Evolutionary Economic Growth Theory of Entrepreneurial Capitalism.	171
Chapter 6. Creating the New Institutional Infrastructure to Support Regional Technology Innovation and Product Commercialization.	201
Chapter 7. Knowledge Creation and Diffusion in U. S. Metro Regional High Technology Industrial Clusters.	233
Chapter 8. The Metro Regional Business Professional Support Network for New Venture Creation.	252
Chapter 9. The Regional Capital Market Institutional Support Structure For Regional New Venture Creation.	279
Chapter 10. Ending The Predatory Global Corporate War on the American Middle Class and Restoring the American Dream of Upward Social Mobility.	318
Bibliography	338

Schedule of Diagrams and Graphics

Chapter 1 Diagram 1. Duke Center on Globalization Smile Diagram. Gereffi, Gary, and Fernandez-Stark, Karina, Global Value Chain Analysis: A Primer, Second Edition, The Duke Center on Globalization, Governance & Competitiveness, 2016. p. 27.

Chapter 1 Diagram 2. The Decline of Labor Share of Income in the U. S, 1950 – 2020. Loecker, Jan De and Eeckhout, Jan, The Rise Of Market Power And The Macroeconomic Implications, NBER Working Paper 23687, 2017, p. 33.

Chapter 1 Diagram 3. Rate of Increase In U. S. Corporate Profits, from 1950 to 2020. Cited in De Loecker and Eeckhout. p. 33.

Chapter 1 Graphic 4. Value of Intermediate and Final Goods, cited in Boehm, Christoph E., et al., Multinationals, Offshoring and the Decline of U. S. Manufacturing, NBER Working Paper 25824, 2019. p. 46.

Chapter 2 Figure 5 Collective Lobbying by Trade Association. Zhang, Hao Commerce, Coalitions, and Global Value Chains: Coordinated and Collective Lobbying on Trade. p. 74.

Chapter 2 Table 8. Imports From China. Autor, David H., Dorn, David, Hanson, Gordon H., The China Syndrome: Local Labor Market Effects of Import Competition in the United States, NBER Working Paper 18054, 2012. p. 76.

Chapter 3 Figure 8. from Islamic Society Review, describes the national geographical alignment between the Western Trading Alliance and BRICs world views. Islamic Society Review. https://islamicsocietiesreview.org/ p. 80.

Chapter 3 Figure 1. Household Survey. Credit: Abraham, Katharine G., Haltiwanger, Sandusky, John, Kristin, Lee, Spletzer, James, Measuring the Gig Economy: Current Knowledge and Open Issues, NBER Working Paper No. w24950, SSRN, 2018. p. 84.

Chapter 3 Table 1: Changes in Employment Shares. Autor, David H., and Dorn, David, The Growth of Low-Skill Service Jobs and the Polarization of the US Labor Market, American Economic Review, 2013. p. 87.

Chapter 3 Table 9. Imports From China. Autor, et al., p. 88.

Chapter 3 Figure 1. Average Changes in Occupations. Autor, David H., Why Are There Still So Many Jobs? The History and Future of WorkplaceAutomation, Journal of Economic Perspectives, 2015. p. 93.

Chapter 3 Figure 2. Trends in Routine and Non Routine Tasks. Autor, David H., et al., The Skill Content Of Recent Technological Change: An Empirical Exploration, NBER Working Paper, 2001. Published in QJE. p. 92.

Chapter 3 Figure 3. Labor Share of Income. Akcigit,Ufuk Ates, Sina T. Ten Facts On Declining Business Dynamism And Lessons From Endogenous Growth Theory, Working Paper 25755 NBER 2019. p. 93.

Chapter 3 Figure 4. Evolution of Labor Share and Market Value. Graphic From Karabarbounis and Neiman, The Evolution of Labor Share and Market Value, 2014. p. 95.

Chapter 3 Table 8. Change in Government Transfers. Autor, David H., Dorn, David, Hanson, Gordon H., The China Syndrome: Local Labor Market Effects Of Import Competition In The United States, NBER Working Paper 18054, 2012. p. 96.

Chapter 3 Figure 5. Wealth and Capital. Kaldor and Piketty's Facts: The Rise of Monopoly Power in the United States, Eggertsson, Gauti B., Robbins, Jacob A., Wold, Ella Getz, NBER Working Paper 24287, 2018. p. 98.

Chapter 3 Table 2. The Innovative Advantage of U. S. Cities. Audretsch, David, The Innovative Advantage of US Cities, 2002. p. 102.

Chapter 3 Table 3. Innovation in Science Based Industry Clusters. Audretsch, David B., Feldman, Maryann P., Innovation in Cities: Science-based Diversity, Specialization and Localized Competition, European Economic Review, 1999. p. 103.

Chapter 3 Figure 1b, Trade Exposure by Commuting Zone. Autor, David H., Dorn, David, Hanson, Gordon H., The Geography Of Trade And Technology Shocks In The United States, NBER Working Paper 18940, 2013. p. 104.

Chapter 3 Figure 1a.Routine Employment Share. Autor, David H., Dorn, David, Hanson, Gordon H., The Geography Of Trade And Technology Shocks In The United States, NBER Working Paper 18940, 2013. p. 106.

Chapter 3 Table 6. Quanitative Experimental Results. Innovation And Trade Policy In A Globalized World, Ufuk Akcigit, Sina, Ates, Giammario, Impullitti, NBER Working Paper 24543, 2018. p. 110.

Chapter 3 Figure 6. Profits as Percent of U. S. GDP. Akcigit, Ufuk, Ates, Sina T.,Ten Facts On Declining Business Dynamism And Lessons From Endogenous Growth Theory, Working Paper 25755, NBER, 2019. p. 112.

Chapter 3 Table 4. Factor Shares of Income. Eggertsson, Gauti B. et al., Kaldor And Piketty's Facts: The Rise Of Monopoly Power In The United States, NBER Working Paper 24287, 2018. p. 113.

Chapter 3 Figure 7. Net Investment. Eggertsson, Gauti B., et al., Kaldor And Piketty's Facts: The Rise Of Monopoly Power In The United States, NBER Working Paper 24287, 2018. p. 114.

Chapter 3 Figure 8. Investment Rate vs. Markup. Loecker, Jan De, Eeckhout, Jan, Global Market Power, NBER Working Paper 24768, 2018. p. 115.

Chapter 3 Figure 9. Evolution of Average Markups. Jan De, Eeckhout, Jan, The Rise of Market Power and the Macroeconomic Implications, NBER Working Paper 23687, 2017. p. 120.

Ending The Predatory Corporate Capitalist War on the American Middle Class:

The American Entrepreneurial Alternative to Totalitarian Corporate Globalism

Copyright © 2024. The Great American Business & Economics Press. GABBY Press.

All rights reserved under Title 17, U.S. Code, International and Pan-American copyright Conventions.

No part of this work may be reproduced or transmitted in any form or by any means, electronic or mechanical, including photocopying, scanning, recording or duplication by any information storage or retrieval system without prior written permission from the author(s) and publisher(s), except for the inclusion of brief quotations with attribution in a review or report. Requests for reproductions or related information should be addressed to the author c/o Great American Business & Economics Press, 620 Kingfisher Lane SW, Sunset Beach, N. C. 28468.

Printed in the United States of America.

ISBN 979-8-218-40203-7

Chapter 3 Figure 10. Evolution of Income Distribution. Jan De, Eeckhout, Jan, The Rise of Market Power and the Macroeconomic Implications, NBER Working Paper 23687, 2017. p. 120.

Chapter 3 Figure 11. Market Concentration. Autor, et al., 2017 b. p. 121.

Chapter 3 Figure 12. Firm Entry and Exit. Haltiwanger, John C., Jarmin, Ron S., Miranda, Javier, Who Creates Jobs? Small Vs. Large Vs. Young, NBER Working Paper 16300, 2010. p. 128.

Chapter 3 Table 7. Basic Structure of Input Output Table. p. 132.

Chapter 3 Figure 13. Value of Intermediate Goods. Akcigit, Ufuk, Ates, Sina, What Happened to U.S. Business Dynamism? NBER Working Paper No. w25756, SSRN, 2023. p. 141.

Chapter 3 Figure 14. Firm Entry and Exits. Haltiwanger, John C., Jarmin, Ron S., Miranda, Javier, Who Creates Jobs? Small Vs. Large Vs. Young, NBER Working Paper 16300, 2010. p. 143.

Chapter 3 Figure 15. Employment Share of Young Firms. Decker, Ryan A., et al., Declining Business Dynamism: What We Know and the Way Forward, American Economic Review, May 2016. p. 144.

Chapter 3 Figure 16. Net Job Creation. Hathaway, Ian, et al., Tech Starts: High-Technology Business Formation and Job Creation in the United States, , Kauffman Foundation Research Series, 2013. p. 144.

Chapter 3 Figure 17. 40 Entrepreneurial Regions. Konczal, Jared, The Most Entrepreneurial Metropolitan Area? Ewing Marion Kauffman Foundation, SSRN. 2013. p. 145.

Chapter 5 Diagram 1. Economy Breaking Away From Equilibrium In Time Period One to Potential Attractor Point in Time Period Two. Vass, Laurie Thomas, The Theory of Technology Evolution, 2019. p. 181.

Chapter 5 Diagram 6. Economy Breaking Away From Equilibirum to Point of Economic Decline. Vass, Laurie Thomas, The Theory of Technology Evolution, 2019. p. 183.

Chapter 5 Diagram 8. Two Possible Pathways of Economy. Vass, Laurie Thomas, The Theory of Technology Evolution, 2019. p. 184.

Chapter 5 Diagram 10, Hypothetical A-B Yellow-Green Parents Created a Blue AB Offspring Product. Vass, Laurie Thomas, The Theory of Technology Evolution, 2019. p. 200.

Chapter 6 Diagram 1. The Small Business Deal Creation Pipeline. p. 211.

Chapter 6 Diagram 2. Graphic from NC Department of Labor, 1982. p. 214.

Chapter 6 Exhibit 2.1 Regional Industrial Clusters. Exhibit 2.1 from Industrial and Regional Clusters: Concepts and Comparative Applications, 2nd ed., 2020. p. 216.

Chapter 6 Exhibit 3.10. Exhibit 3.10. Industrial Cluster Purchasing Patterns Vehicle Manufacturing. Industrial and Regional Clusters: Concepts and Comparative Applications, 2nd ed., 2020. p. 217.

Chapter 6 Exhibit 4.9. Research Triangle, N. C. Industrial Linkages. Exhibit 4.9 from Industrial and Regional Clusters: Concepts and Comparative Applications, 2nd ed., 2020. p. 218.

Chapter 6 Diagram 5. Chronological Sequence of Events of a Radical Innovation Leading to A Potential Market Disruption. p. 222.

Chapter 6 Diagram 2.1. Regional Blockchain New Technology Venture Creation Model. p. 225.

Chapter 6 Figure 3. Young Firm Job Creation. Kaufmann Foundation. p. 230.

Chapter 6 Figure 4. Gross Job Creation and Destruction Rates. Job Creation, Job Destruction, and Productivity Growth: The Role of Young Businesses,The Annual Review of Economics, 2015. p. 231.

Chapter 7 Table 2. High Technology Industries. U. S. Department of Labor Bureau of Labor Statistics. p. 245.

Chapter 7 Table 3. General Benchmark Clusters. National Industry Cluster Templates: A Framework For Applied Regional Analysis, 2000. p. 246.

Chapter 7 Table 4. North Carolina Industry Clusters. High-Tech Clusters in North Carolina, North Carolina Board of Science and Technology, 2000. p. 247.

Chapter 8 Diagram 2. Set of Small Business Analytical Tools. p. 256.

Chapter 8 Diagram 1. Regional Blockchain New Venture Creation. p. 262.

Chapter 9 Diagram 3. Planning and Implementation of a Regional Small Business Innovation System. p.284 .

Chapter 9 Diagram 4. The New Web-Based Business Model. p. 292.

Chapter 9 Diagram 5. The New Internet-Based Model of Raising Capital.p. 293.

Chapter 10 Diagam 1. 2020 Average Market Income by Income Percentile. USAFacts, 2023. P. 235.

Introduction: Hollowing Out America's Middle Class With Corporate Globalism.

A recent Pew Research report indicated that a majority of American citizens suspect that the economy and government economic policies serve to benefit wealthy citizens, to the detriment of middle class citizens. (Most Americans Say the Current Economy Is Helping the Rich, Hurting the Poor and Middle Class. Pew Research Center, December 2019.).

The Pew Research report stated,

"To the extent that current economic conditions are helping particular groups, the public sees the benefits flowing mainly to the most well-off. Roughly seven-in-ten adults (69%) say today's economy is helping people who are wealthy (only 10% say the wealthy are being hurt). At the same time, majorities of Americans say poor people, those without a college degree, older adults, younger adults and the middle class are being hurt rather than helped by current economic conditions."

The survey results are split among the different social classes, with 69% of wealthy citizens stating that the economy is working well for them, while 58% of the middle class respondents stating that the economy is hurting them.

The perception by the middle class of an unfair economic system poses a threat to the social stability of the American society because allegiance to obey the rule of law is based upon the perception of fair rules that benefit all social classes.

The glue that holds the American society together is the allegiance to voluntarily obey the rule of law in an economy where every citizen has a fair opportunity to achieve financial success.

The perception of an unfair economy is supported by the reality of economic and financial data over the past 50 years.

In another Pew Research report, the data indicates that the number of families in the middle class income range decreased, while the share of income in the upper classes increased.

"The middle class, once the economic stratum of a clear majority of American adults, has steadily contracted in the past five decades. The share of adults who live in middle-class households fell from 61% in 1971 to 50% in 2021, according to a new Pew Research Center analysis of government data." (Kochhar, Rakesh, and Sechopoulos, Stella, How the American middle class has changed in the past five decades, Pew Research Center, April 2022.).

The Pew Research found that incomes in the middle class did not increase as rapidly, since 1971, as income growth in the upper income classes.

The report states,

"The median income of middle-class households in 2020 was 50% greater than in 1970 ($90,131 vs. $59,934), as measured in 2020 dollars. These gains were realized slowly, but for the most part steadily, with the exception of the period from 2000 to 2010, the so-called "lost decade," when incomes fell across the board… The rise in income from 1970 to 2020 was steepest for upper-income households.

Their median income increased 69% during that timespan, from $130,008 to $219,572."

The so-called "lost decade of 2010," was not serendipity for the wealthy families in America, or an expected economic outcome of the workings of a competitive free market economic system.

The lost decade was a result of interest rate manipulation by the Federal Reserve Bank, in conjunction with a transition to a globalist economy, which benefitted the wealthy classes to the economic detriment of the majority of American citizens.

Our book is about the cause of the bifurcation of the American society into two categories of social classes.

We describe how the new world order operates, and explain why the outcomes are so detrimental to the American middle class citizens.

As a result of changes in the global trade relationships among large corporations, in collaboration with the operation of western central banks, the upper 20% of citizens are reaping rewards and greater income than the rest of the population.

The middle to lower classes of American citizens are being either squeezed into dead-end gig labor market jobs or else forced into a life-time dependency on government welfare.

This transition to a new world order is a deliberate act by very self-absorbed, selfish global ruling class elites who make decisions that benefit their own social class.

No citizen in America ever voted to implement the new social class stratification. There is no concept of the "consent of the governed" in the operation of the new world order.

The two factors over the past 50 years, the policies of the Fed, and the transition to a global economy, have eroded the concept of American economic sovereignty, from a prior principle that improving the welfare of American citizens is the first priority of government to a current principle that the financial improvement of large corporations and ruling class elites is the mission of government policy.

As we pointed out in A Civil Dissolution: The Best Solution to America's Irreconcilable Ideological Conflict, Madison's constitutional rules were never meant to be fair, but have always operated in collaboration with America's central banks, to benefit the wealthy to the detriment of the middle classes.. (Vass, Laurie Thomas, Gabby Press, 2023.).

In 1832, when Andrew Jackson, the seventh President of the U.S., killed the Congressional reauthorization of the Second Bank, he wrote in his veto message,

"It is to be regretted that the rich and powerful too often bend the acts of government to their selfish purposes. Distinctions in society will always exist under every just government. Equality of talents, of education, or of wealth cannot be produced by human institutions. In the full enjoyment of the gifts of Heaven and the fruits of superior industry, economy, and virtue, every man is equally entitled to protection by law; but when the laws undertake to add to these natural and just advantages artificial distinctions, to grant titles, gratuities, and exclusive privileges, to make the rich richer and the potent more powerful, the humble members of society—the farmers, mechanics, and laborers—

who have neither the time nor the means of securing like favors to themselves, have a right to complain of the injustice of their Government."

There is nothing different in the social class dynamics between the current Federal Reserve Bank, now, with the operation of the central bank in 1832.

Our book goes beyond an analysis and explanation of the new world order to describe how the global economic system is vulnerable to radical technology innovation because the global elites cannot control the pace or direction of radical technical change.

The maintenance of political and economic control by the global ruling class is contingent upon maintaining the status quo distribution of market power, so that the flow of income can be directed to their own social class.

The key to maintaining power for the corporations is to control technology innovation in order to dictate the distribution of benefits from economic growth.

We offer our economic advice to metro and elected state representatives on how a new regional economic development strategy would be a better path for the majority of citizens than the current centralized, undemocratic, unelected operation of the global one-world government.

Our starting economic assumption about a better economic system begins with the observation that the single greatest initial factor endowment of the American society, in 1775, was a concept of individual initiative and entrepreneurial spirit, which was completely different than the social class stratification in Europe.

We argue that this initial factor endowment created an unassailable comparative advantage for the American economy over every other nation in the world.

At that time, the United States had a different set of resources and assets than European nations, and the American culture of individualism gave the economy of the United States a comparative advantage in technology innovation and new venture creation over the static social structure of Europe.

This initial American factor endowment was often called "Yankee ingenuity," which created an economic advantage in trading innovative technology products with European nations.

During the time from 1781 to around 1792, the American society began creating economic and financial institutions, based upon the rule of law, which replaced the rule of the British monarch and British nobility.

The early economic theory of comparative advantage in international trade was based upon the geographically homogeneous nation as a unit of analysis, and global trade was measured in terms of how a nation took advantage of its initial factor endowments to increase national income.

After the implementation of globalism, around 1992, the unit of economic analysis shifted from improvements in the welfare of the nation to the improvement in welfare of large corporations, primarily because globalism seeks to replace national sovereignty, and national borders, with a one-world government.

As explained by David Dollar, Senior Fellow at the John L. Thornton China Center at the Brookings Institution,

"Measuring GVCs [global value chains] in terms of exports, [of a nation] misses a crucial aspect of GVCs: the role of the firm. Fragmented production is not undertaken by [national] economies or economy sectors but by firms [very large firms]. This point is significant for at least three reasons. First, it highlights the concentrated nature of the participation of firms in GVCs. Globally, firms that both import and export (an indication of a GVC firm) comprise *15% of all firms, but they capture 80% of total trade* (World Bank 2020). Second, as Antràs (2020a) argues, GVCs are fundamentally relational. Rather than a global market of impersonal buyers and sellers, production networks are built up by firms that engage in repeated interactions, making them "sticky." And third, MNCs [multi national corporation] course a significant amount of their sales through local affiliates established through foreign direct investment (FDI). When these [revenues] are recorded as domestic activities in host economies, [the revenues of firms in the United States] GVCs tend to be underestimated. (Global Value Chain Development Report 2021: Beyond Production, Asian Development Bank Publication, November 2021.). [italicized emphasis added].

In the prior economic theory of comparative advantage, the rising tide of the welfare benefits of trade floated all the boats, and the economic benefits of global trade were widely distributed to all social classes in the United States.

After the implementation of globalism, with the development of vertically integrated global value chains, the income and financial benefits of globalism are internalized within the legal structure of a large corporation, and the benefits are not distributed to about 80% of the American population.

The American advantage in technology innovation created a faster internal rate of economic growth than the more stagnant rates of economic growth in Europe.

The open upward entrepreneurial path of economic opportunity for individuals is what made America great, and the moral value of American individualism was an exceptional development in human history.

The shared cultural belief in fair economic opportunities served as the glue that held American society together. As long as all citizens continued to believe that American economic sovereignty was the ultimate goal of society, then the social class differences did not cause social class conflict.

Beginning with the transition to a globalist economy, in 1992, the American ruling class elites traded away the initial American factor endowment of individualism, in favor of a global collectivism where all citizens of the world were viewed as economically equal.

The ideological logic of the global ruling class is that American citizens consume too much energy and too much of the world's resources, and that the use of resources must be equalized across the globe to be more fair and more environmentally friendly.

Behind the ruling class rhetoric of global climate change lies a sinister form of authoritarian rule called corporate fascism, which means totalitarian rule by corporations.

David Marcus, in his article, Don't Worry, It's Just Corporate Fascism (The Federalist, January 2021), correctly identifies the global corporate ruling elite as the power behind the collapse of the American middle class.

Marcus writes,

"The basic concept of [corporate] fascism is that everyone marches in the same direction, everyone thinks the same way, and everyone says the same things, all in the name of safety and productivity... Today the greatest threat to American freedom comes not from the government but from corporate actors who seek to control the actions and beliefs of American citizens by with, holding goods and services from those with whom they disagree."

This globalist ideology arose about the same time in American history that the concept of equality changed from equal opportunity to equality in economic outcomes.

The notion of equality of outcomes is attractive to Marxist Democrats in the U. S. because it provides the Marxists with the logic of government control over income distribution.

The two ideologies, globalist corporatism and Marxist collectivism, combine and collaborate in the corrupt crony capitalist political system to undermine the social welfare of the American middle class. (Vass, Laurie Thomas, The American Left's Emerging Social Class Consciousness of Envy In Collusion With the Existing American Ruling Class Consciousness of Greed, SSRN. 2020.).

The future society being proposed by the proponents of globalism has been described as "benevolent authoritarianism," by Von Feigenblatt.

He writes that the future society of corporate globalism looks like the global application of the model of the current Chinese society.

He states,

"The present paper argues that an emerging Asian model combining aspects of corporatism, increasing professional engagement throughout society, and benevolent authoritarianism has shown greater resilience and greater success in protecting the core values that liberal democracies are supposed to be based on, than the open systems favored by the West." (Corporatism and Benevolent Authoritarianism: Viable Antidotes to Populism, SSRN, 2021.).

His language for United States economic sovereignty is "liberal democracies," and his language for the politics of improving middle class welfare is "populism," meaning Trump's America First philosophy.

He embraces the same idea of Madison's constitution that economic decision making for the nation, and one-world government, would be better if only the ruling class natural aristocracy made all decisions.

He writes,

"This leads to the currently controversial conclusion that at the national level decision-making would function better if participation is limited. [to ruling class elites]. Can decision making be limited to those most capable while at the same time increasing empowerment among the rank and file of the population? The answer is yes. The Asian model [Chinese] of benevolent authoritarianism coupled with corporatism

20

satisfies both requirements. Rank and file members actively participate in their unions, guilds, and other sector based organizations while their direct participation in the policy making process is highly restricted."

The entire theoretical edifice of neo-classical equilibrium is obsolete and has been replaced by global monopoly capitalism, where corporations control the allocation of global resources to suit their internal corporate goals.

Neo-classical equilibrium marginal theory is silent on the proposed benefits of global benevolent authoritarianism, and offers a distorted inaccurate description of the operation of global corporatism.

Our book offers a more realistic theory of economic growth based upon the concept of technology evolution in products and the creation of new future markets.

The conventional theory of marginal economics is based upon a canonical vision that supports the social class status quo of globalism. The academic and private economic think tanks, around the world, serve as a type of public relations front to support the virtues of globalism.

The starting assumptions of neo-classical theory do not describe the real world of global trade, instead the assumptions reflect the ideological commitment of economists to support the status quo distribution of political power of global corporations.

In neo-classical marginal analysis, there are many buyers and sellers, who act as price takers in a competitive market.

In globalism, corporations set their prices by marking up marginal costs that they control through vertically integrated supply chains.

In neo-classical theory, all goods produced are identical, without branding or consumer loyalty, to any product.

In globalism, identical products are different because of branding and marketing, which allows corporations discretionary pricing power among consumers in different nations, higher prices for middle class American citizens and lower prices for third-world citizens.

In neo-classical theory, there are many buyers and sellers, in many different markets, each of whom have different tastes and different utility functions.

In globalism, all consumers are seen as the same, with the intent to create a mass global market of citizens all of whom have the same tastes and welfare functions, similar in concept to how the Chinese consumer market operates.

In conventional neo-classical theory, there are many firms in the market, with unlimited entry into the market by new firms.

In globalism, large firms limit entry because new supplier firms need to be members of integrated global value chains and must produce to the standards required by the contractual supply legal agreements with the lead corporation.

In neo-classical marginal theory, all sellers and buyers have complete information about prices, technology, and all other knowledge relevant to the operation of the market.

In globalism, the lead corporations maintain proprietary information about prices, and control the proprietary knowledge about technology innovation and manufacturing production technology.

Neoclassical economists assume that consumer needs drive the economy and the business production that results to fill those needs.

In globalism, the direction of market causation is reversed with large corporations establishing the global market for goods and replacing the consumer-driven competitive market with internal integrated global value chains.

The only factor of production in globalism that is not controlled by the corporations is the unlimited imagination of entrepreneurs to dream up new products, and that factor of production constitutes a threat to the corporate control over the pace and direction of technology evolution.

The starting assumption of neo-classical theory is scarcity of resources in a world of unlimited consumer wants.

The starting assumption of the theory of technology evolution is unlimited technology innovation, in a nation of unlimited human imagination. (Vass, Laurie Thomas, The Theory of Technology Evolution, Gabby Press, 2019.).

We argue that this initial factor endowment of entrepreneurial capitalism created an unassailable comparative advantage for the American economy over every other nation in the world.

Even with the unfair rules of Madison's constitution that benefitted the ruling class, the American middle class prospered because of their ability to innovate and to seize open opportunities for creating new ventures, despite the unfair advantages of the ruling class.

The comparative advantage, then, was created by the insight by Locke, Mason, and Jefferson that the new nation was based upon individualism, which allowed individual entrepreneurs to appropriate their future rewards from innovation.

The strategy to hollow out America's middle class with corporate globalism is deliberate and well-thought out.

The point of attack of the globalist strategy is the destruction of United States national economic sovereignty and the elimination of the American moral value of individualism.

If they are successful in eliminating the philosophy of American individualism, they will eliminate the conditions for entrepreneurial technology innovation.

Our book offers a counter strategy aimed at exploiting the primary vulnerability of globalism, which is radical technology innovation, in a defined geographical territory, in a society where the benefits of economic growth are widely distributed to all social classes.

Chapter 1. New World Order Corporate Globalism.

The term New World Order describes both an economic system of how corporations organize global trade relationships, and an authoritarian one-world political framework for controlling citizens.

The global trade economic component goes under the descriptive term "globalization" which started around 1992 with cross-border supply chain management.

The political control component is described as "global corporatism," or more simply "globalism," where self-selected ruling class global elites impose their concept of global government on formerly sovereign nations.

In the political ideology of globalism, the improvement in the welfare of the world replaces the improvement of welfare of individual nations as the goal of the global corporatism.

The characteristic that is "new" in the new world order is the transition from a world of independent sovereign nations, who trade with each other, to a one world borderless economic order, where large corporations by-pass sovereign nations in order to trade with each other.

As Kevin Sobel-Read points out in his research,

"As of 2006, for instance, there were some 70,000 transnational firms, together with roughly 700,000 subsidiaries and millions of suppliers spanning every corner of the globe…What once was external trade between national economies increasingly has become internalized within firms as global supply chain management, functioning in real time and directly shaping the daily lives of people around the world." (Global Value Chains: A Framework for Analysis, SSRN. 2014.).

Sobel-Read mentions global supply chain management, which was the first iteration of globalization of trade, with the early trade agreements like NAFTA and CAFTA.

The second iteration of globalization was global value chain management, where corporations entered legal agreements with foreign affiliates to produce intermediate goods for assembly into finished goods.

This second iteration ramped up around 2002, after the entrance of China into the World Trade Organization, and the subsequent re-location of intermediate manufacturing production from U. S. locations to China and India.

The third, and most recent iteration of globalization, is vertically integrated value chains, where a single large corporation attempts to consolidate all elements of production and final sales, under the legal entity of a single corporation.

Economists at Duke University have created a diagram of this third iteration of globalization which relates the stage of production with the value-added, or increase in profits, at each step of production, from research and development to final sales of the finished product.

The diagram has the appearance of a smile, because the lower part of the smile is the location of the lower value added components to the entire production process.

At the upper left corner of the smile, value-added, or the addition in profits, is very high, compared to the bottom parts of production, at the bottom of the smile.

At the upper right corner of the smile, at the final sale of the product, value-added is also high, compared to the profits added at the bottom of the smile.

The Duke diagram is reproduced below, as Diagram 1.

Chapter 1 Diagram 1. Duke Center on Globalization Smile Diagram.

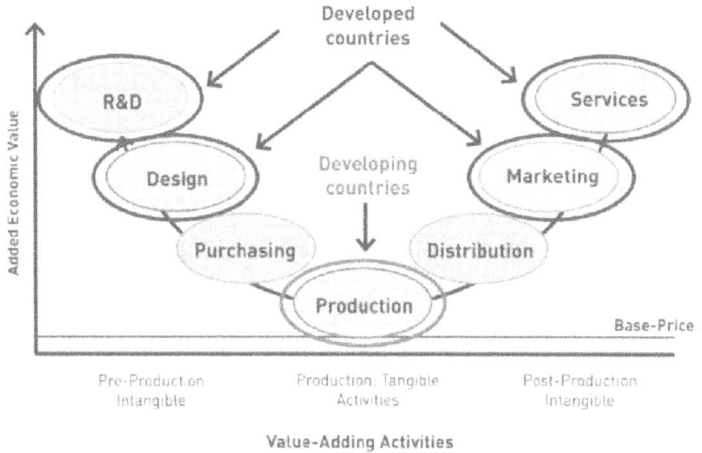

(Credit: Gereffi, Gary, and Fernandez-Stark, Karina, Global Value Chain Analysis: A Primer, Second Edition, The Duke Center on Globalization, Governance & Competitiveness, 2016.).

Gereffi and Fernandez-Stark place their smile diagram into the theoretical context of an input-output matrix of production in order to describe the relationship between the stage of production and the increase in profits at each stage.

The write,

"A [value] chain represents the entire input-output process that brings a product or service from initial conception to the consumer's hands. The main segments in the chain vary by industry, but typically include: research and design, inputs, production, distribution and marketing, and sales, and in some cases the recycling of products after use. This input-output structure involves goods and services, as well as a range of supporting industries. The input-output structure is typically represented as a set of value chain boxes connected by arrows that show the flows of tangible and intangible goods and services, which are critical to mapping the value added at different stages in the chain, and to layering in information of particular interest to the researcher (e.g., jobs, wages, gender, and the firms participating at diverse stages of the chain)."

In addition to describing the relationship between profits and the stages of global production, the Duke diagram also reveals the global New World Order ideology of globalism by describing the difference between so-called developed western alliance countries and developing third world countries.

This terminology of contrasting developed with developing countries is a sleight-of-hand treatment to hide the political power relationships between large global corporations, located primarily in the U. S. and Europe, and production facilities located in the geographical territories under the control of the World Trade Organization of the Western trading alliance.

In the analysis of the New World Order integrated value chains, it is not sovereign nations who trade with each other.

A more accurate description is large corporations, in the Western alliance, who control the production of subordinate affiliates, in the third world, who are locked into legal production contracts with the lead corporation.

Zhang describes the lock-in effects of the third iteration in global integrated corporate value chains in terms of specialization in trade along the global smile diagram.

"According to a recent estimate, input trade now accounts for over three quarters of global trade (World Trade Organization, 2017). Meanwhile, increasing specialization along the GVCs leads to "lock-in" effects for both buyers and sellers, as most firms have to incur significant costs to substitute any of their supply chain partners (e.g., Antras and Staiger (2012); Boehm, Flaaen and Pandalai-Nayar (2019);…As firms cannot easily substitute their immediate value chain partners, their survival heavily relies on the smooth operation of the GVCs—that is, stable delivery of suppliers and timely purchase of the customers. Disruptions to any stage of production would bring severe distress to immediate partners and beyond." (Zhang, Hao, Commerce, Coalitions, and Global Value Chains: Coordinated and Collective Lobbying on Trade, SSRN, 2023.).

In the vertically integrated global value chains, intermediate goods flow back and forth over multiple national borders many times, before the final product is sold.

Dominique Bruhn, in her article, "Global Value Chains and Deep Preferential Trade Agreements: Promoting Trade at the Cost of Domestic Policy Autonomy?" suggests that two-thirds of the world trade in intermediate goods crosses national borders more than once.

She states,

"The importance of trade in parts and components relative to that of trade in final goods has been rising steadily – trade in intermediates now accounts for almost two-thirds of world trade (IMF 2013).This implies that a significant amount of goods crosses borders more than once. UNCTAD (2013d) estimates that in 2010, five trillion USD, representing more than 25% of global gross exports, was double-counted. In a world of global value chains, gross exports are therefore no longer sufficient for studying trade patterns as they mask the underlying structure and overstate export performance through multiple counting in the official statistics. Traditional trade statistics remain relevant as they describe the physical movement of goods across borders, but "the concept of 'value added' is useful in order to understand where economic activity and jobs are generated" (Miroudot / Yamano 2013). (SSRN, 2014.).

As Bruhn points out, the conventional neo-classical trade theory of the benefits of global trade is defective in capturing the dynamics of globalization because the unit of economic analysis is no longer the improvement of welfare in a sovereign nation.

This defect is evident in the data gathering and reporting of the U. S. Department of Commerce trade statistics which continue to be based upon the old unit of analysis of a single nation.

As the OECD notes, the economic assumption that goods and services are produced in one country is theoretically obsolete.

They write,

"Today, most goods and a growing share of services are "made in the world", with different firms and countries specialising in the specific functions and tasks that collectively constitute a GVC. However, many [government domestic] policies are still based on the assumption that goods and services are produced in just one country. (Interconnected Economies: Benefiting From Global Value Chains, OECD Synthesis Report, 2013.).

For example, the U. S. Department of Commerce global trade statistics only record the final stage of finished goods in the gross exports of a country, not the value-added in intermediate production in the corporate global value chain.

The old Ricardo theory of wine for wool description of trade between two sovereign nations is obsolete because the value-added occurs outside of the U. S. borders, but the so-called national economic benefit of trade in the U. S. Department of Commerce data reflects the internal profits of a single large corporation, after the finished good is sold in the final global market.

For example, in the trade statistics between the U. S. and Canada and Mexico, about 60% of the value-added in intermediate production occurs in Canada and Mexico.

The income multiplier benefits of the trade occur in those two countries, but the value-added of the entire intermediate production occurs on the income statement of the U. S. parent corporation, after the U. S. corporation sells the finished good.

That additional 60% of intermediate production in profits is not distributed by the U. S. parent corporation to middle and lower class citizens in the U. S. because the intermediate production occurs in Canada and Mexico.

In other words, the so-called income and jobs benefits of "free trade" ideology is false because middle and lower class citizens in the U. S. never benefit from the income and employment multiplier effects of globalization.

In the vertically integrated global value chains, if there are no factories or factory workers in the United States, then all of the value added from foreign affiliates accrues to the parent U. S. domestic corporation in the form of profits, after they sell the final good.

The U. S. labor share of income goes down, while the GDP goes up because of the increased profits accruing to the U. S. parent corporation.

Diagram 2 describes the historical effect of declining incomes of globalization on U. S. middle and working class citizens. In the graph, the term "labor income" is a reference to the social class of workers who receive wages and salaries, in contrast to the social class of owners of the corporations, who obtain profits.

Chapter 1 Diagram 2. The Decline of Labor Share of Income in the U. S, 1950 – 2020.

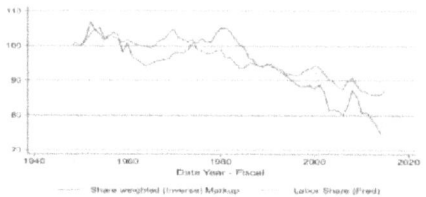

Figure 7. The Evolution of the labor share (BLS), and inverse of the markup (1960-2014) Notes. Labor Share data from BLS. Share of gross domestic income: Compensation of employees, paid. Wages and salary accruals. Disbursements, to persons. 1950=100.

(Citation: Loecker, Jan De and Eeckhout, Jan, The Rise Of Market Power And The Macroeconomic Implications, NBER Working Paper 23687, 2017.).

Diagram 3. below describes the increase in U. S. corporate profits, after the second iteration of integrated global value chains, in 2002. U. S. corporations attained dramatic increases in profits from global value chains, and the increase in profits showed up in national GDP figures as an increase in economic growth.

Chapter 1 Diagram 3. Rate of Increase In U. S. Corporate Profits, from 1950 to 2020.

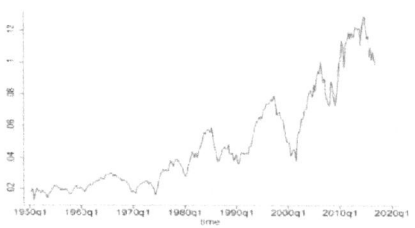

Figure 6: Profit rates. Data from FRED, based on national accounts. Quarterly.

De Loecker and Eeckhout explain that the dramatic increase in corporate profits, after the third iteration of globalization, and the concomitant decrease in the share of U. S. labor income is caused by the ability of large corporations to set their own prices on intermediate goods, inside the integrated global value chains.

Their term for this pricing power is internal "markup" prices, over the corporation's marginal costs of production. They contrast markup pricing as "pure profits," as opposed to ordinary profits obtained in the final sale in a competitive global market.

As the OECD reports,

"If a higher share of domestic value added [in Canada and Mexico] ends up in the final demand of other countries, [the U. S. parent corporation] countries are more vulnerable to demand shocks from abroad. In Mexico and Canada, for example, about 60% of domestic value added destined for exports ends up in final demand in the United States, so that a demand shock [a disruption in global trade] in the United States will have an important impact on these countries [Mexico and Canada]. In most OECD countries, the top five (final) destination countries typically represent around 40% of domestic value added… the likelihood that a local disruption [in Canada or Mexico] will lead to a system-wide failure. This systemic risk follows directly from the system's linkages and interdependencies, as the failure of a single entity or cluster of entities can cause a domino effect that may affect the entire system." (Interconnected Economies: Benefitting From Global Value Chains, OECD Synthesis Report, 2013.).

As Bruhn points out, the conventional neo-classical trade theory of the benefits of global trade is defective in capturing the dynamics of globalization because the unit of analysis is no longer the GDP of a sovereign nation.

Koen de Backer and S. Miroudot raise this issue when they ask:

"The question is: what is the relevant unit?... What is clear is that, as highlighted by Grossman and Rossi-Hansberg, this is "no longer wine for cloth" [Ricardo] and policymakers have to think beyond industries when looking at trade and industrial policies...Today, more than half of world manufactured imports are intermediate goods (primary goods, parts and components, and semi-finished products), and more than 70 percent of world services imports are intermediate services... On average more than half of the value of exports is made up of products traded in the context of global value chains. (Mapping Global Value Chains ECB Working Paper No. 1677. SSRN, 2014.).

The more relevant and accurate unit of economic analysis to explain modern global trade theory is the single global corporation, and the subordinate intermediate production affiliates in the vertically integrated smile diagram value chain.

As Zhang notes,

"Disruptions to any stage of production would bring severe distress to immediate partners and beyond."

The immediate partners Zhang refers to are the lead corporations at the top of the value chain, and the reason for "distress," relates to the ability of the lead corporation to continue to direct the flow of "pure" profits internally to themselves if a disruption occurs anywhere in the extended chain.

As we will describe later, the disruption that large corporations fear the most is the disruptive technological innovation in new products and the emergence of new future markets, which large corporations cannot control in their authoritarian political structure of the New World Order.

Clayton Christensen calls a disruptive technology a superior product or production alternative to the currently dominant know-how in a particular market that devalues the profits of the incumbent industry leaders.

The large corporations are "blind" to the emergence of a disruptive technology because they have a tunnel vision of their political control of the current market.

When the disruptive technology emerges, the large corporations engage in political behavior to maintain their status quo power over pure profit markup pricing.

In the most recent iteration of vertically integrated value chains, the preferred course of action by the large corporations is to avoid a disruption to the status quo by prohibiting technological knowledge from escaping from the flow of innovation inside of the legal entity of the corporation. (The Innovator's Dilemma: When New Technologies Cause Great Firms to Fail, Harvard Business Review Press, 1997.).

Part of the strategy of limiting the escape of technological knowledge is through legal contracts and legal protection of the corporate intellectual property.

The other part of the corporate strategy of limiting the diffusion of technological knowledge is through crony capitalist political power, under the general heading of "free trade."

In the ideology of free trade, the most important part of knowledge creation and knowledge diffusion occurs in the intermediate demand production relations that formerly occurred in U. S. metro industrial clusters.

The free trade legislation in Washington, in 1992, and 2002, allowed those U. S. knowledge creation and diffusion networks to be exported to Mexico, China, and India.

As a consequence of the vertically integrated global value chain, the geographic location in the "developed" world of the U. S. parent corporation in the final demand, finished goods market absorbs most of the value-added profits of goods and services traded, while the role of corporations in the underdeveloped countries providing intermediate inputs upstream is subordinated to the senior corporate partner through legal contracts which lock the intermediate goods partner in binding relationships.

The disruption that the U. S. parent corporation fears the most is the disruption and uncertainty caused by uncontrolled technological innovation, which threatens the flow of 60% value-added to its own income statement.

At the global economic level, a one dollar increase in sales of an intermediate demand foreign affiliate generated an additional 62 cents in revenue for the parent corporation in the U. S. economy. (Multinational Enterprises In Domestic Value Chains OECD Science, Technology And Industry Policy Papers No. 63. March 2019.).

Most of that 62 cents of value added that accrues to the single large corporation in the U. S. is in the form of pure profits obtained by political power over marginal cost pricing markups.

In other words, the smooth operation of the global value chain is extremely important to the large U. S. corporations, and protecting the profits generated in foreign affiliates is an important goal of U. S. foreign and military policy.

The large corporations attempt to control that disruption by controlling the pace and direction of technological innovation through their binding legal contracts with foreign subsidiaries in the corporate value chain.

The trade statistics describe an increase in national income, [GDP] of the United States, but the benefits of income distribution occur in the intermediate production of foreign affiliates, and the profits obtained by the global parent corporation are not distributed to middle class citizens in the United States, because the profits are not reinvested into the domestic U. S. economy.

The profits of the large corporations are invested in strengthening the global value chain of foreign affiliates in China or India, or spent on lobbying Congress for more "free trade" legislation.

From the financial welfare perspective of the parent U. S. corporation, it is more lucrative to earn profits in globally integrated value chains from foreign affiliates and then, to leave the profits in the foreign nation, rather than repatriating the profits by transferring the profits to the domestic U. S. economy for reinvestment.

As described by the Asian Development Bank, leaving the U. S. profits in Asia benefits the Asian economies, rather than the U. S. domestic economy.

They write,

"First, MNCs [U. S. Multi National Corporations] may dilute their [taxable income in the U. S.] (most of which is gained from their IPs) [intellectual property at the left top corner of the Duke value chain] from subsidiaries operating in low-tax countries (which may not be the countries where the IP creation and value occurred) with income from subsidiaries in high-tax countries. This is to avoid taxation through international transfer pricing and other measures. Second, MNCs have strong incentives to strengthen IP rights protection and to encourage innovation, given both the relatively low cost of illegal copying or reproducing IP and the higher costs of R&D investment to create and maintain control of their IP. This is the reason most factoryless goods producers do not license their IP to third parties. And third, IP protection is no longer simply a matter of encouraging innovation. These days it is more importantly about protecting a new source of bread and butter for the home countries of MNCs." (Global Value Chain Development Report 2021: Beyond Production, Asian Development Bank Publication | November 2021.).

The new source of bread and butter technology innovation could possibly arise from the "learn-by-doing" in the third world country, gained through the intermediate production process governed by binding legal contracts that protect U. S. corporate intellectual property rights.

The Asian Development Bank continues by using the Apple iPhone as an example for its explanation of leaving U. S. corporate profits in the Asian nations.

They write,

"From an accounting point of view, Apple's subsidiaries [intermediate production affiliates] are earning profits in the PRC [Peoples Republic of China] using [Apple's] IP to organize production, sales, and servicing there. Apple, [the parent corporation] in the US is the ultimate owner of those profits, but there are tax advantages to booking the profits overseas and leaving them there. As of September 2021, 131 countries had agreed to a new global tax regime [New World Order] with a minimum corporate profit tax…The firms [U. S. corporations] specializing in [technology innovation] tasks beyond production have control over the geographic allocation of tasks. Taking the iPhone X as an example, it is Apple Inc. that organizes, operates, and expands the iPhone value chain. As a result, Apple alone captures the largest share of the iPhone X's value added: 59%." [the same percentage of profits of 60% found by De Loecker and Eeckhout.].

In "Analytical Frameworks for Global Value Chains: An Overview Global Value Chain Development Report, Satoshi Inomata describes the connection between the smooth operation of global trade and U. S. foreign policy related to vertical integration in the global value chains.

Inomata explains,

"The vertical integration type of GVC is based on the hierarchical structure [of a single corporation] that assumes an absolute and unidirectional control of the parent company over its subsidiaries. The activities and performance of subsidiaries are strictly monitored and assessed in line with their headquarter management strategies." (SSRN. 2017.).

The control over the corporate subsidiaries in foreign countries has become an important U. S. foreign policy consideration because U. S. government political control allows the parent U. S. corporation to direct income to itself, protected in the corrupt rent seeking/rent extraction political process by the U. S. military, or the FBI/CIA.

The successful, smooth operation of the economic trading component of globalization in the New World Order depends upon the authoritarian political control component of globalism to enforce foreign affiliate compliance with the rules of the Western trading alliance.

In the U. S., the language to describe the foreign policy political component of the new world order is the "global nation," or sometimes, one-world government.

In his 1992 article, "The Birth of the Global Nation," Strobe Talbott described how the military might of the U. S. military was deployed to enforce the rules of global trade in the Western trading alliance.

Talbott, at that time, was a foreign policy advisor to President Clinton, and served as the deputy secretary of state from 1994 to 2001. After leaving government, he was the Director of the Yale Center for the Study of Globalization.

Talbott wrote,

"Countries are . . . artificial and temporary. . . . Within the next hundred years . . . nationhood as we know it will be obsolete; all states will recognize a single, global authority. A phrase briefly fashionable in the mid-20th century "citizen of the world" will have assumed real meaning by the end of the 21st." (The Birth of the Global Nation, Time Magazine, 1992.).

In Talbott's conception of the New World Order, the U. S. military acts as the policeman of the world, to enforce the rules based trading order of American foreign policy.

In the political ideology of free trade globalism, there is no difference between the rights of citizens in the U. S. and non-citizens. In that logic, all illegal immigrants coming across the U. S. border are entitled to all of the same economic, social and legal privileges of citizens the world over.

The free trade ideology of the New World Order is described by the 2019 policy document of the World Economic Forum (WEF), where they describe the role of the U. S. as policeman of the world, and how Trump's election threatens the operation of the New World Order.

The WEF writes,

"In a globalized world, we are only as secure and prosperous as the least secure and least prosperous societies around us. The UN Sustainable Development Goals, or SDGs, which set universal goals of ending poverty, protecting the planet, and achieving gender equality among others, are a recognition of this reality… As a political ideology, "globalism", or the idea that one should take a global perspective, is on the wane. And internationally, the power that propelled the world to its highest level of globalization ever, the United States, [Trump] is backing away from its role as policeman and [free] trade champion of the world. (A Brief History of Globalization, WEF, Jan 17, 2019.).

The WEF uses the derisive term "populist," to describe political opposition to the New World Order agenda.

As they note,

"Populists on both the left and the right have promoted the false notion that because charity begins at home, it should end at home, too. But an open global economy cannot be maintained while we have such closed politics. Both the head and the heart should recognize that addressing humanitarian crises and supporting fragile states like Yemen, Nigeria, the DRC, and Iraq is both morally right and pragmatically sound."

The WEF could have also added that the main beneficiaries of the head and heart strategy are large corporations that fund the WEF globalist propaganda. Yemen, Nigeria, the DRC, and Iraq operate in the global value chains as subordinate partners to the global military power of the U. S. foreign policy free trade objectives.

When a country like Iraq disobeys the rules of U. S. foreign policy, Iraq gets invaded by the U. S. military, acting in its capacity of policeman of the world.

Zhang describes the foreign policy political activity in the U. S. that coordinates the global free trade ideology.

Zhang writes,

"This proposition demonstrates that the optimal tariff [for large corporation] is co-determined by domestic [U. S.] upstream, midstream, [intermediate goods] and downstream [final sales] producers that have different interests and constraints. Specifically, we can derive the following three implications.

- First, domestic upstream [large U. S. corporations] producers would demand a lower tariff as they [low tariffs] add more value [profits] to the foreign imported product (what I define as high "forward participation").
- Upstream producers face competing [domestic political] priorities, but if they [large U. S. corporations] add more value to the foreign [third world intermediate] midstream production as opposed to the [former U. S. intermediate demand] domestic midstream production, the first term [low tariff free trade] will dominate the second term [political interests of small U. S. manufacturers] and vice versa.
- With the strengthening of GVCs linkages in recent decades (i.e., increasing forward participation and backward dependence via the common foreign partner), both upstream and downstream producers rely on the stable delivery of foreign imports, [smooth operation] which induces interdependencies in their [free trade] policy preferences. In other words, they [large U. S. corporations] now care about not only their own product but also the foreign import along the same GVC. Whereas their [large U. S. corporations] preferences are aligned [with third world intermediate demand] via GVC linkages, the midstream producers [formerly small U. S. manufacturers] are excluded from the GVC and harmed by outsourcing." (Zhang, Hao, Commerce, Coalitions, and Global Value Chains: Coordinated and Collective Lobbying on Trade, SSRN, 2023.).

What Zhang means by his term that former small U. S. manufacturers are "harmed by the outsourcing" of U. S. intermediate production to third world countries, is that the intermediate demand formerly produced in the U. S. was the source of technology innovation and entrepreneurship in the domestic U. S. economy.

That initial factor of production in the American society was destroyed by the free trade policies, and it is the re-emergence of that source of technological innovation that constitutes the biggest threat to the large corporations in the smooth operation of the vertically integrated global value chains.

Kevin Sobel-Read, cited earlier, writes,

"More than two-thirds of all transnational trade is conducted by means of multinational corporations. [large corporations]. And a full half of that trade – that is, over one third of all transnational trade – is performed between corporate subsidiaries. In order to fully understand the form, function, and effects of global value chains, the inquiry must begin with the value chains themselves – as the unit of analysis – drawing on each of the many relevant legal disciplines as appropriate." (Global Value Chains: A Framework for Analysis, SSRN, 2014.).

The large U. S. corporations import over 90% of all intermediate inputs from their foreign affiliates in the global supply chain. The 90% of the intermediate inputs now imported by the large U. S. corporations was formerly produced in metro regional intermediate manufacturing plants in the U. S.

Boehm et al., point out,

"We find that foreign sourcing of intermediate inputs is a striking characteristic of multinationals. Over 90% of overall U.S. intermediate imports in our sample are imported by multinationals. Moreover, the fraction of U.S. multinationals sourcing inputs from developing countries nearly doubled from 1993 [the first iteration of vertically integrated value chains] to 2011 [the third iteration of GVC].. To illustrate the link between these high and increasing intermediate imports by multinationals and the observed employment declines, we return to the event study. We show that the relative employment declines in transitioning plants [formerly U. S. production plants] are accompanied by large increases in imports of intermediates by the parent firm. The increase in imports is largest when the [U. S. domestic] plant is shut down." (Boehm, Christoph E., et al., Multinationals, Offshoring And The Decline Of U.S. Manufacturing, NBER Working Paper 25824, 2019.).

They provide a graphic to describe the increase in intermediate production imported by large U. S. corporations.

Chapter 1 Graphic 4. Value of Intermediate and Final Goods.

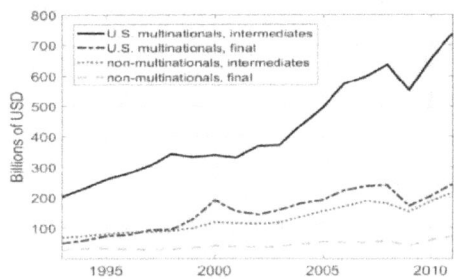

Figure 1: Value of intermediate and final goods imports by firm type

Notes: The data are from the LFTTD, DCA, and UBP as explained in text. The figure shows the value of intermediate and final goods imports by firm type. The value of imports of foreign multinational firms is excluded from this figure.

Citation: Value of Intermediate and Final Goods, cited in Boehm, Christoph E., et al., Multinationals, Offshoring and the Decline of U. S. Manufacturing, NBER Working Paper 25824, 2019.

They write,

"Figure 1 illustrates the growth of intermediate input imports, where we have split the sample into U.S. multinationals and other non-multinational U.S. firms. The rise in intermediate input imports of U.S. multinationals is striking. [after 2002]… In contrast, the share of multinational firms sourcing from developed countries [U. S. domestic manufacturing firms] has only increased about 10 percentage points during our sample period. Although non-multinational [U. S. domestic manufacturing plants] firms have also experienced increases in foreign input sourcing, the levels are roughly an order of magnitude smaller and they account for a small fraction of foreign input sourcing in the data." (Boehm, Christoph E., et al.,).

Antras and Staiger describe the binding legal lock-in effect that the large corporation exert over the foreign intermediate supply affiliates.

They write,

"Intermediate input purchases tend to be associated with significant lock-in effects for both buyers and sellers. For example, differentiated intermediate inputs are frequently customized to the needs of their intended buyers [large U. S. corporations] and hence embody a disproportionate amount of relationship specific investments, which may be hard to recoup when transacting with alternative parties. Moreover, offshoring often involves the costly search for suitable foreign suppliers or foreign buyers, which makes separations costly and thereby provides another source of lock in." (Antràs, Pol and Staiger, Robert W., Offshoring and the Role of Trade Agreements, American Economic Review, 2012.).

Compliance with the terms of the legally binding contracts between U. S> domestic parent corporations and third world intermediate production affiliates includes compliance with the intellectual property rights of the U. S. parent corporation.

The OECD reports that it is a very small set of very large corporations that dominate integrated global value chains.

They state,

"The new evidence indicates that MNEs account roughly for one-half of international trade, one-third of output and GDP and one-fourth of employment in the global economy." (Multinational Enterprises In Domestic Value Chains, OECD Science, Technology And Industry Policy Papers No. 63. March 2019.).

The U. S. corporate strategy to limit the spread of technology innovation is based upon access to foreign knowledge through strategic relationships with foreign affiliates and control over the creation of new technical knowledge in the U. S. metro regions, that previously accounted for tacit knowledge creation and diffusion.

The OECD reports,

"Another motivation for the spread of GVCs is access to knowledge. Companies increasingly make investments abroad to gain access to strategic knowledge assets, whether these are skilled workers, universities, research centres or other sources of expertise. Proximity to competitors and suppliers is another factor in the growth of GVCs, as it enables firms to learn from others." (Interconnected Economies: Benefiting From Global Value Chains, Oecd Synthesis Report, 2013.).

Antràs and Chor cite the importance of tacit knowledge diffusion, or face-to-face communication, in the close proximity of location of the U. S. corporation operations and the foreign intermediate demand production affiliates.

They write,

"In such settings, the link between a buyer and its supplier is "built-up over time", with these repeated interactions often accompanied by an exchange of tacit knowledge. This generates a "mutual dependence" in the GVC link that makes "the costs of switching to new partners high" (Gereffi et al., 2005, p.86).43." (GLOBAL VALUE CHAINS, Antràs, Pol and Chor, Davin, NBER Working Paper 28549, 2021.).

Prior to the third iteration of integrated global value chains, those close, personal, face-to-face knowledge relationships occurred in U. S. metro regional industrial clusters.

In the politics of free trade, those U. S. domestic networks of knowledge creation and diffusion were destroyed when the U. S. intermediate production was moved to third world countries.

We extend the legal scholarship work of John P. Esser, who suggested that each price-based transaction that occurs between a U. S. parent corporation and the foreign production affiliates in the integrated global value chain constitutes an economic legal exchange. (Esser, John P.,

Institutionalizing Industry: The Changing Forms of Contract, Law & Social Inquiry Vol. 21, No. 3, 1996.).

In our application of Esser's scholarship, the legal transaction is captured by the input-output coefficients in the global A matrix of the global value chain.

In other words, the A matrix describes a price-based relationship between the parent corporation and the foreign affiliates. The price-based transaction is also a surrogate indicator of an on-going, semi-permanent legal relationship between the parent corporation and the affiliate.

In our extension of Esser's work, we assert that the price-based transaction in the A matrix is also a surrogate indicator of a knowledge exchange between the parent corporation and the affiliates.

In contrast to Paul Krugman's assertion that knowledge flows are invisible, we assert that the coefficients in the A matrix describe the visualization of both knowledge creation and knowledge diffusion, in addition to the evidence of a legal transaction between the trading partners.

Krugman wrote,

"Knowledge flows are invisible; they leave no paper trail by which they may be measured and tracked, and there is nothing to prevent the theorist from assuming anything about them that she likes" (Krugman, Paul, Increasing Returns and Economic Geography, 1991.).

We agree with Sobel-Read, cited earlier that the exchange of intellectual property and technological knowledge in global value chains is one important strategy for parent U. S.

corporations to control the escape of technological knowledge from inside of the corporation.

Sobel-Read notes,

"In the traditional view, vertical integration is most desired "[w]hen technological advances are rapid and where knowledge about production remains tacit…There is no question that global value chains are becoming a primary conduit for the transfer of intellectual property globally. At the same time, as Berman makes clear, "the creators of intellectual products are relying less on traditional intellectual property regimes to enable them to limit access to their material, and more on a combination of contractual rights and technological protections." [SSRN 2014.).

Ronald J. Gilson, et al., also cite the importance for large U. S. corporations controlling knowledge creation and diffusion in global value chains. (Gilson, Ronald J. et al., Contracting for Innovation: Vertical Disintegration and Interfirm Collaboration, Columbia Law and Economics Working Paper No. 340, 2009.).

They write,

"The pressure toward vertical integration will be especially powerful in rapidly innovating industries where swift technological change produces uncertainty in supply relationships; that is, where the future states of those relationships cannot be predicted probabilistically. In the presence of uncertainty, [created by uncontrolled technological innovation] contemporary contract theory offers no general solution to the problem of assuring both efficient levels of transaction-specific investment ex ante and adjustment to an efficient outcome ex post after uncertainty is resolved…we suggest that the change in the boundary of the firm [across national boundaries in integrated global value chains] has given rise to a new form of contracting between firms - what we call contracting for innovation. This pattern braids explicit and implicit contracting to support iterative collaborative innovation by raising switching costs."

What Gilson means by the term "raising switching costs," is that the cost imposed on the foreign affiliates by the global U. S. parent corporation are too great for the foreign affiliate to break away from the binding legal contracts.

And, in the rare case where the foreign firm does manage to break away by creating new technology, there is always the presence of the U. S. policeman of the world, waiting just around the corner to enforce global order.

Chapter 2. The Political Ideology of U. S. One World Authoritarian Corporatism.

In order to direct the global value chain flow of income to themselves, the large U. S. corporations bend U. S. foreign and economic policy to their own financial interests, independent of any conception of democratic citizen consent.

Large corporations who happen to be domiciled in the geographic territory of the United States no longer see themselves as citizens of the U. S., producing value for the citizens of the nation.

Rather, the large corporations see themselves as citizens of the world, and use the foreign policy of the U. S. military to protect their dominant status in the global western trading alliance of the New World Order.

The two components of the New World Order, the globalization in trading relationships, and the political ideology of one-world globalism, work in tandem to benefit large corporations.

The authoritarian component of New World Order corporatism replaces the free choices of citizens in both free market economics and free democratic choice of citizens in government.

As described by David Marcus, in his Federalist article, "Don't Worry, Its Just Corporate Fascism,"

"The basic concept of corporate fascism is that everyone marches in the same direction, everyone thinks the same way, and everyone says the same things, all in the name of safety and productivity." (The Federalist, 2021.).

The social governing model for America corporate fascism is a society that functions just like the communist society of China, where a totalitarian regime makes all of the major social and political decisions.

In "Corporatism and Benevolent Authoritarianism: Viable Antidotes to Populism," Otto Federico von Feigenblatt, et al., suggest that the Chinese model is superior to the national sovereignty model because well-educated elites make better decisions than common citizens in a representative democracy.

They write,

"The present paper argues that an emerging Asian model [China] combining aspects of corporatism, [fascism] increasing professional engagement throughout society, [elite decision-making] and benevolent authoritarianism [all citizens are treated the same] has shown greater resilience and greater success in protecting the core values that liberal democracies are supposed to be based on, than the open systems [citizen consent] favored by the West…Corporatism in this study refers to the representation of different sectors or social groups as discreet entities [social group identities] in public policy making. Rather than direct participation by the individual, [citizen democratic participation] corporatism favors indirect representation of the group [social class] to which the individual belongs. (SSRN. 2021.).

One of the elements that is "new" in the New World Order is the transition in the U. S. from a representative republic, where elected representatives represent the interests of the constituents who elected them, to a crony capitalist system of rent seeking by the corporations and rent extraction by the elected representatives.

Richard D. Wolff, in his Salon article, "How racism became the essential tool for maintaining a capitalist order," explains that around 1985, the large U. S. corporate leadership had a type of collective "eureka" moment.

Wolff writes,

"So in this [1985] eureka moment capitalists [large U. S. corporations] said, "What are we doing here in Western Europe, North America and Japan? It's much more profitable if we produce in China, India and Brazil." And there begins what we're still in the middle of: the exodus, the abandonment of the places of origin of capitalism by the capitalists. If you go from high wages in the United States to low wages in China, the bottom line is that the [U. S.] people earning wages are earning a lot less than they used to. It's not just that they're not Americans; they're Chinese, but they can't buy back what you're building." (Salon, June 26, 2020.).

The initial stages of global corporatism involved innovative political strategies by corporate lobbyists to gain Congressional authorization to move production facilities to low cost nations. (Vass, Laurie Thomas, Searching for Signs of Technological Innovation in the Ruins of the American Economy, SSRN, 2008.).

In other words, after the 1985 eureka moment, the U. S. corporations reached a collective political decision that domestic U. S. economic sovereign interests were not as relevant or significant, to their global operations.

The corporations began to implement policies and obligations of citizenship to all citizens in the nations where they conducted intermediate production.

As Leonard Lynn and Hal Salzman note in "Collaborative Advantage,"

"U. S. multinationals are weakening their national identities, becoming citizens of the countries in which they do business and providing no favors to their country of origin. This means that the goal advocated by some U.S. policymakers of having the United States regain its position of leadership in all key technologies is simply not feasible, nor is it clear how the United States would retain that advantage when its firms are only loosely tied to the country." (Issues In Science and Technology, Winter, 2006.).

As we explained in A Civil Dissolution, Madison's constitution did not state that the mission of the nation was to advance the economic interests of all citizens, but instead was meant to balance and check the majority power of the common citizens from invading the property rights of the natural aristocracy. (Vass, Laurie Thomas, A Civil Dissolution: The Best Solution to America's Irreconcilable Ideological Conflict, Gabby Press, 2023.).

After 2002, when the large U. S. corporations moved their regional intermediate supply chains to China, they disconnected themselves from the national economy, and functioned more as "citizens of the world" than American corporate citizens, with an allegiance to improving the welfare of the U. S. economy.

Stephen Haber emphasizes the legal change in property rights granted to the participants in the global corporate crony system that skews the benefits exclusively to those agents.

Haber states,

"The preferential subsidies, monopoly rights or protection from international competition benefits global corporations by establishing a legal system that provides access to bank credit,, property rights protection between incumbents and new entrants and favorable trade agreements, like NAFTA." (Haber, Stephen, Introduction: The Political Economy of Crony Capitalism, 2015.).

After the entrance of China to the World Trade Organization, global U. S. corporations created a corporate political alliance with the Chinese Communist Party, facilitated by a corporate political lobbying agency called, the U.S. China Business Council.

Both the US China Business Council and a second corporate lobbying agency, domiciled in the U. S., called the Business Roundtable, are primarily responsible for implementing the trade agreements with China, and for instructing their lobbyists to write the subsequent legislation that allows American companies tax-advantaged benefits from production in China.

The USCBC is a private, nonpartisan, nonprofit organization of approximately 200 American companies that do business with China.

As they modestly state on their website, the mission of the USCBC is to "Help Shape the World's Most Important Relationship."

Their membership overlaps with the members of the U. S. Business Roundtable, which provides added political muscle to implement their political activities in Washington. About 75% of the 200 USCBC member companies are also members of the Business Roundtable, which has branch affiliates in major metro regions in the United States.

We place the political power of this small group of corporations into a political theoretical framework called global corporate cronyism.

In our theoretical framework, the political influence of rent seeking and rent extraction of globalism replaces the prior framework of Madison's representative republic.

Cronyism, as a political influence, is a component of the one-world authoritarian ideology called corporatism, which is form of fascist alliance between corporations and the agencies of the U. S. government.

Michael Munger, of Duke University, describes this form of global governance "corporatism."

He writes,

It [corporatism] is a social system where the government intervenes aggressively into the economy, typically with political instruments that benefit large corporations and enterprises to the detriment of smaller businesses and private citizens. Such instruments include subsidies, tariffs, import quotas, exclusive production privileges such as licenses, antitrust laws, and compulsory cartelization designs… Thus, nobody [in the representative republic] has a strong vested interest in promoting [middle class citizens] and defending free markets" (Munger, Michael C., and Villarreal-Diaz, Mario, The Road to Crony Capitalism, The Independent Review, Winter 2019.).

Global corporatism seeks to replace the concept of United States national sovereignty in order to implement a one-world authoritarian government.

The political goal of global corporatism is to eliminate the concept of the rule of law in the U. S. national constitution in favor of a ruling class tyranny that enforces a private, for-profit "rules-based-governance" of corporate control over citizens.

Under the original concept of the American rule of law, the basic promise citizens made to each other, in 1775, was not to destroy America's heritage of liberty in order to gain personal financial advantage.

The operation of vertically integrated global value chains violates that initial promise of the rule of law because the large corporations subordinate the liberty of citizens to their own selfish motives of directing the flow of income to themselves.

Global crony corporatism, as currently practiced in America, only benefits the few large corporations and those ruling class elites privileged to participate in the flow of money and profits.

As we estimated in Civil Dissolution, the current U. S. operation of global crony corporatism benefits about 15% of the U. S. population.

Under the prior rule of law, American citizens had some reasonable expectation that elected representatives and agents of government would protect the commonwealth.

Even though citizens may not understand how the Treasury controls the supply of money, or how the Federal Reserve regulates the interest and credit markets, citizens had some legitimate expectation that the money supply and interest rates would be set to benefit the broad social good.

In other words, under the prior American Rule of Law, citizens trusted the agents of government to do the right thing for all social classes.

In the new crony corporatism, large corporations and elected representatives collude to benefit themselves, and not the commonwealth.

The economic interests of middle class citizens are not represented in the crony corporatist framework because Madison's constitution did not require those citizens to be represented, under the new iteration of globalism.

Todd Zywiki has described the first component of New World Order globalism as crony corporate capitalism.

Zywiki writes,

"Crony capitalism thus rests on an implicit guarantee by the]U. S.] government that it will protect certain politically-connected firms from the rigors of competition, thereby guaranteeing those firms and industries a certain flow of revenues. In (implicit) exchange for this guaranteed flow of revenues, the firm promises to share some of that surplus with politically-favored groups, [the Big Guy] such as labor unions or favored interest groups (such as environmental groups), and with the politicians themselves through campaign contributions and other means of support." (Rent Seeking Crony Capitalism, and the Crony Constitution, SSRN, 2015.).

The U. S. government's guarantee of protection of the corporate foreign market interests is a component of the ordinary and usual every day corruption of shared plunder rent seeking in the American political system.

Ruling class shared plunder has always been a key element of the functioning of the U. S. political system, since the days of Madison's constitution and Hamilton's first national bank.

The difference in the concept of shared plunder, after the corporate eureka moment in 1985, is the replacement of national sovereignty with the concept of a one-world, borderless government, controlled by large corporations.

Zywicki explains that there are two different financial exchanges in the crony capitalist system:

• Rent seeking by corporations who need the protection of the U. S. military, and agents of the deep state to bend public policy to their own interests, and

• Rent extraction by elected representatives, and the agents of the deep state, who financially benefit from the corruption.

The new financial plunder political model of corporate cronyism is a three step exchange:

First, the U. S. government collects taxes to fund global military operations. The U. S. military industrial complex sells military equipment to both the U. S. military, and also to foreign governments, who are members of the WTO western trading alliance.

Second, the special interest military lobbying system wheedles government elected representatives for a piece of the tax revenues when the government pays for both the domestic and foreign military equipment.

Third, during the rent seeking negotiations between lobbyists and elected representatives, the rent extractors set their price for rent extraction, in exchange for government protection of the large corporation in U. S. foreign policy.

Zywicki writes,

"Finally, crony capitalism can also occur through rent-extraction by politicians: in this scheme, politicians threaten to impose harm or take away benefits currently held by various firms or industries, which those firms can avoid by paying tribute to the politician. In this situation, the [military-indsutrial] firms lobby not for gain, but to avoid losses that are larger than their rivals." (SSRN, 2015.).

This tradeoff for government protection is characteristic of the Mafia organized crime protection racket. In exchange for preferential governmental treatment, favored large corporations become agents and private accomplices of implementing U. S. government foreign policy.

Stefan J. Padfield, in Crony Stakeholder Capitalism, explains,

"Crony capitalism is a political-economic system wherein government protects and subsidizes powerful corporations and in (implicit) exchange, the government uses those businesses to carry out government policies outside of the ordinary [representative republic] processes of government." (SSRN, April 23, 2023.).

What Padfield means by his term "outside of the ordinary process of government," is that the crony corruption occurs outside of the democratic representative republic election system of U. S. citizen consent.

The two parties to the crony capitalist exchange are agents of government, and corporations, in their capacity of executing United States foreign government policy.

Ordinary American middle class citizens are not parties to the negotiations in this crony capitalist exchange model.

There may be other "stakeholder parties" at the negotiation table during rent extraction, but common citizens do not have their own "special interest group," to plead for a share of the plunder.

Both the elected representatives in D. C., and the CEOs of corporations have their own internal financial welfare functions that they maximize in secret negotiations, to the exclusion of any democratic concept of the will of the people, or consent of the governed.

We agree with James Buchanan that no imaginary grand U. S. social welfare function exists that elected representatives consult in making decisions about military expenditures or economic policy. (Buchanan, James M., and Tullock, Gordon, The Calculus of Consent: Logical Foundations of Constitutional Democracy, Liberty Foundation, 1962.).

Neither is there a grand social welfare utility function that the U. S. Federal Reserve Bank consults in making decisions about money supply and interest rates.

Buchanan highlighted that many public finance scholars treat all activities of the state as if it were an all knowing "fiscal brain."

In the fiscal brain [Keynesian] model there is no concern for cronyism by assumption. The state does exactly what is necessary to maximize social welfare, no more and no less.

Most social scientists invoke a similar notion of the "defense brain" where it is assumed that the state is purely protective and there is no cronyism associated with its security activities making the concern irrelevant. (Buchanan, James M., "Rent Seeking and Profit Seeking," In, James M. Buchanan, Robert Tollison, and Gordon Tullock (eds). Toward a Theory of the Rent-Seeking Society, 1980.).

In the New World Order those political and financial decisions benefit the American Ruling Class, and elected representatives.

In "Cronyism: Necessary for the Minimal, Protective State," Christopher J. Coyne and Abigail R Hall explain that the way Madison's U. S. Constitution is written makes the crony corruption inevitable. (GMU Working Paper in Economics No. 18-26. SSRN, 2018.).

They write,

"Decisions [in Congress] are not made based on the "national interest" or to provide for the "common defense" of the nation." Instead, the foundation and operation of the industry is based on political relationships, favors, and privilege… These gatekeepers [in Congress] can extract rents from private defense firms who are dependent on government funding. For example, the House Subcommittee on Defense, which is a permanent subcommittee of the United States House Committee on Appropriations, controls the flow of military-related funding and is therefore central to the profitability of private defense firms. As such, the members of this committee are able to extract rents from private firms for their own narrow benefit…As Schweizer (2013: 37) notes, the final report of the subcommittee is "the sort of document that can make or break the programs of defense contractors, both large and small." This control over the budget allows the [elected representatives] gatekeepers to seek favors from firms who are incentivized to comply."

As Coyne and Hall point out,

"Rent seeking expenditures are best understood as legal bribes whereby [corporate] donors [to elected representatives] seek to establish or maintain favorable terms with political actors in exchange for future benefits. As Higgs (2012: 214) notes, "[b]oth the givers and receivers understand these payments in exactly the same way that they understand illegal forms of bribery, even though they never admit this understanding in public." (SSRN. July 2018.).

The origination of the modern version of the corrupt crony corporatism in the U. S. government coincided with the emergence of the political ideology of authoritarian globalism.

Both components, crony corruption and globalism, ramped up after the enactment of NAFTA, around 1992.

Prior to 1992, the production and operation of U. S. domiciled corporations spread income benefits throughout American middle and working classes, as a result of the income multiplier in the inter-industrial trade among U. S. domiciled corporations.

Those inter-industrial income flows no longer exist in the U. S. economic structure because production of intermediate goods now occurs in China or India.

The political ideology of one-world authoritarian globalism and crony corporate capitalism work together to insure a smooth flow of income to the large corporations.

In order to protect the flow of global profits to themselves, the U. S. corporations require the protection of the U. S. military to enforce trade agreements that favor U. S. domiciled corporations.

The trade agreements are reached in secret by members of Congress, who benefit from the rent extraction in crony capitalism, and corporate executives who seek government protection.

The U. S. corporations become surrogate agents of U. S. foreign policy, through the operation of the U. S. military-industrial complex that depends on perpetual wars.

The enforcement of trade agreements is called "rules-based-governance" of corporate behavior.

Currently, the leadership and management of the New World Order corporatism is under the jurisdiction of a global nongovernment agency called the World Economic Forum.

The WEF advocates for one-world global corporatism because independent nation states do not cooperate to stop global climate change.

As they state in their 2019 policy document,

"Pollution in one part of the world leads to extreme weather events in another. And the cutting of forests in the few "green lungs" the world has left, like the Amazon rainforest, has a further devastating effect on not just the world's biodiversity, but its capacity to cope with hazardous greenhouse gas emissions." (A Brief History of Globalization, WEF, Jan 17, 2019.).

In the propaganda logic of the WEF, global climate change is the primary issue that supports implementing a one-world government, but climate change is linked to other important goals that can only be achieved in a one-world government,

The WEF states,

"The UN Sustainable Development Goals, or SDGs, which set universal goals of ending poverty, protecting the planet, and achieving gender equality among others, are a recognition of this reality."

According to the WEF, the main threat to attaining a one-world government is the old idea of American national sovereignty.

The Asian Development Bank identifies the narrow vision of sovereign independent nations [the U. S.] with the more globalist ideology of a one-world government that can address these global concerns.

They state,

"At the level of international relations, countries must avoid the exclusive unilateral [sovereign national] pursuit of relative gains via GVCs and unfair trade practices. Rather, they need to reignite international collaboration that fosters reciprocity, trust, and transparency via multilateral institutions [non-democratic] and converge on a [one-world government] regime that tackles rising cybersecurity risks." (Global Value Chain Development Report 2021: Beyond Production. Asian Development Bank Publication, November 2021.).

They cite the same climate change risks as the WEF cites that can only be addressed from a globalist perspective that incorporates a "virtuous, synergistic circle."

They write:

"International collaboration to develop a global cost-sharing instrument ahead of the next pandemic could enable a fairer distribution of the costs of monitoring, containing, and suppressing pandemics while strengthening incentives for early action. The proliferation of extreme weather events worldwide makes clear that new technology must privilege renewable energy and decarbonization. Measures that go beyond the Paris Agreement may be required, including the elimination of global fossil fuel subsidies for both production and consumption, an agreement on a globally negotiated minimum carbon tax adjusted to gross domestic product, improved carbon emission standards, and other urgent measures toward net zero. Urgent cooperation on environmental risks may help soften the rough edges of geopolitical and pandemic-related ones, thus reinforcing mutual commitments across all three domains in a virtuous, synergistic circle.

The U. S. Federal Reserve Bank in Dallas echoes these globalist concerns and adds unlimited immigration across national borders as an important step towards global collaboration.

The Dallas Fed writes,

"Globalization has important political implications because a country's policies determine the level of interaction between a nation and the rest of the world. Restrictive [U. S.] immigration laws limit the movement of people. Trade policies such as [Trump's] tariffs or quotas restrict the flow of goods and services between nations. Capital controls limit the amount of financial capital that moves across the globe." (Globalization: The Dallas Fed, No Date.).

The OECD cautions that the globalist agenda will impose costs on the standard of living of middle and working class citizens in the United States due to the disproportionate use of energy and other natural resources in the United States, compared to other less developed nations.

They write,

"Greater international co-operation will increasingly be needed to help reconcile national policies [the U. S.] with the global nature of economic activity. Given the broad welfare implications of GVCs, governments, enterprises and other stakeholders [not based upon democratic citizen consent] need to remain mindful of their respective roles and responsibilities with respect to the governance of GVCs.... International competition in GVCs will entail adjustment costs, [such as a decline in U. S. middle class welfare] as some activities grow [in China] and others decline [in U. S. intermediate manufacturing] and as activities [intermediate demand production] are relocated across countries. Policy [one world government] needs to facilitate the adjustment process through well-designed labour market and social policies and through investment in education and skills. Structural policies also help strengthen the flexibility of economies and their resilience against future shocks. [covid]" (Interconnected Economies: Benefiting From Global Value Chains, Oecd Synthesis Report, 2013.).

In order to facilitate the transition from a representative republic to an authoritarian corporatist system, the large U. S. corporations have created an elaborate global lobbying framework to engage in rent seeking and rent extraction.

Hao Zhang, in Commerce, Coalitions, and Global Value Chains: Coordinated and Collective Lobbying on Trade, describes how the new globalist strategy works.

He writes,

"I offer direct evidence that GVC partners tend to lobby together, lobby on the same bill, hire the same lobbyist, and even mobilize wider support through trade associations... I show that GVC coalitions drive the formation and depth of preferential trade networks. These results provide micro foundations for new coalitional politics under GVCs and challenge the common assumption about industries and firms as isolated political actors." (SSRN, 2023.).

What is new in the New World Order corporatism is that the GVC political coalitions include the foreign affiliates of the large global U. S. corporations, combining to make a truly global one-world government coalition, based upon the U. S. military acting as policeman of the world.

Zhang continues,

"In terms of trade politics, the most important type of production linkages are GVC linkages that two [U. S.] domestic firms form through the same foreign partner. [in the vertically integrated value chain]. These GVC linkages foster common interests in trade liberalization [so-called low tariffs of free trade ideology] and bring a variety of domestic firms into small groups of repeated interactions and political collaboration. Therefore, domestic firms with GVC linkages (hereafter termed as "GVC partners") are most likely to coordinate their political activities."

In the new American corporatism, as Munger points out, no political lobbying group, and no political party, represents the interests of middle and working class American citizens in representing the sovereign economic interests of the nation.

It is an extremely small powerful set of corporations who are controlling national economic and foreign policy decisions.

Zhang writes,

"Indeed, my data show that over 80% of US public firms have less than 6 value chain partners that are also public firms. Furthermore, their suppliers, if more than 1, often provide different products or services.. Overall, these estimates suggest that if there is one more active GVC partner for all firms, hundreds more firms would engage in lobbying, and millions more would be invested in politics. In addition, these estimates only refer to the direct effect of GVC partner lobbying, and if higher-order effects (such as lobbying of a firm's GVC partner's GVC partner) are considered, the total network effect would be even larger."

The corporate power is exercised through the power of extended trade association coalitions that extend around the WTO western trade alliance.

Zhang provides three examples of industrial sector trade associations in his research that combine resources, under the general ideological heading of "free trade."

The American Apparel and Footwear Association includes:

• Cotton Incorporated (Upstream Producer)
• Designer Brands (Fashion Designer)
• BSI Supply Chain Services and Solutions (Supply Chain Manager)
• Bureau Veritas (Quality Control Service)
• Ascena Retail Group (Distribution Center)
• Intertek China (Foreign Subsidiary)
• Adidas (Foreign Production)

The Semiconductor Industry Association includes:

• NVdia (Design and Upstream Production)
• Applied Materials (Production Equipment Supplier)
• Corning (Specialty Glass and Ceramics Production)
• Littlefuse (Circuit Protection)
• EMD Electronics (Display and Coating)

- International Business Machines Corporation (Design and Downstream Production)
- Rochester Electronics (Distribution and Recycle)
- Samsung (Foreign Production)

The Pharmaceutical Research and Manufacturers of America includes:

- ABS Global (Upstream and Material Supply)
- Biogen (Neuroscience Research and development)
- Pfizer (Vaccine Production)
- Cooley (Legal Service)
- Alexandria Real Estate Equities (Investment)
- Aisling Capital (Investment and Commercialization)
- Agri-Energy (Waste Management)
- Pfizer Canada (Foreign Subsidiary)

Zhang notes,

"Through trade associations, these lead firms can mobilize even more resources, increase diversity/representativeness of the coalition, strengthen their leadership positions, and bypass contribution limits. As risks and benefits propagate through value chains, smaller firms may agree to be jointly represented. Meanwhile, trade associations play a key role in facilitating information flows from large to smaller firms (Kowal, 2018; Selling, 2020) and providing a social environment that is often characterized by mimicry, cue-taking, and bandwagon effects (Baumgartner and Leech, 1998; Scott, 2013)."

Zhang provides his Figure 5 to show the increase in the trade association coalition political spending, from 2004 – 2019.

As Zhang notes in his comments on Figure 5, the collective lobbying expenditures on behalf of the 'free trade coalition" during this time period represented 30% of the entire lobbying expenditure for all governmental lobbying, on all issues.

The trade association lobbying expenditures dramatically increased after 2005, coinciding with the period of time that U. S. corporations were moving intermediate demand production from the U. S. to China.

Chapter 2 Figure 5. Collective Lobbying by Trade Association.

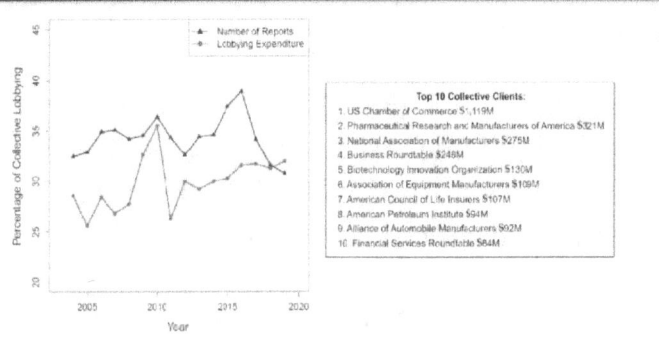

Figure 5: **Collective Lobbying by Trade Associations:** This figure summarizes lobbying activities by trade associations (2004-2019) and the top 10 trade associations in terms of lobbying expenditure. Collective lobbying through trade associations have consistently occupied about 30% - a nontrivial portion - of the total lobbying activities.

Credit: Figure 5. Zhang, Hao Commerce, Coalitions, and Global Value Chains: Coordinated and Collective Lobbying on Trade.

This period of time marks the beginning of the third iteration of global value chain operation to the most recent iteration of vertically integrated global value chains.

As the crony capitalist rent seeking-rent extraction political activity of the free trade coalition increased, from 2001 – 2019, the number of U. S. citizens who entered a permanent life time dependency on government welfare also went up.

David H. Autor, et al., explain that increased trade with China cost the average American citizen about $549 in annual income for every $1000 increase of imports from China, during the second iteration of global value chains, from 1990 – 2007.

Middle and lower class citizens who previously had worked and obtained wages and salaries prior to the implementation of the trade agreements with China could not find jobs and applied for government welfare payments.

This is an example of what the OECD meant in their statement that the implementation of the New World Order would require "some adjustment" to the standard of living of middle and working class citizens in America.

The ideological logic of global corporatism is that U. S. citizens consume too much of the world's resources, and that the unfair disparity can only be remedied by a one-world government that brings the standard of living in America down to the standard of living in the so-called developing nations.

In other words, to paraphrase David Marcus, in his article about corporate fascism, in the New World Order authoritarian corporatism, all citizens in the world must be the same, economically.

Chapter 2 Table 8. Imports From China.

Table 8. Imports from China and Change of Government Transfer Receipts in Commuting Zones, 1990-2007; 2SLS Estimates.
Dep Vars: 10-Year Equivalent Log and Dollar Change of Annual Transfer Receipts per Capita (in log pts and US$)

	Total Individ Transfers (1)	TAA Benefits (2)	Unemp- loyment Benefits (3)	SSA Re- tirement Benefits (4)	SSA Disability Benefits (5)	Medical Benefits (6)	Federal Income Assist (7)	Other Income Assist (8)	Educ/ Training Assist (9)
A. Log Change of Transfer Receipts per Capita									
(Δ Imports from China to US)/Worker	1.01 **	14.41 ~	3.46 ~	0.72 ~	1.96 **	0.54	3.04 **	1.08	2.78 *
	(0.33)	(7.59)	(1.87)	(0.38)	(0.69)	(0.49)	(0.96)	(2.20)	(1.32)
R²	0.57	0.28	0.48	0.36	0.52	0.27	0.54	0.37	0.33
B. Dollar Change of Transfer Receipts per Capita									
(Δ Imports from China to US)/Worker	57.73 **	0.23	3.42	10.00 ~	8.40 **	18.27	7.20 **	4.13	3.71 **
	(18.41)	(0.17)	(2.26)	(5.45)	(2.21)	(11.84)	(2.35)	(4.44)	(1.44)
R²	0.75	0.28	0.41	0.47	0.63	0.66	0.53	0.30	0.37

Notes: N=1444 (722 commuting zones × 2 time periods), except N=1436 in column 2, panel A. Results for TAA benefits in column 2 are based on state-level data that is allocated to commuting zones in proportion to unemployment benefits. Unemployment benefits in column 3 include state benefits and federal unemployment benefits for civilian federal employees, railroad employees, and veterans. Medical benefits in column 6 consist mainly of Medicare and Medicaid. Federal income assistance in column 7 comprises the SSI, AFDC/TANF, and SNAP programs while other income assistance in column 8 consists mainly of general assistance. Education and training assistance in column 9 includes such benefits as interest payments on guaranteed student loans, Pell grants, and Job Corps benefits. The transfer categories displayed in columns 2 to 9 account for 96% of total individual transfer receipts. All regressions include the full vector of control variables from column 6 of Table 3. Robust standard errors in parentheses are clustered on state. Models are weighted by start of period commuting zone share of national population. ~ p ≤ 0.10, * p ≤ 0.05, ** p ≤ 0.01.

Credit: Table 8. Autor, David H., Dorn, David, Hanson, Gordon H., The China Syndrome: Local Labor Market Effects Of Import Competition In The United States, NBER Working Paper 18054, 2012.

As Autor, et al., explain,

"Overall, Table 8 suggests that through its effects on [U. S.] employment and earnings, rising import exposure [from China] spurs a substantial increase in government transfer payments to citizens in the form of increased disability, medical, income assistance, and unemployment benefit payments. These transfer payments vastly exceed the expenses of the TAA program, which specifically targets workers who lose employment due to import competition."

In order to direct the global value chain flow of income to themselves, the large U. S. corporations bend U. S. foreign and economic policy to their own financial interests, independent of any conception of democratic citizen consent.

Income that previously had been earned by middle and working class citizens in U. S. intermediate production has been successfully diverted to the large corporations, via the vertically integrated global value chains.

The decrease of $549 per adult in middle class income as a result of trade with China is not simply a zero sum loss for U. S. workers and a net gain increase in profits for the large corporations.

Imposing the loss of income upon middle class American citizens was a necessary outcome for the corporations to implement the one-world authoritarian model of government in order to obtain the global market power to mark up prices over marginal costs to obtain "pure profits."

The pricing power of the corporations to markup prices over marginal costs of production is a reflection of the political power of the ideology of one world authoritarian corporatism, which replaced free consumer choice in markets and free political choice in a democratic representative constitution.

The two forces at work in the New World Order corporatism are the ideology of one world government, and the crony corporate power to bend U. S. economic and political power to serve their own corporate financial interests in the rent seeking/rent/extraction political process.

The goal of the one-world government authoritarian corporatism is a world where all citizens are the same, economically. That future society for American citizens looks just like the Chinese communist society today.

Chapter 3. The Destructive Economic Power of the New World Order Western Globalist Trading Alliance On American Middle and Working Class Citizens.

The implementation the New World Order Western Trading Alliance is the cause of domestic U. S. race and social class violence, as the U. S. ruling class seeks to create civil chaos as the pretext for imposing an authoritarian police state government in the U. S. that maintains the power and privileges of the American ruling class.

The U. S. domestic economy is not creating enough economic growth, and the income distribution in the shrinking economy is being diverted to large corporations in the vertically integrated global value chains.

Middle and working class U, S, citizens are being squeezed out of the economic system, and are facing a future of reduced standards of living because of the operation of the Western Global Corporate Trading Alliance.

Middle and working class citizens have sought to protect their financial welfare by electing politicians who promise to restore national economic sovereignty.

The restoration of national economic sovereignty, and the election of conservative populists, is a threat to the smooth operation of the Western Global Trading Alliance.

The smooth operation of the trading relationships in global vertical value chains depends on an authoritarian regime to force U. S. citizens to comply with western rules based global order that allow the ruling class to continue to direct the income and wealth of the global trading relations to their own social class.

The logic of authoritarian corporate globalism is that the management of the world economy, where large U. S. and Western alliance corporations own and manage production and sales facilities all over the world, is easier if U. S. citizens are forced to behave the same way as other citizens, all over the world.

The economic chaos and anxiety created by globalism for middle and working class U. S. citizens contributes to the effectiveness of the ruling class propaganda of race hatred and social class polarization, which leads citizens to seek social stability in authoritarian regimes that promise social stability in exchange for citizen independence and liberty.

As the U. S. economy contracts, and the flow of income of the shrinking economic pie is diverted from the middle class to the ruling class, middle and working class citizens become desperate to survive, and the authoritarian police state will force citizen compliance with the rules of the New World Order.

We focus the Western New World Order Corporate Trading Alliance, in contrast to a new perspective of non-western nations composed of Brazil, Iran, Russia and China, commonly called BRICs.

Chapter 3 Figure 8. from Islamic Society Review, describes the national geographical alignment between the Western Trading Alliance and BRICs world views.

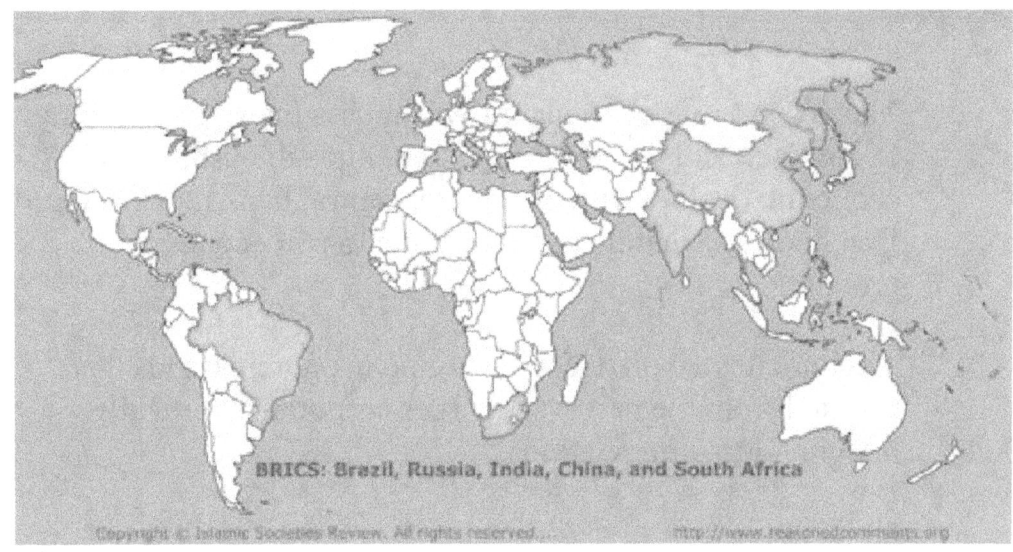

Credit: Islamic Society Review. https://islamicsocietiesreview.org/

The authoritarian political and economic police state model being pursued by U. S. corporations is a U. S. society that looks and functions just like the current totalitarian society of China, where a small ruling class make all of the social and economic decisions.

The implementation of this global production and sales institutional framework has caused economic damage to the United States middle and working class economic structure that existed, prior to 1992.

The economic destruction of the former U. S. economy can be categorized into several related topics.

For example, Ufuk Akcigit places the damage to the U. S. economy under the general topic category as "loss of U. S. business dynamism," meaning a loss of domestic economic growth, since the beginning of the globalization of trading patterns.

The absence of economic growth causes the U. S. economy to contract, and the government attempts to cushion the economic decline with ephemeral central bank monetary and fiscal policies that do not contribute to real economic growth.

Akcigit cites 10 different damaging economic trends that resulted from the new world order corporatist vertically integrated trading relations.

He writes,

"We focus on 10 specific trends: (i) market concentration has risen, (ii) average markups have increased, (iii) the profit share of GDP has increased, (iv) the labor share of output has gone down, (v) the rise in market concentration and the fall in labor share are positively associated, (vi) productivity dispersion of firms has risen, (vii) firm entry rate has declined, (viii) the share of young firms in economic activity has declined, (ix) job reallocation has slowed down, and (x) the dispersion of firm growth has decreased…Decker et al. (2016b) document that other measures of business dynamism, such as gross job reallocation, reverberate with this post-2000 pattern, again especially in high-tech sectors. In this regard, our post-2000 findings tell a coherent story with these empirical regularities, suggesting a concurrent slowdown in knowledge diffusion and business dynamism." (Akcigit, Ufuk, Sina, Ates, What Happened to U.S. Business Dynamism? NBER Working Paper No. w25756, SSRN, 2023.).

Boehm, et al., also describe the damaging effect of globalization on the U. S. economy in terms of the loss of the intermediate production in manufacturing sectors.

They add that the damage to the economy requires government intervention to help displaced middle class American workers adjust to the new lower standards of living which result from globalization.

They write,

"Our results add to the mounting evidence, that international trade differentially exposes [U. S.] manufacturing workers to competition from abroad. [global wage and income equalization]. This suggests that policy interventions that assist displaced workers may be desirable." (Boehm, Christoph E., Flaaen, Aaron, Pandalai-Nayar, Nitya, Multinationals, Offshoring And The Decline Of U.S. Manufacturing, NBER Working Paper 25824, 2019.).

We add to both the Akcigit and Boehm analyses of the damaging effect of globalization of trade in vertically integrated corporate value chains by categorizing the damaging effects into six broad topic categories, primarily on the permanent income and welfare damage to middle and working class American citizens.

Our six categories of economic damage of globalization are:

1. Economic and income decline of the U. S. middle and working classes and increased social class polarization between the wealthy haves, and the unlucky have-nots.
2. Regional economic decline in metro and rural regions affected by global trade.

3. Decline in national economic growth rates caused by declining capital investment and reinvestment of corporate profits.
4. Corporate monopoly pricing power and the increase of pure monopoly profits.
5. Loss of technological innovation related to the loss of domestic intermediate input production.
6. Increased macro economic instability in the transition of the U. S. economic free enterprise economy to the communist state owned crony corporatism Chinese economic model.

Chapter 3 Topic Category #1: Economic and income decline of the U. S. middle and working classes and increased social class polarization between the wealthy haves, and the unlucky have-nots.

One of the most important damaging effects of globalization on U. S. middle and working class citizens was the loss of jobs that had upward occupational career paths, paid decent wages and had health benefits.

The increase in homelessness and increased government welfare payments to displaced workers was caused by workers who lost their jobs because of globalization, then lost their homes, and became homeless because they could not find any jobs, other than jobs in what is known as the "gig" labor market.

In their article, "Measuring the Gig Economy: Current Knowledge and Open Issues," Katharine G. Abraham, et al., define the gig labor market as,

"[The] growth in the number of people working in contingent or precarious jobs, positions in which workers had no long-term connection to a particular business, but were employed to complete a specific task or for a defined period of time – or under other non-standard employment arrangements...the number of workers in the gig labor market with no formal employer-employee relationship is large and growing. Both media sources and scholars have adopted the term "gig economy" to refer broadly to these less structured work arrangements as well as more narrowly to the subset of flexible jobs mediated through various online platforms. The latter have been viewed as yielding an increasingly "on demand" economy where goods and services can be acquired through apps on smartphones and other web based applications."

They provide a table, described as Figure 1 below, to describe the growth of the gig lablor market, after the inception of the globalization in trade.

Chapter 3 Figure 1. Household Survey.

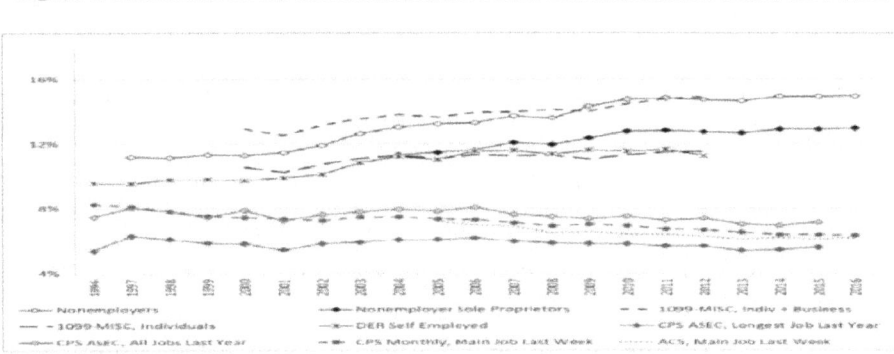

Credit Figure 1: Abraham, Katharine G., Haltiwanger, Sandusky, John, Kristin, Lee, Spletzer, James, Measuring the Gig Economy: Current Knowledge and Open Issues, NBER Working Paper No. w24950, SSRN, 2018.

After the entrance of China into the WTO, in 2001, the U. S. gig labor market increased from around 10% of the U. S. labor market to around 14% of the labor market.

At the same period of time, jobs in the formal labor market, with stable wages and health benefits declined from around 8% of the labor market to around 4.5%.

The divergence in the labor market trend lines in Figure 1is an indicator of the polarization in the American economy caused by globalization in trade.

We estimate that about 15% of the U. S. labor market benefits from global trade, while about 85% of the labor market have either dropped out of the labor force, or now work in the 6 gig service sectors, in restaurants, hair salons, and house cleaning custodial jobs.

As Abraham points out,

"Gig workers do not enjoy the legal rights and protections afforded under the unemployment insurance system, the workers compensation system, the Fair Labor Standards Act and other laws and regulations written with more traditional employment arrangements in mind (Harris and Krueger 2015). Further, those who rely primarily or exclusively on self employment are markedly less likely to have health insurance or to have a retirement plan (Jackson, Looney and Romnath 2017) and may have hours and earnings that are substantially more variable and less predictable."

In the chronological sequence of events in the implementation of globalization, first, the U. S. middle and working classes lost their regular formal jobs in the labor market, which they had prior to 1992, before globalization.

Then, after the implementation of globalization, they entered the gig labor market.

When they lose their unstable gig job, they lose their homes, and become homeless.

Appendix Table 1, from Autor and Dorn, describes both the loss of middle class jobs and decline in hourly wages for production workers, with modest job increases for corporate managers, whose jobs were connected to the global trade relationships.

The large increase in service sector jobs of 53%, from 1980 to 2005, documents the trend that many middle class workers who lost their jobs in manufacturing went to work in the service sector gig labor market.

The gig labor market is not connected to global value chain trade relationships.

During that same period from 1980 to 2005, jobs in the corporate professional occupations, which are connected to the global value chains, increased by 4%, and their incomes increased 5.3%.

Chapter 3 Table 1. Changes in Employment Share.

APPENDIX TABLE 1—LEVELS AND CHANGES IN EMPLOYMENT SHARE AND MEAN REAL LOG HOURLY WAGES BY MAJOR OCCUPATION GROUPS AMONG WORKERS WITHOUT COLLEGE EDUCATION, 1950–2005

	Level						Growth rate (%)	
	1950	1970	1980	1990	2000	2005	1950–1980	1980–2005
Panel A. Share of employment (%pts)								
Managers/prof/tech/finance/public safety	14.5	13.4	14.5	15.9	14.2	15.0	−0.1	3.9
Production/craft	5.7	5.7	6.0	4.9	5.5	4.5	6.1	−25.8
Transport/construct/mech/mining/farm	33.8	27.8	29.5	29.2	30.2	31.3	−12.7	6.2
Machine operators/assemblers	14.8	17.1	14.7	12.5	10.4	8.5	−0.8	−42.5
Clerical/retail sales	19.1	22.6	22.4	22.0	21.8	20.9	17.7	−6.6
Service occupations	12.2	13.3	12.9	15.6	17.9	19.8	5.8	53.2
Panel B. Mean log hourly wage (2004$)								
Managers/prof/tech/finance/public safety	2.16	2.69	2.63	2.59	2.68	2.76	15.8	5.3
Production/craft	2.23	2.71	2.70	2.64	2.62	2.63	15.8	−2.9
Transport/construct/mech/mining/farm	2.04	2.55	2.59	2.52	2.56	2.57	18.5	−1.0
Machine operators/assemblers	2.03	2.45	2.46	2.42	2.47	2.48	14.3	0.7
Clerical/retail sales	1.96	2.38	2.37	2.35	2.41	2.45	13.6	3.2
Service occupations	1.47	1.99	2.07	2.08	2.17	2.18	20.3	4.2

Notes: Sample includes persons who were age 18–64 and working in the prior year. Occupation categories are defined according to Census classification. Hourly wages are defined as yearly wage and salary income divided by the product of weeks worked times usual weekly hours. Employment share is defined as share in total work hours of workers without college education. Labor supply is measured as weeks worked times usual weekly hours in prior year. All calculations use labor supply weights.

Source: Census 1 percent samples for 1950 and 1970; Census 5 percent samples for 1980, 1990, 2000; American Community Survey 2005.

Credit: Appendix Table 1: from Autor, David H., and Dorn, David, The Growth of Low-Skill Service Jobs and the Polarization of the US Labor Market, American Economic Review, 2013.

Table 9, below, also from Autor, et al., describes the loss of income for the hypothetical U. S. worker, as a result of trade with China.

They show that the average decline in U. S. economic growth is 1.48% per year, from 1990 to 2007.

The average U. S. worker lost 2.14% in wages during that period.

Private capital investment in domestic U. S. economy declined ½% per year.

Welfare payments went up 2.21% per year as a result of increased imports from China.

Chapter 3 Table 9. Imports From China.

Table 9. Imports from China and Change in Household Income, 1990-2007: 2SLS Estimates. Dependent Variable: 10-Year Equivalent Relative Growth and Absolute Dollar Change of Average and Median Annual Household Income per Working-Age Adult (in %pts and US$)

	Average HH Income/Adult by Source				Median HH Inc./Ad.	
	Total (1)	Wage-Salary (2)	Business Invest. (3)	SocSec +AFDC (4)	Total (5)	Wage-Salary (6)
A. Relative Growth (%pts)						
(Δ Imports from China to US)/Worker	-1.48 **	-2.14 **	-0.51	2.12 **	-1.73 **	-2.32 **
	(0.36)	(0.59)	(0.74)	(0.58)	(0.38)	(0.51)
R²	0.69	0.43	0.76	0.52	0.53	0.52
B. Dollar Change						
(Δ Imports from China to US)/Worker	-492.6 **	-549.3 **	40.1	17.3 **	-439.9 **	-476.5 **
	(160.4)	(159.4)	(116.7)	(4.3)	(112.7)	(122.2)
R²	0.63	0.40	0.72	0.51	0.49	0.48

Notes: N=1444 (722 commuting zones x 2 time periods). Per capita household income is defined as the sum of individual incomes of all working age household members (age 16-64), divided by the number of household members of that age group. Total income comprises wage and salary income, self-employment, business and investment income, social security and welfare income, and income from other non-specified sources. Social security and welfare income in column 4 includes social security retirement, disability, and supplementary income, aid to families with dependent children (AFDC), and general assistance. All regressions include the full vector of control variables from column 6 of Table 3. Robust standard errors in parentheses are clustered on state. Models are weighted by start of period commuting zone share of national population. ~ p ≤ 0.10, * p ≤ 0.05, ** p ≤ 0.01.

Credit Table 9: Autor, David H., Dorn, David, Hanson, Gordon H., The China Syndrome: Local Labor Market Effects Of Import Competition In The United States, NBER Working Paper 18054, 2012.

This outcome for U. S. middle class citizens is not the rosy panacea promised in 1992 by crony corporate proponents of globalism during the debates in Congress about enacting NAFTA.

That corporate political propaganda from 1992 was based upon econometric models that held U. S. labor class income constant in order to describe the welfare improvements generated by lower import prices for finished goods.

The logic of the corporate propaganda was that U. S. middle and working class citizens would benefit from lower prices resulting from global trade, if their incomes after the implementation of NAFTA were the same as their incomes before the passage of NAFTA.

Instead of constant middle class incomes, after the passage of NAFTA, incomes of middle and working class citizens decreased as imports of both finished goods and intermediate demand goods increased.

Then, 10 years later, prices on finished goods imports increased due to corporate monopoly power to markup prices on intermediate goods 67% over marginal costs.

The recent inflation in the U. S. economy is caused by price increases in global trade and is also caused by the money and interest rate manipulation by the Fed, which causes asset bubbles in real estate and hard assets, which serves to benefit bankers and wealthy citizens.

Maarten De Ridder provides a more accurate analysis in the sequence of events following the implementation of global trading patterns, after 1992, than the corporate propaganda of the benefits of NAFTA and globalization.

In his analysis, in the first stage of globalization, prices on imported finished goods into the U. S. decline, but the increase in intermediate demand imports also causes a decline in U. S. middle class incomes, as intermediate demand networks are moved to China, and U. S. workers lose their decent jobs and enter the gig labor market.

After the global economy adjusts to the new trading patterns, prices for finished goods go up, because of the increased market power of large corporations to markup prices in the intermediate demand networks.

The higher wages that previously were paid to U. S. middle class citizens were subsequently paid as slave labor wages in China, and the difference in wages was diverted to global elites, in the form of increased "pure profits."

Large corporations control the markup prices in closed vertically integrated value chains through their legal contracts with foreign affiliates in the intermediate demand value chains.

De Ritter explains,

"As the [global] economy transitions to the new balanced growth path, [a new lower Nash equilibrium] there is an initial increase in productivity [lower finished goods prices] as firms deploy more intangible inputs. [computer automated production and internet logistics] This does not lead to an increase in wages, [in the U. S. labor markets] however, as the higher productivity is offset by higher markups. Firms [existing firms in the U. S.] without an increased intangible input efficiency [caused by globalization] have less incentive to innovate, as they are unable to offer a sufficiently low price [over intermediate demand marginal cost] if they enter new markets. (Market Power and Innovation in the Intangible Economy, Working Paper, University of Cambridge, 2019.).

In other words, existing U. S. firms in the former domestic intermediate demand networks that are left behind after the implementation of globalization are in a permanent competitive disadvantage to global corporations because the remaining firms cannot match the internal marginal costs of the large corporations, based upon the Chinese slave labor wages codified in corporate legal contracts..

Autor, in Figure 1 below, provides another graphic to show the labor market polarization between middle and working classes and corporate professional classes, during the period 1980 – 2010.

From 1980 to 2010, middle and working class occupations lost jobs. Generally, those occupations were filled by workers with a community college degree or a high school diploma.

Corporate managers and professional occupation jobs increased.

Chapter 3 Figure 1. Changes in U. S. Occupational Employment/.

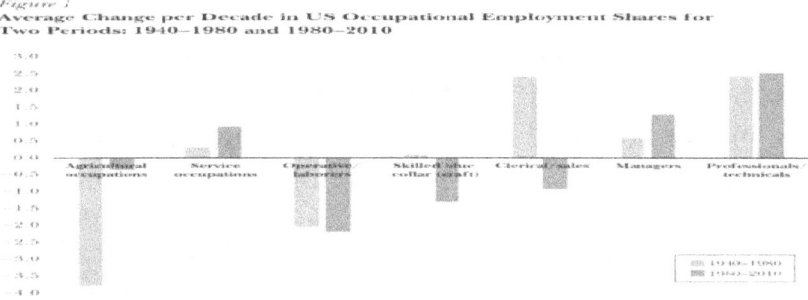

Credit: Figure 1 cited in Autor, David H., Why Are There Still So Many Jobs? The History and Future of WorkplaceAutomation, Journal of Economic Perspectives, 2015.

The polarization between social classes in America can be seen in Figure 3, below, with nonroutine corporate managerial jobs increasing over time, after 2000, while routine U. S. middle class jobs declined.

Chapter 3 Figure 2. Trends In Routine and Nonroutine Tasks.

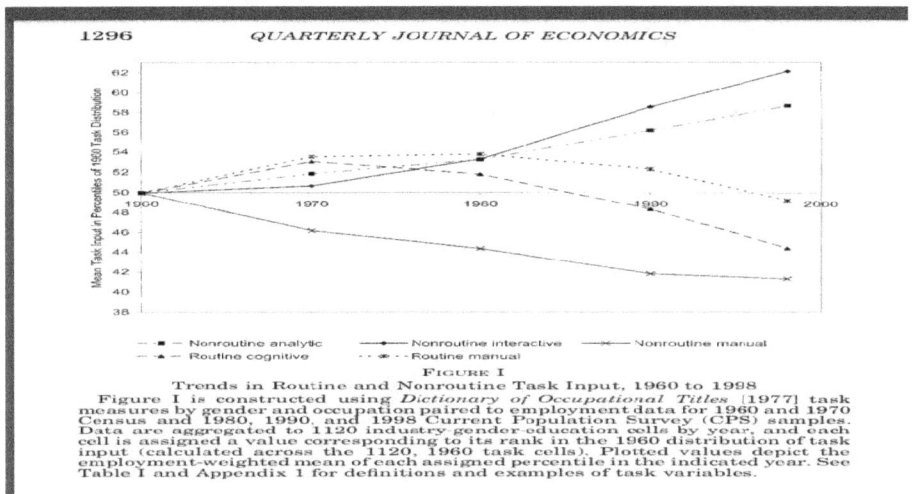

Figure 2 from Autor, David H., et al., The Skill Content Of Recent Technological Change: An Empirical Exploration, NBER Working Paper, 2001. Published in QJE.

As a result of the implementation of globalization in trade relations, the share of income obtained by U. S. middle and working class citizens declined, from about 67% of GDP, in 1980 to about 60%, in 2010.

The rate of decline in working class income is especially severe after 2001, when China was admitted to the WTO, as a "developing nation," with most favored trade status.

The prices of intermediate input prices in the global value chains are set internally by the large U. S. corporations because they legally control the trade relations of their foreign intermediate demand affiliates.

In other words, inside of the vertically integrated global value chains, prices on semi-finished goods are insulated from market forces, and not determined by supply and demand competition.

Chapter 3 Figure 3. Labor Share of Income.

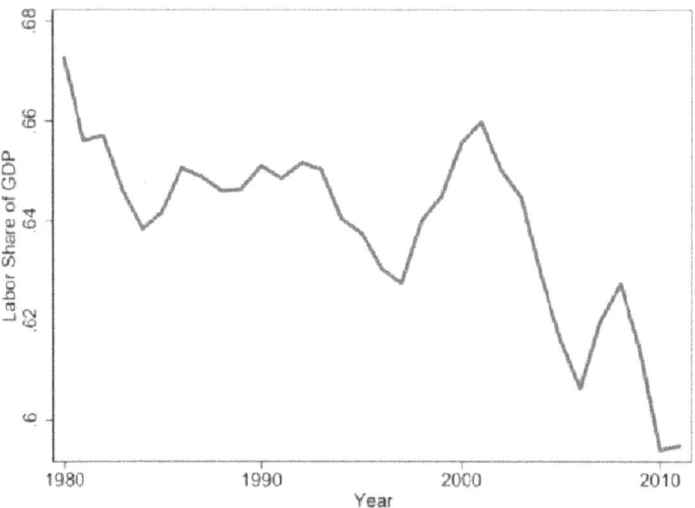

Source: Karabarbounis and Neiman (2013)

Figure 4: LABOR SHARE.

Credit: Figure 3 cited in Akcigit,Ufuk Ates, Sina T. Ten Facts On Declining Business Dynamism And Lessons From Endogenous Growth Theory, Working Paper 25755 NBER 2019.

Large corporations have the power to markup intermediate inputs to derive "pure profits," that are not profits obtained through free market competition.

The component of GDP comprised of pure profits, which was previously earned by middle class citizens in domestic. U. S. production, prior to 1992, has been shifted from the middle and working classes to the executives and owners of the large corporations.

The share of U. S. GDP composed of pure profits increased from 3% of GDP, in 1985, to 17% of GDP, in 2015. (Eggertsson, Gauti B. et al., Kaldor And Piketty's Facts: The Rise Of Monopoly Power In The United States, NBER Working Paper 24287, 2018.).

In other words, from a conventional canonical economic theory interpretation of GDP, the increase in GDP should have translated into an improvement in the welfare of working class citizens.

The increase in GDP in 2015 did not benefit middle class workers because the 17% increase in pure profits were generated in foreign locations, and the pure profits were never re-invested in the domestic U. S. economy.

During the same period of time that pure profits were increasing, the labor share of middle and working class income in the GDP declined from 63% in 1985 to 57% in 2015.

The portion of middle class income that used to be distributed to U. S. citizens, prior to 2001, was in the form of income and employer multiplier effects of intermediate demand production in the domestic U. S. economy, and that component of income is no longer obtained by the U. S. workers because the intermediate demand networks were moved to China and India.

The graph, in Figure 5 below, describes, that as pure profits increase in the globalization of trade, the share of income obtained by middle and working class citizens goes down.

The trends in pure profits in the first graph are inverted in order to describe the statistical relationship between the increase in pure profits and decline of middle class incomes.

The decline in middle class income is especially prevalent after the 2002 entrance of China into the WTO.

The trend lines in the second part of the graph describe the relationship between the increase in pure profits, and the monopoly concentration of corporate power of the vertically integrated global value chains.

As pure profits increase, especially after 2002, the market concentration of large corporations increases, which means that more and more of the world economy is controlled by legal contracts and is not subject to market supply and demand competitive forces.

Chapter 3 Figure 4. Evolution of Labor Share and Market Value.

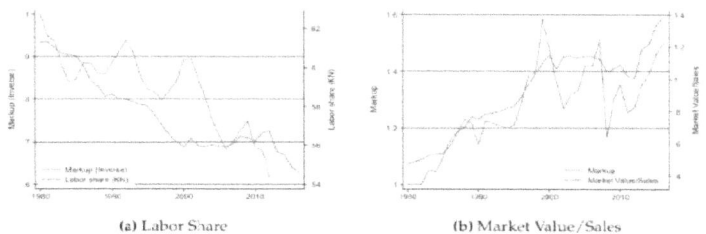

Figure 5: The Evolution of Labor Share and Market Value/Sales with Global Markups. Labor share data, for the corporate sector, from Karabarbounis and Neiman (2014).

Credit: Figure 4 Graphic From Karabarbounis and Neiman, The Evolution of Labor Share and Market Value, 2014.

Boehm, et al., cited earlier in their categorization of the damage caused by the implementation of globalization in trading relationships, suggested that government intervention in increased welfare payments to middle and working class citizens may offset some of the loss of income for displaced workers.

Table 8 below, from Autor, et al., describes the increase in U. S. government welfare payments, after China was admitted to the WTO, in 2001.

Chapter 3 Table 8. Change in Government Transfers.

Table 8. Imports from China and Change of Government Transfer Receipts in Commuting Zones, 1990-2007: 2SLS Estimates.
Dep Vars: 10-Year Equivalent Log and Dollar Change of Annual Transfer Receipts per Capita (in log pts and US$)

	Total Individ Transfers (1)	TAA Benefits (2)	Unemployment Benefits (3)	SSA Retirement Benefits (4)	SSA Disability Benefits (5)	Medical Benefits (6)	Federal Income Assist (7)	Other Income Assist (8)	Educ/ Training Assist (9)
A. Log Change of Transfer Receipts per Capita									
(Δ Imports from China to US)/Worker	1.01 **	14.41 **	−3.46	−0.72	1.96 **	0.54	3.01 **	1.08	2.78 *
	(0.33)	(7.59)	(1.87)	(0.38)	(0.69)	(0.49)	(0.96)	(2.20)	(1.32)
R²	0.57	0.28	0.48	0.36	0.32	0.27	0.54	0.37	0.33
B. Dollar Change of Transfer Receipts per Capita									
(Δ Imports from China to US)/Worker	57.73 **	0.23	3.42	10.00	−8.40 **	18.27 **	7.20 **	4.13	3.71 **
	(18.41)	(0.17)	(2.26)	(5.45)	(2.21)	(11.84)	(2.35)	(4.44)	(1.44)
R²	0.75	0.28	0.41	0.47	0.63	0.66	0.53	0.30	0.37

Notes: N=1444 (722 commuting zones x 2 time periods), except N=1436 in column 2, panel A. Results for TAA benefits in column 2 are based on state-level data that is allocated to commuting zones in proportion to unemployment benefits. Unemployment benefits in column 3 include state benefits and federal unemployment benefits for civilian federal employees, railroad employees, and veterans. Medical benefits in column 6 consist mainly of Medicare and Medicaid. Federal income assistance in column 7 comprises the SSI, AFDC/TANF and SNAP programs while other income assistance in column 8 consists mainly of general assistance. Education and training assistance in column 9 includes such benefits as interest payments on guaranteed student loans, Pell grants, and Job Corps benefits. The transfer categories displayed in columns 2 to 9 account for 96% of total individual transfer receipts. All regressions include the full vector of control variables from column 6 of Table 3. Robust standard errors in parentheses are clustered on state. Models are weighted by start of period commuting zone share of national population. ~ p ≤ 0.10, * p ≤ 0.05, ** p ≤ 0.01.

Table 8 Graphic From Autor, David H., Dorn, David, Hanson, Gordon H., The China Syndrome: Local Labor Market Effects Of Import Competition In The United States, NBER Working Paper 18054, 2012.

The lower part of Table 8 describes that for every dollar of increased imports from China, a hypothetical U. S. worker obtained an additional $57 in welfare payments.

We would add to this research result that the increase in welfare payments to the middle and working classes indicates a transition from a life of earning a living by working to a life-time dependency on government welfare because the economic damage caused by globalization has eliminated economic growth.

The U. S. economy does not create enough new jobs to employ the unemployed workers, and consequently, they drop out of the labor force, into a life of forced idleness and permanent welfare income.

The transition of the U. S. society from a society of citizens who work to earn an income to a society of government welfare dependency is consistent with the political globalist ideology of forcing all citizens to be the same, with equal poverty-level incomes throughout the world.

As cited earlier, Figure 5, below, in Autor, et al., describe that between 1990 and 2007, the average U. S. worker lost 2.14% in wages each year, during that period.

The absolute annual dollar decline in middle and working class income between 1990 and 2007 was $497, as a result of increased trade with China.

As a result of the implementation of vertically integrated global value chains, the American ruling class has successfully diverted a large portion of income and wealth previously earned by the middle class and working classes to themselves.

The share of wealth in American social classes became more concentrated, while the rate of capital investment in the U. S. domestic economy declined.

The rate of personal savings, a surrogate indicator of wealth for middle and working class citizens declined, as middle class citizens consumed their savings in order to survive the destructive economic consequences of the New World Order global trading relations.

As described in Figure 1, from Eggertsson, et al., the personal savings rate of middle class citizens has declined from around 11% of GDP, to a low of 2%.

When the U. S. personal savings rate declines to 0%, middle class American citizens will no longer have a cushion of savings to absorb the economic destruction of the New World Order, and they, too, like the current labor force of gig workers, can look forward to a future of poverty, government welfare dependency, and homelessness.

Chapter 3 Figure 5. Wealth and Capital.

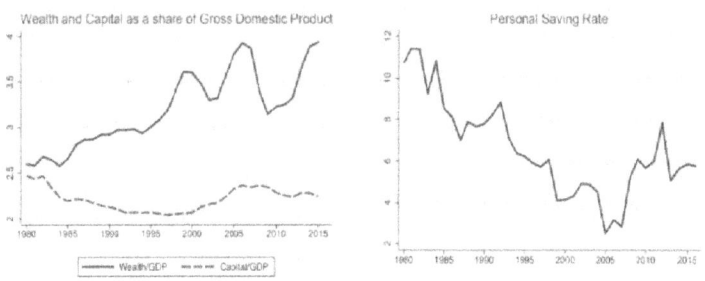

Figure 1: Wealth and capital as a share of gross value added

Citation Figure 5: Kaldor and Piketty's Facts: The Rise of Monopoly Power in the United States, Eggertsson, Gauti B.,

Robbins, Jacob A., Wold, Ella Getz, NBER Working Paper 24287, 2018.

Chapter 3 Topic Category #2. Regional economic decline in metro and rural regions affected by global trade.

Prior to 1992, the metro regional economies in 350 U. S. metro regions performed two important economic functions.

First, as a result of the employment and labor markets within each intermediate demand manufacturing network, middle and working class citizens obtained good, high wage jobs, with upward occupational career paths.

Citizens not directly employed in the metro manufacturing industrial sectors obtained income and employment benefits from the indirect and induced income and employment multipliers of economic transactions within the regional economy.

A dollar spent within the metro regional manufacturing industrial sectors was spent and re-spent many times within the regional intermediate demand economy, generating wealth and income for regional citizens.

The second great economic benefit of the regional economic structure, prior to 1992, was the creation and diffusion of technological knowledge within each regional intermediate demand technology cluster of firms who traded with each other.

All of the engineers, technicians, sales staff, and scientists, in each region, met and talked to each other about their industry. These informal discussions in each metro region were a form of tacit knowledge creation and diffusion.

Tacit knowledge creation and diffusion in each metro regional industrial cluster caused a high rate of new technological ventures to be started, as workers left their prior jobs to start their own firm.

All net new job creation in the U. S. economy was caused, prior to 1992, by new ventures, less than 5 years old.

The implementation of the New World Order corporate globalization destroyed the intermediate demand economic industrial clusters in the U. S. regional economies, and consequently, destroyed the tacit knowledge networks that were the cause of new venture creation.

Not only did middle class workers lose their good jobs, with the implementation of the New World Order trading patterns, the loss of intermediate industrial production also caused the destruction of the networks of tacit knowledge creation and diffusion, and the subsequent elimination of technology new venture creation in 350 metro regional economies.

The current high level of violence and racial conflict in American cities is a result of the implementation of the New World Order, as citizens can no longer find decent jobs, and the desperate citizens are politically manipulated by the ruling class propaganda of race hatred, as a pretext for implementing an authoritarian government.

The small amount of technological innovation in American metro regions, after 1992, became concentrated in just 5 metro regions, which were connected to globalization trade patterns in vertically integrated global value chains.

The remaining large metro regions did not sustain enough technological innovation, and consequently, did not generate enough new jobs in new venture creation, to offset the loss of jobs in the former regional intermediate demand clusters.

Those metro regions that are not connected to globalization trading patterns have the highest rates of violence and crime, as desperate citizens seek to survive the economic chaos created by globalization.

Amy Liu, Vice President and Director of the Metropolitan Policy Program at the Brookings Institution, testified before Congress, in 2021, about the metro geographical impact of globalization.

Liu testified,

" Specifically, between 2005 and 2017, just five metro areas (San Francisco, San Jose, Seattle, San Diego, and Boston) captured 90 percent of the nation's growth in innovation jobs. Other Brookings analyses found similar regional divergence, in which large metro areas outperformed small- and midsized metro areas this past decade, all metro areas grew jobs, and while micropolitan and rural areas lost jobs or barely stabilized. In response, some argue that the nation needs to facilitate people-based policies that provide working families the choice to move to higher opportunity regions." (The Future of Regional Economic Development and Implications for U.S. Economic Development Administration Programs Testimony submitted to the United States Senate Committee on Environment and Public Works, November 1, 2021.).

Table 2 below, describes the different technology industrial clusters for technological innovation in different metro regions.

The Congressional testimony of Liu is supported by the appearance of these same 5 metro regions in Table 2 below, prepared by Audretsch, across a wide set of industrial sectors, categorized by Standard Industrial Classification (SIC codes).

Chapter 3 Table 2. The Innovative Advantage of U. S. Cities.

Table 2: The Innovative Advantage of U.S. Cities (MSA and Count)

SIC	Industry	N	Most Innovative MSA
3573	Electronic Computing Machinery	787	San Jose (166); Boston (48); Los Angeles (48); Anaheim (35)
3823	Process Control Instruments	464	Boston (45); Philadelphia (31); Chicago (26)
3662	Radio/TV Equipment	311	San Jose (58); Boston (25); New York (17); Los Angeles (14)
3674	Semiconductors	168	San Jose (53); Boston (10); Dallas (10); Los Angeles (10)
3825	Instruments to Measure Electricity	114	San Jose (22); Boston (20)
2834	Pharmaceuticals	116	Newark (27); Philadelphia (11); New York (10)
3842	Surgical Appliances	101	Newark (20); Nassau-Suffolk (10); Bergen-Passaic (8); Philadelphia (6)
3494	Values and Pipe Fittings	81	Anaheim (6); Los Angeles (6); Cleveland (6); Cincinnati (5)
3679	Electronic Components	72	San Jose (19); Anaheim (7); Boston (6)
3561	Pumps and Pumping Equipment	68	Philadelphia (8); Aurora-Elgin (7)
3861	Photographic Equipment	57	Rochester (8); Minneapolis (7)
3579	Office Machines	54	New York (11); Philadelphia (7); Stamford (5)
3622	Industrial Controls	51	San Jose (7); Cleveland (4)
3841	Surgical and Medical Instruments	51	Nassau-Suffolk (10); Bergen-Passaic (8)

Credit: Audretsch, David, The Innovative Advantage of US Cities, 2002.

Audretsch and Feldman, in Table 3 below, show a relationship between technology industrial clusters and mean industry innovation per 100,000 workers in each industrial cluster, in each of the important metro regions.

We add our insight to the two tables by Audretsch and Feldman, that those technology innovation workers no longer exist in the former U. S. innovative metro regions because the cause of innovation in those metro regions was tacit knowledge creation and diffusion that previously existed in the metro regional intermediate demand clusters that were moved to China, after 2002.

Chapter 3 Table 3. Innovation in Science Based Industry Clusters.

Table 3: Innovation in Science-Based Industry Clusters

Cluster	Prominent Cities	Mean Industry Innovations per 100,000 workers
Agra-Business	Atlanta	92.40
	Dallas	41.15
	Chicago	33.03
	St. Louis	91.74
Chemical Engineering	Dallas	38.09
	Minneapolis	66.67
	San Francisco	43.89
	Wilmington	85.47
Office Machinery	Anaheim-Santa Ana	92.59
	Minneapolis	31.86
	Rochester	72.20
	Stanford	68.40
Industrial Machinery	Anaheim-Santa Ana	54.95
	Cincinnati	66.01
	Cleveland	141.51
	Passaic, NJ	90.90
High-Tech Computing	Boston	73.89
	Houston	62.08
	San Jose	44.88
	Minneapolis	181.74
Biomedical	Boston	38.71
	Cleveland	68.76
	Dallas	35.22
	New York	188.07

Source: Feldman and Audretsch (1999)

Credit: Audretsch, David B., Feldman, Maryann P., Innovation in Cities: Science-based Diversity, Specialization and Localized Competition, European Economic Review, 1999.

The geographic impact of job loss from increased trade with China is described in Figure 1b, below, from Autor et al.

Autor describes commuting zones within 50 miles of a metro region. He describes that the highest rates of job loss were in the Rust Belt and Sun Belt large metro regions.

The initial job losses were the direct immediate loss of jobs in manufacturing and then later, the subsequent indirect job losses in the metro regional intermediate demand industries that serviced and supplied the primary manufacturing industrial sectors.

Both the direct and indirect job losses were compounded by the induced loss of jobs and incomes, as the regional jobs and incomes multipliers were destroyed by globalization trade patterns.

Chapter 3 Figure 1b, Trade Exposure by Commuting Zone.

The total direct, indirect and induced job losses took place over an extended period of time, generally from 1992 to 2002.

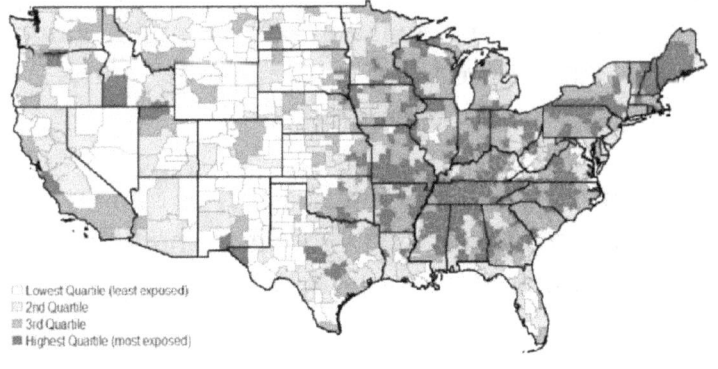

Figure 1b. Trade Exposure by Commuting Zone, 1990-2007

Citation Figure 1b. Autor, David H., Dorn, David, Hanson, Gordon H., The Geography Of Trade And Technology Shocks In The United States, NBER Working Paper 18940, 2013.

The map in 1b describes the economic relationship between metro regions, and the surrounding rural areas, where citizens lived, and commuted to work, within the metro industrial clusters.

After the intermediate input industrial sectors were moved to China and India, both metro and rural regional economies suffered permanent economic damage.

As Autor et al., write,

"Growth in import exposure per worker differs by more than factor of six across Census divisions, increasing, for example, by an average of $4,000 per worker per decade in the East South Central division between 1990 and 2007 versus a relatively modest $620 per worker per decade in the Mountain division…As expected, many manufacturing-intensive regions appear among the most trade-exposed CZs, including substantial parts of the Northeast and South Central U.S., where labor-intensive goods manufacturing, such as furniture, rubber products, toys, apparel, footwear and leather goods, is [was] concentrated."

They note the dual negative economic effect of trade with China occurring at the same time as the implementation of computer integrated manufacturing techniques.

They provide a second map, 1a below, which combines the negative technology automation effect with the job loss trade effect of trade with China.

We would add our analysis to both of the maps that the loss of workers in manufacturing, resulting from automation, compounds the destruction to the tacit technology knowledge creation networks, because those workers, especially the high skill industrial workers, were a source of knowledge when they met each other in bars and in trade shows, to discuss how their regional economies functioned, and subsequently, left their jobs to create new technology ventures.

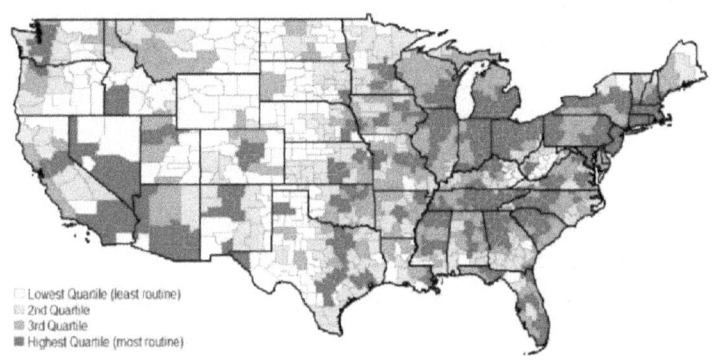

Figure 1a. Routine Employment Share by Commuting Zone in 1990

Citation Figure 1a: Autor, David H., Dorn, David, Hanson, Gordon H., The Geography Of Trade And Technology Shocks In The United States, NBER Wor 18940, 2013.

In a second research effort on the economic consequences of trade with China, Autor, et al., estimate the total loss of jobs in the two decades after 1990, in the metro commuting zones.

They write,

"Rising exposure [to trade with China] increases [U. S.] unemployment, lowers labor force participation, and reduces wages in local labor markets. Conservatively, it explains one-quarter of the contemporaneous aggregate decline in U.S. manufacturing employment. Transfer benefits payments for unemployment, disability, retirement, and healthcare also rise sharply in exposed [commuting zone] labor markets... For the mainland U.S. working-age population, these estimates imply a supply-shock driven net reduction in U.S. manufacturing employment of 548 thousand workers between 1990 and 2000 and a further reduction of 982 thousand workers between 2000 and 2007."

Our additional insight is that those 1.5 million U. S. workers are no longer creating and diffusing technical knowledge, and are no longer creating new technology ventures, in metro regional economies.

The intermediate demand industrial production networks, which were the incubator nurseries for technology innovation in U. S. metro regions, no longer exist in the United States, and from the perspective of the authoritarian one-world government of the ruling class, it is essential that those tacit knowledge networks never again exist in the American society.

The spread of tacit knowledge cannot be controlled by the large corporations, and uncontrolled tacit knowledge creation is a threat to the smooth operation of the New World Order in directing the global flow of income to themselves.

The key causal factor of American new venture creation in tacit knowledge creation is an individualist social moral value that allows any individual to create a new venture and to obtain future rewards in profits and income.

That type of individualist social culture is a threat to the smooth operation of the New World Order authoritarian structure that directs income to the global ruling class, which is why the totalitarian collectivist society of China is so attractive as a model to the global corporate ruling class, in implementing a world where all citizens look and act the same.

The implementation of that future collectivist global society depends on corporate control over technology innovation inside of the vertically integrated global value chains, where codified technological knowledge is insulated from open, uncontrolled flows of tacit knowledge in the 350 metro regional intermediate demand industrial clusters that existed, prior to 1992.

Chapter 3 Topic Category #3. Decline in national economic growth rates caused by declining capital investment and reinvestment of corporate profits in the domestic U. S. economy.

The economic term most often used by academic scholars to describe the decline in economic growth rates in the U. S. economy, after 1992, is "decline of business dynamism."

For example, Akcigit et al., note that most of the academic community of economist agree that,

"The [scholarly economic] literature has more or less agreed that there is a broad weakening of business dynamism in the United States." (Akcigit, Ufuk, Ates Sina,, Ten Facts On Declining Business Dynamism And Lessons From Endogenous Growth Theory, Working Paper 25755, NBER, 2019.).

The term "endogenous growth theory," means economic growth caused by factors that are internal to the U.S. domestic economy, such as the rate of private capital investment in new firms, or new production techniques.

In their research on the decline of domestic economic growth rates, they cite the important missing ingredient of knowledge diffusion, which combines with the lack of free entry of new ventures in the economy as the primary reason they cite for lack of business dynamism.

They write,

"We demonstrate theoretically that a decline in knowledge diffusion implies higher concentration with higher markups and profits, in line with empirical findings in the literature (Facts 1, 2, and 3). It also generates a decrease in the labor share of output (Fact 4).… the decline in the intensity of knowledge diffusion is the only margin [factor] that can explain all observed trends both qualitatively and quantitatively."

In other words, of all the possible factors they investigated that could cause a decline in domestic economic growth, the single greatest factor that explained all of the observed trends of economic decline was a decline in knowledge diffusion.

They place all of the possible factors that could cause a decline in U. S. economic growth into a statistical method to disaggregate the different causes of economic decline, in Table 6 below.

Under their topic category of lower knowledge diffusion, they describe the links and relationships between lower knowledge diffusion and 3 other important factors of economic decline.

These other 3 factors are the power to markup prices over marginal costs, (84% statistical relationship), increased rate of both market profits and pure profits (78% statistical relationship, and increased monopoly concentration of corporate revenues (96%).

Chapter 3 Table 6. Quanitative Experimental Results.

Table 6: Quantitative experiment results (contributions as in equation 30)

Channel i	Lower corporate tax	Higher R&D subsidies	Higher entry cost	Lower knowledge diffusion
Entry	-8.2%	-0.4%	17.9%	50.6%
Labor	-9.0%	-7.7%	3.6%	78.7%
Markup	7.6%	10.8%	3.6%	84.2%
Profit	-9.0%	-7.7%	3.6%	78.7%
Concentration	4.3%	7.1%	-7.2%	96.2%
Young firms	-13.2%	-7.7%	-1.3%	71.2%
Prod. gap	7.2%	10.5%	3.5%	83.8%
Reallocation	-6.9%	0.2%	13.6%	48.5%
Dispersion	32.7%	29.2%	-44.6%	136%

Notes: Percentage values measure the share of the contribution from the specific channel to the total model-generated deviation between 1980 and 2010. Negative values mean that adding the specific channel moves the model-generated variable in the opposite of the empirical counterpart. A value larger than 100% means that the difference between the hypothetical and empirical paths is larger than the observed variation.

Citation Table 6: taken from Innovation And Trade Policy In A Globalized World, Ufuk Akcigit, Sina, Ates, Giammario, Impullitti, NBER Working Paper 24543, 2018.

We extend their conclusion about lower knowledge diffusion by broadening the term to include both knowledge creation, and knowledge diffusion, which we place into the theoretical structure of technology evolution, which occurred in the intermediate demand networks in the 350 U. S. metro regions, prior to 1992. (Vass, Laurie Thomas, The Theory of Technology Evolution, Gabby Press, 2019.).

Akcigit et al., cite the obvious, common sense relationship between the rate of private capital investment in the domestic economy, and the rate of economic growth.

Private capital investment in the U. S. economy, prior to 1992, was derived from a portion of corporate profits.

In that prior time period, as profits in U. S. corporations went up, generally there was a stable rate of profit investment, which would eventually lead to an increased rate of economic growth, generally about 3 – 5 years after the initial investment.

After 1992, the rate of U. S. corporate profits went up, but the rate of capital investment went down, leading to a prolonged decline in the rate of U. S. economic growth, or more commonly, business dynamism..

Profits made by corporations that led to capital investment in the U. S. domestic economy were shifted to investments in foreign countries in the location of the vertically integrated global value chain affiliates.

The response to the decline of capital investment by the U. S. Federal Reserve Bank and the U. S. Department of the Treasury was to increase government spending on so-called public investments, which did not generate economic growth, but contributed to the creation of asset bubbles in real estate and hard assets, primarily owned by members of the ruling social classes.

Akcigit et al., explain,

"The profit share of GDP has been on the rise, as shown in Figure 3. Some recent papers investigate the implications of this trend. Gutiérrez and Philippon (2016) argue that higher within-industry concentration measured in terms of profitability is associated with weak investment. This result resonates with the findings of Eggertsson et al. (2018), who explore mechanisms that can give rise to higher profitability and lower investment-to-output ratio, along with several other changes. In a different approach, Aghion et al. (2018) explore the link between innovation and top income inequality in the United States and show evidence of the tight association between innovative activity per capita and profit share of output."

They provide a graphic, in Figure 6 below, to describe the increase in U. S. corporate profits after 1992.

Chapter 3 Figure 6. Profits as Percent of U. S. GDP.

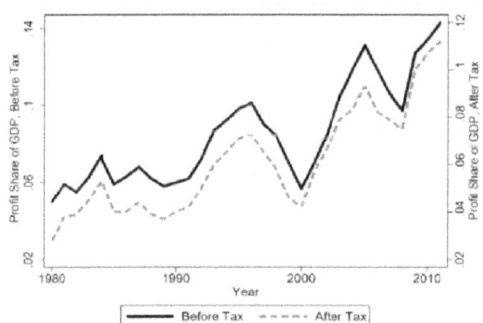

Source: Authors' own calculation using the BEA NIPA Table 1.15. The figure shows corporate profits of nonfinancial domestic U.S. firms adjusted for inventory valuation and capital consumption.

Figure 3: PROFITS AS A FRACTION OF GDP OVER TIME.

Figure 6. Graphic From Akcigit, Ufuk, Ates, Sina T., Ten Facts On Declining Business Dynamism And Lessons From Endogenous Growth Theory, Working Paper 25755, NBER, 2019.

The rate of increase in U. S. corporate profits is especially evident after 2001, when China entered the WTO.

Much of the increase in profits, after 1992, is related to the portion of profits contributed by "pure profit," which is the portion of profits derived from internal corporate margin price markups on intermediate goods that are not subjected to competitive market forces inside the vertically integrated global value chains

Pure profits, as a percentage of total U. S. GDP, increased from 3% of GDP, in 1985, to 17% of GDP in 2015.

The labor share [middle and working class] of income in the GDP declined from 63% in 1985 to 57% in 2015.

The capital share of GDP, which is the portion of profits was previously derived from sales in the U. S. intermediate demand competitive market, declined to 17% of GDP, indicating that global corporations replaced that prior part of profits with the portion of profits derived from "pure profits" in the global trade economy.

Chapter 3 Table 4. Factor Shares of Income.

Factor share	1985	2015	Change (%)
Labor Share (%)	63	57	- 6
Capital Share (%)	26	17	- 9
Tax Share (%)	8	9	+1
Pure Profit Share (%)	3	17	+14

Table 1: Factor shares. 5-year moving averages

Table 4 Graphic from Eggertsson, Gauti B. et al., Kaldor And Piketty's Facts: The Rise Of Monopoly Power In The United States, NBER Working Paper 24287, 2018.

Eggertsson, et al., show in Figure 5, that the rate of investment of gross profits in the U. S. domestic economy declined dramatically, after 2000.

Chapter 3 Figure 7. Net Investment.

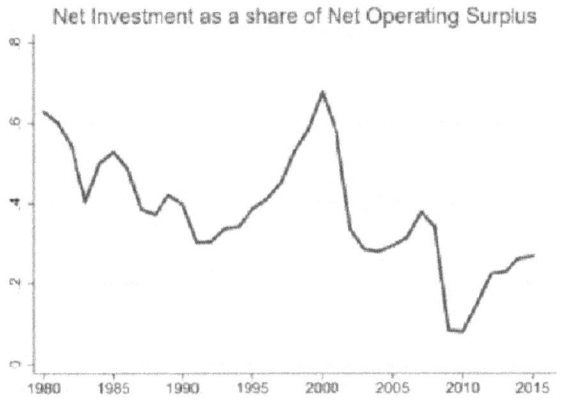

Figure 5: Net investment as a share of net operating surplus

Figure 7 Graphic from Eggertsson, Gauti B., et al., Kaldor And Piketty's Facts: The Rise Of Monopoly Power In The United States, NBER Working Paper 24287, 2018.

In a sophisticated statistical method, Loecker and Eeckhout show the relationship between the increase in the rate of pure profits from markup pricing in intermediate demand inputs and the decline in the rate of corporate capital investment.

In their Figure 8, they show that as corporate pure profit markups go up, the rate of domestic capital investment goes down.

Chapter 3 Figure 8. Investment Rate vs. Markup.

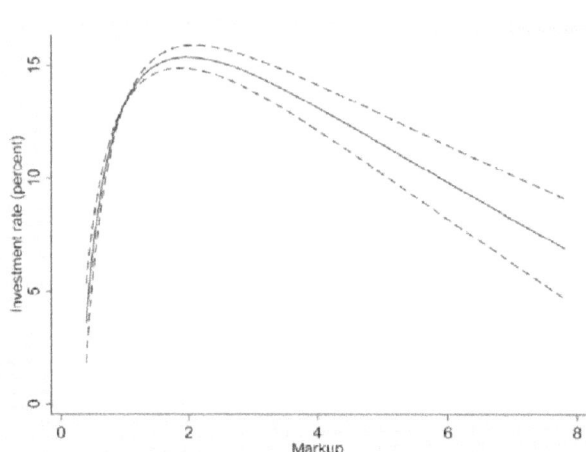

Figure 8. Investment Rate vs. Markup

Note: Figure reports fitted value of investment rate vs. markup across sample range of markup based on estimates reported in Table 2 (column 1). Dashes indicate 90 percent confidence interval.

Figure 8 graphic from Loecker, Jan De, Eeckhout, Jan, Global Market Power, NBER Working Paper 24768, 2018.

In the initial phase of globalization, in 1992, the markups over marginal cost were modest, in the range of 2%, and investment initially increased during the initial economic phase, leading to a lower Nash equilibrium in the global economy.

As markups over marginal costs increased, over 2%, the rate of corporate investment declined.

Díez, et al., describe the time lag between the rise in markups over marginal costs and the subsequent decline in capital investment.

They write,

"At higher levels of markups, however, increases in markups become associated with lower investment, as indicated by the negative coefficient in the second row. This finding is consistent with the "inverted-U" relation between competition and investment posited by Aghion and others (2005), where pre-innovation rents rise faster than post-innovation rents at high levels of market power, implying weaker incentives to invest…. As of 2016, higher markups are associated with lower investment for 8, 17, and 6 percent of U.S. publicly listed firms, across the three specifications, respectively. In contrast, no firms had a negative association between higher markups and investment as of 1980." (Díez, Federico J., Leigh, Daniel and Tambunlertchai, Suchanan, Global Market Power and its Macroeconomic Implications, IMF Working Paper, WP/18/137, 2018.).

They also cite the relationship between the increase in pure profits and the decline of middle and working class incomes, as a portion of GDP.

They write,

"the relation between higher markups and the labor share features a negative and statistically significant coefficient estimate of ♯ (column 1, row 1) and the relation is monotonic. As the level of market concentration increases, the negative relation between markups and the labor share grows stronger. Overall, these results are consistent with the conjecture of Autor and others (2017) that a rise in market power reduces the labor share."

Currently, markups over marginal costs in intermediate demand production in U. S. corporations are 67% higher than they were in 1992.

Eggertsson, et al., write

"De Loecker and Eeckhout (2017) use firm level data and techniques from industrial organization to estimate a new time series of markups. These results show a massive increase in markups, from 18% in 1980 to 67% in the present, a much larger increase than our results." (Eggertsson, Gauti B. et al., Kaldor And Piketty's Facts: The Rise Of Monopoly Power In The United States, NBER Working Paper 24287, 2018.).

Eggertsson, et al., are confused and puzzled by this theoretical anomaly in the relationship between historic rates of profits and subsequent levels of investment of working capital, derived from corporate sales in the finished goods market.

They write,

"While 50% of net operating revenue was used for investment in the early 1980s, it has fallen to about 25% in the present. Net investment as a share of gross value added [profit] shows a similar decline. This decrease in investment is somewhat puzzling, given historically low interest rates."

We help them solve this seeming puzzle by explaining that the higher markups and declining rates of investment are an indication of both the increase in pure profits, as a portion of

U. S. GDP, which is not being reinvested, and also an indication of the increasing monopoly power of large corporation in controlling the New World Order, as more and more parts of the vertically integrated global value chains escape the force of price competition in competitive markets.

The low interest rates and increased money supply that Eggertsson, et al., cite are the Fed's effort to fill in the capital gap of missing investment capital with superficial government spending and monetary policy that does not produce real economic growth.

Chapter 3 Topic Category #4. Corporate monopoly pricing power and the increase of pure monopoly profits.

The economic power of global corporations to set prices has eliminated the theoretical justification for the concept of price competition leading to a general equilibrium.

The logical justification of the welfare benefits for both the Heckscher-Ohlin theory of global trade, and the theory of general equilibrium of economic stability related to price competition, are no longer valid economic concepts to explain vertically integrated global value chains.

The economic term for this corporate economic power to set prices in order to obtain profits from setting price markups is "pure profits."

The ability of large corporations to obtain pure profits is an indicator of global corporate monopoly power in the vertically integrated global value chains.

Antras and Chor explain why the former theoretical frameworks are no longer valid. As we described earlier, the older theories of trade and equilibrium were based upon the independent welfare sovereignty of nations.

With the corporate monopoly power of price markups, large corporations by-pass market competitive forces through their long-term legal contracts with foreign trade affiliates.

Antras and Chor write,

"World trade flows are dominated by a small number of large firms that actively participate in GVCs and that capture large market shares in their sector's exports and imports. In more plain words, it is not countries or 'country-sectors' that participate in GVCs, but it is rather individual firms in those country-sectors that choose to do so…An extreme version of this type of relational contracting arises when parties involved in a GVC altogether by-pass the market mechanism and decide to transact within firm boundaries..the internalization of transactions in a GVC is just one of the many organizational responses to the contractual vagaries associated with cross-border transactions." (Antràs, Pol, Chor, Davin, Global Value Chains, NBER Working Paper 28549, 2021.).

Instead of the prediction of general equilibrium theory, the global corporate power to set prices leads to the social class polarization and macro economic instability, whose frequency of recessions is increasing over time, from 1992, to the present.

Figure 9, below, describes that the increase in average corporate markups is related to the concentration of GDP market share of sales in a very narrow spectrum of large corporations.

Chapter 3 Figure 9. Evolution of Average Markups.

Figure 1: The Evolution of Average Markups (1960 - 2014). Average Markup is weighted by marketshare of sales in the sample.

Figure 9 Graphic From Loecker, Jan De, Eeckhout, Jan, The Rise of Market Power and the Macroeconomic Implications, NBER Working Paper 23687, 2017.

De Loecker and Eeckout show, in Figure 10, below, that at the 90th percentile of market share, the largest corporations enjoy a markup of 2.5 times price over marginal costs.

Chapter 3 Figure 10. Evolution of Income Distribution

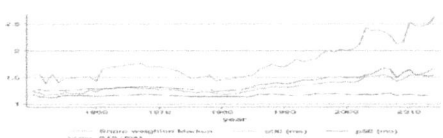

Figure 3: The Evolution of the Distribution (Percentiles) of Markups (1950 - 2014). (The percentiles of the Markup distribution are weighted by marketshare of sales in the sample.)

Figure 10 Graphic From Loecker, Jan De, Eeckhout, Jan, The Rise of Market Power and the Macroeconomic Implications, NBER Working Paper 23687, 2017.

In other words, the greatest portion of global corporate monopoly price power occurs in a very small set of very large corporations.

In Figure 11, below, Autor, et al., describe that the top 20 largest corporations have
the same level of market concentration, in 2010, as the top 4 largest corporations. The figure describes the rapid rise in monopoly power in U. S. corporations, after 2002.

Chapter 3 Figure 11. Market Concentration.

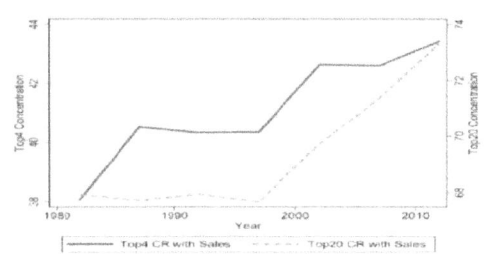

Citation Figure 11. Autor, et al., 2017 b. p. 79.
The vertically integrated global value chains are comprised of a very small set of foreign value chain affiliates, who are locked into long-term legal contracts with the U. S. senior large corporate value chain partner.

Zhang notes in his research,

"In short, GVCs have increasingly "stretched thin" with only a few large firms delivering customized products at each stage. Indeed, my data show that over 80% of US public firms have less than 6 value chain partners that are also public firms. Furthermore, their suppliers, if more than 1, often provide different products or services…Indeed, my analysis shows that among public firms in the US, the average length of value chain relationships is over 4 years, and more than 80% of them are longer than one year, the typical threshold for stable GVC linkages (Alfaro-Urena, Manelici and Vasquez, 2022)." (Zhang, Hao, Commerce, Coalitions, and Global Value Chains: Coordinated and Collective Lobbying on Trade, SSRN, 2023.).

Diez, et al., also describe the relationship between the large corporation's power to markup prices over marginal costs and monopoly power in a very small set of U. S. corporations.

They write,

"For 2016, the U.S. firms in the sample have sales equivalent to 79 percent of U.S. GDP. We find a strong positive relation between markups and broad measures of profitability at the firm level, suggesting that the rise in measured markups has been associated with increased market power. On average, for firms in the United States and other advanced economies, a 10 percentage point rise in markups is associated with, respectively, 19 and 13 percentage point increases in the ratio of dividends to sales…As of 2016, higher markups are associated with lower investment for 8, 17, and 6 percent of U.S. publicly listed firms, across the three specifications, respectively." (Díez, Federico J., Leigh, Daniel, Tambunlertchai, Suchanan, Global Market Power and its Macroeconomic Implications, IMF Working Paper, WP/18/137, 2018.).

The research of Teresa Fort suggests that out of the total 243,700 domestic U. S. global manufacturing firms, in 2017, that only 1200 corporations dominate total global sales in the vertically integrated global value chains.

Fort writes,

"Of the 243,700 US manufacturing firms, (in 2017), only 1,700 have majority-owned foreign establishments. Among these 1,700 multinationals, 1,200 firms own US and foreign manufacturing plants, versus 350 firms with just domestic plants, and only 150 firms with exclusively foreign in-house manufacturing. Firms with both domestic and foreign manufacturing plants are thus the most prevalent type of US multinational manufacturing enterprise…(The) 1,200 out of the total of 243,700 global (GVC) firms had global sales of $6.7 trillion (in 2017). (Fort, Teresa C., The Changing Firm And Country Boundaries Of Us Manufacturers In Global Value Chains, NBER Working Paper 31319, 2023.).

Fort notes that 150 large U. S. corporations do not produce any goods within the U. S. domestic economy, because they only maintain production facilities in foreign affiliate nations.

Fort describes these 150 corporations as "factoryless" firms because their major work in the U. S. domestic economy is to design the technology of their products in the U. S. and then, to conduct all other manufacturing operations in foreign affiliate nations.

To recall the earlier "smile diagram" of the Duke researchers of vertically integrated global value chains, these 150 corporations conduct operations in the top left portion of the smile in technology research and development.

Fort explains,

"Factoryless goods producers differ from in-house manufacturers because they outsource all physical transformation activities to other firms. Although this type of firm includes examples as prominent as Apple, Nike, and Qualcomm, they are hard or even impossible to identify using standard datasets…a majority of factoryless goods producers in 2017 design the goods they sell, and those that design are more likely to contract with foreign suppliers. These patterns are all consistent with the premise that factoryless goods producers tend to focus on pre-production manufacturing stages [top left of the smaile] in the United States, while locating physical transformation tasks [bottom of the smile] outside both the firm and the country."

All of the net sales revenues of these large factoryless corporations are pure profits from marginal cost markups in the intermediate and final demand production networks.

These 150 corporations successfully lobby Congress for tax benefits and pro-free trade legislation, yet they contribute nothing of economic value in the way of jobs or income for U. S. middle and working class citizens.

The welfare contribution of manufacturing in the U. S. economy, prior to 1992, occurred in the intermediate demand networks in 350 metro regions, and the welfare benefits were due to jobs, income and tacit knowledge creation in those metro regions.

Those intermediate demand networks were moved to China and India, and no longer exist in the domestic U. S. economy.

Boehm, et al., note that over 90% of all imports by large U. S. corporations are in the intermediate demand networks that formerly were produced in the U. S. domestic economy. (Boehm, Christoph E. Flaaen, Aaron, Pandalai-Nayar, Nitya, Multinationals, Offshoring And The Decline Of U.S. Manufacturing, NBER Working Paper 25824 2019.).

They write,

"We find that foreign sourcing of intermediate inputs is a striking characteristic of multinationals. Over 90% of overall U.S. intermediate imports in our sample are imported by multinationals. Moreover, the fraction of U.S. multinationals sourcing inputs from developing countries nearly doubled from 1993 to 2011."

In the political globalism operation of the New World Order, the large corporations whose headquarters are located in the United States, benefit from the military protection of the U. S. military to protect global trade routes, and enforce U. S. economic dominance in the Western Trading lliance, and also benefit financially by sales to corporations in the U. S. military-industrial complex.

The income that was previously distributed to U. S. middle and working class citizens in the intermediate demand networks no longer is obtained by U. S. citizens because the large corporations have successfully diverted 90% of the intermediate demand income, to themselves.

The increase in normal market profits, and the increase in pure profits, after 1992, in the vertically integrated global value chains are not re-invested in the domestic U. S. economy.

Most of the overseas profits are never repatriated to the domestic economy because the corporate Congressional lobbying effort by large corporations makes it more lucrative to book the profits overseas, in order to avoid paying U. S. corporate income taxes.

Those overseas profits show up in U. S. GDP statistics as an increase in domestic economic GDP, but that part of the U. S. GDP does not contribute to the financial welfare of middle and working class citizens.

The diversion of income from the American middle class to the corporate ruling class increases income inequality in America, which provides the context for fomenting political race hatred and social class polarization to implement the authoritarian police state.

In our analysis of vertically integrated global value chains, the U. S. military protects and enforces global trading rules of the Western trading alliance, while the authoritarian police state enforces citizen obedience to the new levels of income inequality, lower standards of living, poverty and homelessness, for middle and working class citizens.

De Loecker and Eeckhout explain that the corporate markups over marginal costs in the intermediate demand networks increases income inequality.

They write,

"This establishes that higher markups lead to higher [pure] profits, and that they [the markups] are not driven by higher overhead [marginal production] costs. This further confirms the fact that the increase in markups brings about a [income] distributional change with more of the surplus [profits] going to the owners of the firms and less to the workers." (Loecker, Jan De, Eeckhout, Jan, Global Market Power, NBER Working Paper 24768, 2018.).

They explain why canonical economic theory is no longer valid in explaining the transition of the U. S. domestic economy to the New World Order globalist economy.

They explain,

"In the absence of competitive [market price] pressure, firms grab market power which in turn allows them to sell goods at higher prices. Market power naturally leads to redistribution of resources [income] from workers and consumers to the owners of firms: the profit share is higher, [in GDP statistics] while the labor share to workers [in GDP] is lower and the goods are sold at higher prices to consumers [inflation]. Market power also has welfare effects: due to higher prices, consumption is lower and a suboptimal number of consumers are priced out of the market [into poverty and homelessness] (Harberger (1954)), and market power stifles innovation and investment (Aghion, Bloom, Blundell, Griffith, and Howitt (2005))."

The economic damage to middle and working class citizens is not simply the permanent loss of income, jobs, and personal savings.

The diversion of profits from the domestic U. S. economy to the location of the foreign affiliates permanently destroys the ability of the U. S. economy to generate new jobs in new technology ventures.

Since 2001, the rate of job creation in new ventures has not be sufficient to overcome the loss of jobs in the former U. S. economy.

As we describe in the next category of economic destruction, all net new jobs are created by new firms, less than 5 years old. That part of the U. S. economy has been destroyed by the implementation of the New World Order globalist regime.

Haltiwanger, et al., in Figure 7 below, describe the impressive rate of decline in U. S. firm entry and exit rates, especially after 2002.

Chapter 3 Figure 12. Firm Entry and Exit.

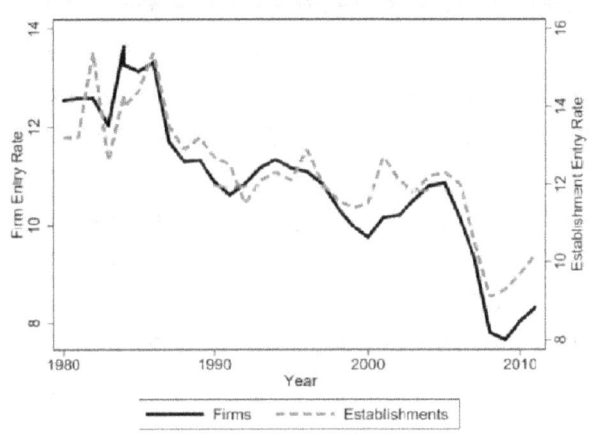

Source: Authors' calculations from BDS database [see also Decker et al. (2016)].

Figure 7: FIRM ENTRY AND EXIT RATES IN THE UNITED STATES.

Figure 12 from Haltiwanger, John C., Jarmin, Ron S., Miranda, Javier, Who Creates Jobs? Small Vs. Large Vs. Young, NBER Working Paper 16300, 2010.

Chapter 3 Topic Category #5. Loss of U. S. technological innovation related to the loss of U. S. domestic intermediate input production.

Prior to 1992, technological innovation in the U. S. created the conditions for entrepreneurial new venture creation, as workers left their old jobs to start new ventures.

New ventures create new flows of future income in new intermediate demand networks, which did not exist in the old economic structure.

The new intermediate demand markets create entirely new future markets, where the new finished good in the final demand markets are sold.

The creation of new future markets disrupts the flow of income to incumbent large corporations, who depend on the status quo arrangement of political and economic power to continue to divert global monopoly profits to themselves.

The key important strategy for large corporations to maintain the flow of monopoly profits derived from the vertically integrated global value chains is to control the creation and diffusion of tacit technological knowledge, so that new technology ventures are not created by nascent American entrepreneurs.

Without the ability to control the pace and direction of technological innovation to suit their internal needs, the large corporations are vulnerable to the forces of "creative destruction." (Schumpeter, Joseph, Capitalism, Socialism, and Democracy, 1942.).

By eliminating the former metro regional tacit knowledge networks, by moving those intermediate demand networks to China, the large corporations successfully crippled the entrepreneurial rate of new venture creation in the domestic U. S. economy.

The police state authoritarian control over U. S. citizens by the large corporations is a necessary component of the New World Order to maintain the status quo distribution of income inequality that results from the control over the pace and direction of technology innovation.

Prior to 1992, the high rate of new venture creation in 350 U. S. metro regions was a result of the tacit knowledge flows within each intermediate demand networks, primarily in the nine high technology industrial clusters in each region.

Metro regions that contained extensive inter-industry relationships, experienced high rates of new venture creation which resulted from high rates of tacit knowledge creation and diffusion.

We use North Carolina as an example to explain the relationship between tacit knowledge flows in intermediate demand networks and a high rate of entrepreneurial new venture creation.

Feser and Renski applied factor analysis to the intermediate demand coefficients of a modified national U. S. input-output table to derive the nine high technology clusters in the North Carolina economy. (Feser, Edward J., Renski, Henry, High-Tech Clusters in North Carolina, North Carolina Board of Science and Technology, 2000.).

Each cell in the modified input-output table contains a numerical coefficient that describes three underlying economic relationships related to transactions among member firms in each industrial cluster.

The first relationship is a price-based relationship of sales of intermediate goods among member firms, within the major metro regions of the North Carolina economy.

The numerical coefficient of the second relationship describes a legal contractual relationship among member firms that codifies the social/institutional legal relationships underlying each sales transaction.

The third, and most important relationship, of the numerical coefficient describes the existence of a flow of tacit knowledge between the staff of the firms engaged in an input-output transaction.

The research of Bergman and Renzi uncovered technological affinities in production among the electronic sectors and biotech sectors located in the Research Triangle metro region.

The Research Triangle Region experienced one of the nation's highest rates of new venture creation, over the 30 year period from about 1970 to 2000.

As a way of illustrating this concept of tacit knowledge flows represented by numerical coefficients in an input output table, we use a hypothetical model provided by Table 1 below, of the economy of China.

Chapter 3 Table 7. Basic Structure of Input Output Table.

Table 1. Basic structure of an economic input-output table in China.

		Industrial use				Final use		Foreign
		Sector 1	Sector 2	...	Sector n	Consumptive	Gross capital formation	Export
Intermediate inputs	Sector 1	$z^L_{1,1}$	$z^L_{1,2}$		$z^L_{1,n}$	d^L_1		e_1
	Sector 2	$z^L_{2,1}$	$z^L_{2,2}$		$z^L_{2,n}$	d^L_2		e_2
	...							
	Sector n	$z^L_{n,1}$	$z^L_{n,2}$		$z^L_{n,n}$	d^L_n		e_n
Imported industrial inputs	Sector 1	$z^I_{1,1}$	$z^I_{1,2}$		$z^I_{1,n}$	d^I_1		
	Sector 2	$z^I_{2,1}$	$z^I_{2,2}$		$z^I_{2,n}$	d^I_2		
	...							
	Sector n	$z^I_{n,1}$	$z^I_{n,2}$		$z^I_{n,n}$	d^I_n		
Net economic Inputs (Value added)	Wages, taxes, surplus, etc.	w_1	w_2		w_n			

https://z-cm.blogspot.com/2014/12/input-output-tables.html

This very simplified model only describes intermediate production relationships between two industrial sectors in China.

Sector 2, in the model, buys intermediate products from Sector 1, described by coefficient Z 21. Those firms in industrial sector 1 and 2, shown in the top left quadrant are geographically located in China.

Those firms may be members of an extended vertically integrated global value chain, but the intermediate inputs that they buy and sell to each other are located in China.

The income and employment multiplier effects of the intermediate trade between sector 1 and 2, occurs in China.

The Chinese executives and scientific staff in sector 1 and 2 meet with each other and share tacit knowledge about how their economy operates and how to resolve issues related to the legal contractual relationship, evidenced by the coefficient, $Z\,21$.

In China, the tacit knowledge creation and diffusion does not lead to the creation of entrepreneurial new technology ventures by the executive and scientific staff because all decisions about capital investment are made by the ruling class elites in the Chinese Communist Party.

China, like all collectivist totalitarian societies in the world, does not allow an entrepreneurial individualist moral social value for the creation of new ventures.

Prior to 2002, those intermediate goods, described by coefficient $Z\,21$, were made in the United States, and the coefficient would have described knowledge flows between the scientific and engineering staff in the metro regional production relationships between U. S. industrial sectors 1 and 2.

In the case of the Research Triangle of North Carolina, the high rates of technology knowledge creation and diffusion caused a high rate of entrepreneurial new venture creation because the social institutional moral values in the United States encourage entrepreneurship.

After 2002, those hypothetical intermediate demand sectors were moved by large corporations from the U. S. to China.

The former tacit knowledge networks in the U. S. metro regions were destroyed.

Returning to Table 7 of the hypothetical input-output model of China, the coefficient in the lower left quadrant Z^{21}, describes foreign inputs from sector 1 that are imported from firms outside of China and purchased by Chinese sector 2.

The firms in the lower left quadrant are members of a vertically integrated global value chain, with Chinese firms acting as the foreign affiliates of the parent global corporation which is using Chinese labor to produce intermediate goods for trans- shipment of the semi-finished goods to other locations for final assembly.

The technology of the parent corporation is codified, proprietary knowledge with very limited "spill-over" effects to the Chinese affiliate firms.

At each step of production of intermediated demand in the Chinese production, the U. S. parent corporation obtains pure profits, as value added, until the finished good is finally sold in the global final demand market.

In the vertically integrated global value chains, the large U. S. corporations engage in "factoryless" production, represented by the top left corner of the Duke smile diagram.

In other words, the technology innovation and research and development in the global value chains now occurs inside the U. S. corporate global value chain, and the actual production occurs in the intermediate demand production networks in China.

The Chinese command and control collectivist society steals the U. S. technology and invests their share of value-added by creating Chinese firms which contribute to the nine Chinese "champion" industrial sectors in China.

The stolen U. S. technology does not lead to entrepreneurial new venture creation in China because there is no social or political concept of individualism in China.

The stolen U. S. technology does not lead to entrepreneurial new venture creation in U. S. metro regions because the tacit knowledge creation and diffusion networks were destroyed when the large corporations moved the intermediate demand production networks to China.

This New World Order technology transfer process constitutes a win-win-win for both the Chinese communist regime and the U. S. parent corporations in the vertically integrated global value chains.

First, the U. S. corporations destroy the source of tacit technology flows in the U. S., and cripple the threat posed by technology innovation in entrepreneurial ventures in the U. S. which would disrupt the status quo distribution of income to the large corporations.

By eliminating the threat of uncontrolled technology innovation derived from tacit knowledge flows, the large U. S. corporations can more easily control the pace and direction of technology innovation to suit their own internal corporate goals of extending the life of their proprietary technology.

Second, the U. S. corporations obtain pure profits by raising prices on intermediate goods over marginal costs, currently at 67% pure profits over marginal costs of production.

Third, the Chinese regime steals the U. S. technology for free, and then shares profits with U. S. parent corporations from the sale of intermediate goods, denoted by the coefficient $Z^\wedge$, back to the U. S. corporations, at the legally established price for the intermediate goods.

The inter-industry relationships between the U. S. parent corporations and the Chinese affiliates are codified in legal contracts that insulate the transactions from competitive market exchange.

In his article, "Contracting for Innovation: Vertical Disintegration and Interfirm Collaboration," Gilson calls this new form of technology transfer "contracting for innovation."

Gilson writes,

"We suggest that the change in the boundary of the firm [in vertically integrated global value chains] has given rise to a new form of contracting between firms, [the parent U. S. corporations and the Chinese intermediate demand production affiliates] in the what we call contracting for innovation." (Gilson, Ronald J., et al., Columbia Law and Economics Working Paper No. 340, 2009.).

Gilson explains the motive of contracting for innovation, from the perspective of the U. S. parent corporations in the global value chains.

He writes,

"The pressure toward vertical integration will be especially powerful [for large U. S. corporations] in rapidly innovating industries where swift technological change [caused by tacit knowledge] produces uncertainty in supply relationships; that is, where the future states of those relationships cannot be predicted probabilistically. In the presence of uncertainty, contemporary contract theory offers no general solution to the problem of assuring both efficient levels of transaction-specific investment ex ante and adjustment to an efficient outcome ex post after uncertainty is resolved [through the legal contract]… Vertical integration was a response to the threat of disruption to the production process. [and to the flow of income]. Because achieving economies of scale entailed large specific investments [by U. S. corporations] in production equipment [in China] that had little or no value unless used for the purpose to which it was dedicated, interruptions in the flow of production [and to the flow of global income] could be ruinous. [to the large U. S. corporations]."

In other words, in contrast to Thomas L. Friedman, who suggests that economic knowledge flows leave no trace, we counter that the appearance of a coefficient in the intermediate demand matrix is evidence of a social/business network of knowledge flows.

Prior to 1992, as the research by Bergman shows, U. S. metro regional economies with high inter-industry relationships exhibited a high rate of new venture creation in high technology industrial networks.

After the intermediate demand networks were moved to China, the U. S. economy experienced declining rates of economic growth and dramatic declines in the rate of new venture creation.

Bergman and Feser characterized these types of knowledge creation and diffusion regional inter-industry relationships, prior to 2002, as metro regions that have an "innovation environment." (Bergman, Edward M., Feser, Edward J., Industrial and Regional Clusters: Concepts and Comparative Applications, 2nd ed., West Virginia University Regional Research Institute, 2020.).

They write,

"Enterprises do not conduct business in isolation, they do not innovate in isolation. The innovation environment constitutes research that attempts to the characteristics of "learning economies," economies that help sustain the perpetual research and innovation necessary to continually generate new products and open new markets. According to Roelandt and den Hertog (1999, p. 1): In modern innovation theory the strategic behaviour and alliances of firms, as well as the interaction and [tacit] knowledge exchange between firms, research institutes, universities and other institutions, are at the heart of the analysis of innovation processes. Innovation and the upgrading of productive capacity is seen as a dynamic social process that evolves most successfully in a network in which intensive interaction exists between those 'producing' and those 'purchasing and using' knowledge [tacit knowledge exchange]… Industry clusters and networks can serve as mechanisms whereby firms exchange knowledge and information that cannot be codified. Such tacit forms of knowledge are viewed as increasingly important given the rapidly changing global economic environment. Tacit knowledge must also be exchanged between individuals, not business entities, reinforcing advantages to spatial clustering (Lundvall 1999). Such advantages are likely to be strongest for technology-intensive firms, yet even traditional, design-oriented sectors such as furniture and apparel, may seek to improve flexibility and ability to innovate by clustering in particular regions."

As the rate of intermediate inputs from China increased, after 2002, the rate of new venture creation in the U. S. decreased.

As Boehm, et al., cited earlier explains,

We find that foreign sourcing [by U. S. parent corporations] of intermediate inputs is a striking characteristic of multinationals. Over 90% of overall U.S. intermediate imports in our sample are imported by multinationals. Moreover, the fraction of U.S. multinationals sourcing inputs from developing [third world] countries nearly doubled from 1993 to 2011. To illustrate the link between these high and increasing intermediate imports by multinationals and the observed employment declines, we return to the event study. We show that the relative employment declines in transitioning plants [in the U. S. intermediate input networks] are accompanied by large increases in imports of intermediates by the parent firm. The increase in imports is largest when the plant [in the U. S.] is shut down." (Boehm, et al., Multinationals, Offshoring And The Decline Of U.S. Manufacturing, NBER Working Paper 25824, 2019.).

In their explanation of the decline in U. S. economic growth rates, after 2002, Akcigit and Ates cite the rise of intermediate inputs as part of the cause of the decline.

They provide Figure 13 below, showing the dramatic rise of intermediate inputs, after 2002.

They explain,

"With knowledge diffusion [in U. S. metro regions] slowing down, the direct effect is that market leaders [large parent corporations in the vertical integrated global value chains] are protected from being imitated. [in their proprietary codified technology] As a result, the technology gaps start widening, presenting market leaders a stronger market power. Market concentration and markups rise on average. Profit share [pure profit] of GDP increases, and labor share [middle and working classes] decreases. Larger gaps also discourage the followers, [latent potential entrepreneurs] causing the productivity gap between them and the leaders to open up. The strengthening of leaders also discourages forward-looking entrants; hence, firm entry and the employment share of young firms go down. Discouraged followers and entrants exert smaller competitive pressure on market leaders; as a result, market leaders relax, and they experiment innovate less [in order to extend the life of the incumbent technology] less. Hence, overall dynamism and experimentation decrease in the economy…A large literature has argued that geographical proximity to the knowledge source [metro regional intermediate demand networks] plays a very crucial role in knowledge diffusion [Jaffe et al. (1993), Audretsch and Feldman (1996), Porter (2000)]. If the ability to utilize spillovers from other firms depends on the geographical proximity to these knowledge-source firms, it would be natural to expect a reduction in knowledge diffusion from leaders to followers in the United States if the leaders do most of their economic activity abroad. This would in turn depress domestic flow of knowledge."

Chapter 3 Figure 13. Value of Intermediate Goods.

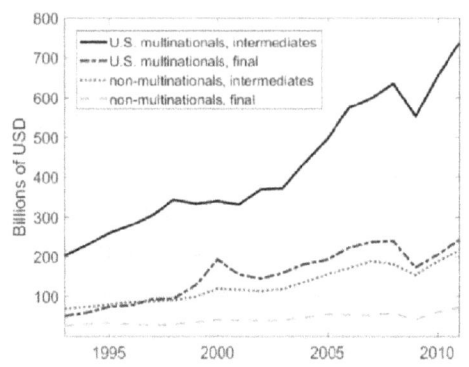

Figure 1: Value of intermediate and final goods imports by firm type

Notes: The data are from the LFTTD, BCA, and UBP as explained in text. The figure shows the value of intermediate and final goods imports by firm type. The value of imports of foreign multinational firms is excluded from this figure.

Citation Figure 13: Akcigit, Ufuk, Ates, Sina, What Happened to U.S. Business Dynamism? NBER Working Paper No. w25756, SSRN, 2023.

In other words, after 2002, when the U. S. intermediate demand networks were moved to China, the former innovative regions lost the ability to innovate because the intermediate demand networks no longer existed in the U. S.

Akcigit cite the importance of new venture creation in the high tech industrial sectors as one of the reasons for the declining U. S. economic growth rates.

They write,

"While several measures of business dynamism have indicated a slowdown in most sectors of the U.S. economy since the 1980s, the decline in the high-tech sector has become most visible in the 2000s (Decker et al., 2016b). As shown in Figure 12, the dispersion of firm growth in high-tech sectors started to decline steadily around 2000. Decker et al. (2016b) document that other measures of business dynamism, such as gross job reallocation, reverberate with this post-2000 pattern, again especially in high-tech sectors. In this regard, our post-2000 findings tell a coherent story with these empirical regularities, suggesting a concurrent slowdown in knowledge diffusion and business dynamism." (What Happened to U.S. Business Dynamism? NBER Working Paper No. w25756).

Haltiwanger, et al., explains that in the absence of new venture creation in the U. S. economy, that the rate of job creation is negative.

Haltiwanger writes,

"This pattern implies that, excluding the jobs from new firms, the U.S. net employment growth rate is negative on average. This simple comparison highlights the importance of business startups to job creation in the United States… In short, firms aged five or younger are key drivers of new job creation, a fact that is especially true in high-tech. Sustaining a robust rate of net new job creation requires a constant supply of firm births each year." (Haltiwanger, John, Jarmin, Ron S., Miranda, Javier, Business Dynamics Statistics Briefing: Jobs Created from Business Startups in the United States, Business Dynamics Statistics Briefing, SSRN, 2009.).

They show, in Figure 14 below, that the rate of new venture creation for firms less than 5 years old, has declined, after 2002, when the U. S. intermediate demand networks were moved to China.

Chapter 3 Figure 14. Firm Entry and Exits.

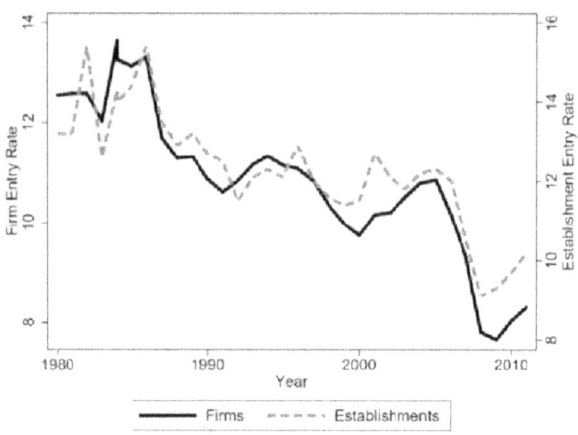

Source: Authors' calculations from BDS database [see also Decker et al. (2016)].

Figure 7: FIRM ENTRY AND EXIT RATES IN THE UNITED STATES.

Citation Figure 14: from Haltiwanger, e al., Who Creates Jobs? Small Vs. Large Vs. Young, NBER Working Paper 16300, 2010.

Ryan A. Decker, et al., describe that the rate of new venture creation of young firms was gradually declining in the U.S., after around 1990, but accelerated after 2002.

Chapter 3 Figure 15. Employment Share of Young Firms.

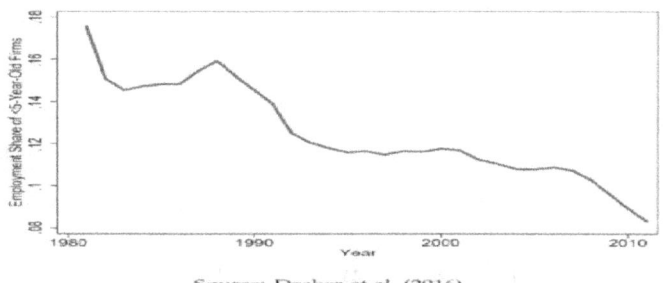

Figure 8: EMPLOYMENT SHARE OF <5-YEAR OLD FIRMS.

Credit Figure 15: Decker, Ryan A., et al., Declining Business Dynamism: What We Know and the Way Forward, American Economic Review, May 2016.).

Ian Hathaway, in Figure 16 below, describes the importance of high tech startups, who are less than 5 years old, as the main source of net job creation in the U. S.

Chapter 3 Figure 16. Net Job Creation.

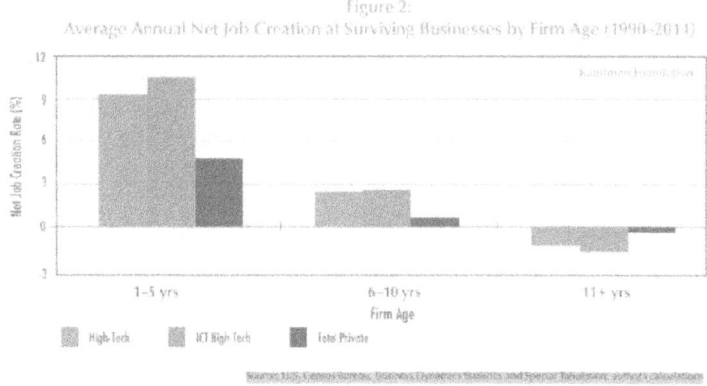

Figure 16 citation: Hathaway, Ian, et al., Tech Starts: High-Technology Business Formation and Job Creation in the United States, , Kauffman Foundation Research Series, 2013.

The reason that a high rate of new venture creation is required to sustain job growth in America is that most new technology ventures die in the first five years

The source of new high tech ventures in the U. S. is the metro regional intermediate demand networks, where technology knowledge is created and diffused, leading to a high rate of new venture creation when entrepreneurs leave their jobs to create a new venture.

Konczal shows, in Figure 17 below, that the rate of new venture creation for U. S. metro regions, of all sizes, began generally declining from 1990, with significant declines in all metro population sizes, after 2005.

Chapter 3 Figure 17. 40 Entrepreneurial Regions.

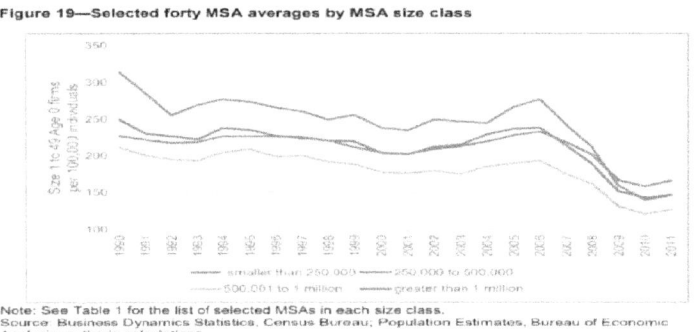

Credit Figure 17: Konczal, Jared, The Most Entrepreneurial Metropolitan Area? Ewing Marion Kauffman Foundation, SSRN. 2013.

As we describe in later chapters of this book, the threat of tacit knowledge creation and diffusion, and the subsequent rate of entrepreneurial new ventures, constitutes the biggest single threat to the smooth operation and continued corporate control of the vertically integrated global values chains.

The restoration of those former United States tacit knowledge networks in each of the 350 major metro regions is the single best strategy to disintegrate the vertically integrated global value chains, and to re-establish the concept of American national economic sovereignty.

Chapter 3 Topic Category #6. Increased macro economic instability and increased social class conflict in the transition of the U. S. economic free enterprise economy to the communist state owned crony corporatism Chinese economic model.

The logic of authoritarian corporate globalism is that the management of the world economy, where large U. S. and Western alliance corporations own and manage production and sales facilities all over the world, is easier if U. S. citizens are forced to behave the same way as other citizens, all over the world.

The economic chaos and anxiety created by corporate globalism for middle and working class U. S. citizens contributes to the effectiveness of the ruling class propaganda of race hatred and social class polarization, which leads citizens to seek social stability in authoritarian regimes that promise social stability in exchange for citizen independence and liberty.

The U. S economy does not function as a free market economy, but as a centrally managed and administered planned crony corporate capitalist economy.

The main difference in operation between the U. S. economic model and the Chinese Communist economic model is that a small set of ruling class elites in China make all the decisions, whereas a seven member Board of Governors of the U. S. Federal Reserve System manage and administer the economy to benefit the American ruling class.

The seven members of the Federal Reserve board are all members of the American ruling social class, and all of them are former bank executives in major U. S. private commercial banks.

The decisions they make are not guided by some grand social welfare function, or any constitutional provisions about whose social welfare they seek to maximize.

The social welfare they seek to maximize is the financial welfare of their own social class, and the financial welfare of the outside private commercial banks who are member banks of the Reserve system.

Their operation and performance in the management of the U. S. economy has been a dismal failure for U. S. middle and working class citizens.

On the other hand, their performance in manipulating interest rates and the money supply has been a raging success for the crony corporate capitalist system, as evidenced by the rapid increase in corporate profits, after 2001, when China was admitted to the WTO.

The function of the U. S. Federal reserve is to coordinate U. S. economic and foreign policy with the other central banks in the Western Global Trading Alliance member states to achieve consolidated global management of the New World Order.

The economic and financial instability of the U. S. economy contributes to the ruling class propaganda of race hatred and social class polarization, as desperate U. S. citizens seek social stability in an authoritarian totalitarian regime.

The U. S. macro economic instability is caused by a predictable sequence of events, beginning with a period of a rapid increase in money supply and an increase in fiscal spending and debt issuance.

The loose money policies cause a period of asset speculation and inflation. The speculation leads to a gigantic bubble in assets and the creation of synthetic investment instruments, which then burst, causing aggregate demand to collapse and asset values to plummet.

Agents in the U. S. Treasury and the Federal Reserve Board chairman then proceed to manipulate interest rates and money supply, primarily to the benefit of banks and corporations.

In the period of the bubble burst, common citizens lose their houses and their farms to the elite, due to the way the creditor/debtor laws are written to benefit the bankers.

Bankers, and creditors, then proceed to foreclose on the property and assets of common citizens, who cannot make their debt payments. During the period of asset speculation, the rate of private capital investment collapses, causing economic decline in the 3 to 5 year horizon.

Investment capital is shifted from productive investments that lead to long-term capital gains and economic growth, to speculative short-term capital gains for wealthy citizens who can afford to take the risks of asset speculation.

The shift in capital investment to short-term speculative investments causes the U. S. economy enter into a period of recession.

One consequence of the control over banking by the elites is that they use the government to insulate themselves from the damage that they inflict on common citizens by bailing out the banks and wealthy citizens with U. S. tax dollars.

During the period of economic collapse, the common middle class citizens become financially destitute, and the concentration of wealth, and the distribution of income, becomes more and more concentrated in the hands of the few.

The monetary and interest rate performance of the Fed, since around 1985, has led to a general economic collapse about every 7 years.

On October 19, 1987, the Black Monday Stock Market Crash occurred. The cause of the crash was banking collusion with agents of the deep state, asset speculation, insider trading and program trading by 5 large global securities firms.

In 1991, the speculative real estate bubble, and the leveraged buy-out bubble, both burst at the same time, causing the recession of 1991.

Beginning in 1991, the American economy began to enter a series of speculative bubbles caused by government banking policy intervention. The frequency of economic collapse shortened from every 10 years to about every 5 years.

The capital gains and profits from the exits in IT bubble investments, initially made in 1992, were ploughed back into short-term speculative early stage IPO investments, in 1997.

Speculation and collusion in the IPO market dumped hundreds of millions of worthless IT securities into the public markets for ordinary American investors to buy.

The government intervention and increased spending, in 2001, did not create lasting economic growth benefits because domestic markets and the global corporate economy were no longer integrated.

The income and employment multiplier effects of government spending occurred in the nations of the foreign corporate affiliates in the integrated global value chains.

After the Islamic terrorist attack, on September 11, 2001, the US. stock market collapsed again. The U. S. economy entered a prolonged recession.

Again, the U. S. government tried stimulus spending, which ended up primarily benefitting special financial interests in foreign counties and domestic real estate speculation in the U. S.

In 2002, U. S. trade and tax policies were changed to facilitate more offshoring of technology innovation and R&D. The primary beneficiary of the new trade polices was China, admitted to the World Trade Organization, as an undeveloped nation.

The changes in regulation of corporations led to a series of Enron-type collapses and wide-spread corporate financial accounting fraud and political corruption in the U. S. government.

In the period from 2003 to 2008, the U. S. rate of job creation was lower than the rate of job destruction.

Beginning in 2003, the U. S. rate of domestic direct investment declined, and U. S. foreign direct investment increased.

In 2004, the U. S. rates of profit for the 1500 largest global corporation increased to record levels.

As a result of U. S. trade and tax policies, those record profits were not repatriated, or reinvested, in U. S. domestic value chains. The record profits were reinvested in foreign global value chains, primarily in China.

The trade policies and increased foreign capital investment had created a bifurcated domestic economy. A large part of the domestic economy and labor market did not benefit from transactions in the global corporate value chains.

At the same period of time, in 2004, the operation of the U. S. representative republic became more and more disconnected from the consent of the governed, and more and more corrupt in the operation of the global crony corporate New World Order.

Beginning in March, 2008, speculation in oil and gas increased the price of a barrel of oil from $43 per barrel to $145 per barrel. The asset speculation was a result of collusion between oil corporations and government officials, aided and abetted by a useless war in Iraq and Afghanistan.

The rapid increase in oil prices caused a sharp contraction in consumer spending. The decreased consumer spending caused a prolonged economic recession.

In September 2008, the mortgage debt bubble, directly caused by U. S. loose money government banking and interest rate policies, burst, and the U. S. economy collapsed again.

As a result of that collapse, and coincident with the 2008 election of a socialist president, the U. S. economy did not experience growth for the next 8 years.

Beginning in 2009, the Federal Reserve performed its usual function of bailing out the world's central bankers, and the large corporations, with trillions of U. S. tax dollars.

In the absence of economic growth, between 2008 to 2016, middle and working class citizens became attracted to the ideology of socialism, which resulted in 65 million citizens voting for the Democrat socialist candidate for President, in 2016.

After the 2020 economic collapse, the entire sequence of interest rate manipulation and asset speculation began again.

The history of U. S. economic collapse and social instability is repeating, with thousands of citizens homeless and in poverty.

As we describe below, in Chapter 5, The New Evolutionary Economic Growth Theory of Entrepreneurial Capitalism, there is only one economic pathway out of this dysfunctional New World Order for the economic destruction being experienced by middle and working class U. S. citizens.

and more corrupt in the operation of the global crony corporate New World Order.

Beginning in March, 2008, speculation in oil and gas increased the price of a barrel of oil from $43 per barrel to $145 per barrel. The asset speculation was a result of collusion between oil corporations and government officials, aided and abetted by a useless war in Iraq and Afghanistan.

The rapid increase in oil prices caused a sharp contraction in consumer spending. The decreased consumer spending caused a prolonged economic recession.

In September 2008, the mortgage debt bubble, directly caused by U. S. loose money government banking and interest rate policies, burst, and the U. S. economy collapsed again.

As a result of that collapse, and coincident with the 2008 election of a socialist president, the U. S. economy did not experience growth for the next 8 years.

Beginning in 2009, the Federal Reserve performed its usual function of bailing out the world's central bankers, and the large corporations, with trillions of U. S. tax dollars.

In the absence of economic growth, between 2008 to 2016, middle and working class citizens became attracted to the ideology of socialism, which resulted in 65 million citizens voting for the Democrat socialist candidate for President, in 2016.

After the 2020 economic collapse, the entire sequence of interest rate manipulation and asset speculation began again.

The history of U. S. economic collapse and social instability is repeating, with thousands of citizens homeless and in poverty.

As we describe below, in Chapter 5, The New Evolutionary Economic Growth Theory of Entrepreneurial Capitalism, there is only one economic pathway out of this dysfunctional New World Order for the economic destruction being experienced by middle and working class U. S. citizens.

Chapter 4. The Vulnerability of Rules-Based Corporate Globalism to Regional Radical Technology Innovation.

In his recent article, "How Yemen changed everything: In a single move, Yemen's Ansarallah has checkmated the west and its rules-based order," Pepe Escobar compares the vulnerability of global rules-based authoritarian corporatism to a move by a pawn, late in a chess game. (The Cradle.com, December 28, 2023.).

In Escobar's analogy, the U. S. military is the world's chess queen, acting in its role as the policewoman of the world to keep the shipping lanes open at the entrance to the Red Sea.

The Houthis rebels are the pawns, whose single chess move forward, by firing drones and rockets on commercial shipping vessels, brings the supply chains of the Western Global Trading Alliance to a halt.

After the recent guerilla attack on a Maersk container ship, Maersk said it was suspending operations in the Red Sea.

The Western Corporate Global Trading Alliance is vulnerable to many external threats, among them the blocking of the Suez Canal, low water in the Panama Canal, inability to offload cargo at U. S. ports, the elimination of the U. S. dollar as the global reserve currency, the unleashing of bio-terrorism by China, and global military confrontations, like the ones in Ukraine and Gaza.

Escobar continues his chess analogy by writing,

"This [move by the pawn] is a quantum shift on the [Western Trading Alliance globalist] chessboard. It means West Asian powers [BRICs] will frame the new regional architecture [multipolar, not unipolar] from now on, not US Navy projection… a chokepoint Hormuz-Bab al-Mandeb combo blockade might skyrocket the price of oil to at least $500 a barrel, triggering the implosion of the $618 trillion derivatives market and crashing the entire [Western Global Trading Alliance] international banking system."

Escobar correctly identifies the central banks in the Western Trading Alliance as components in the application of power in the globalist authoritarian regime.

The Western Alliance central banking regime attempted to punish Russia with monetary sanctions because Russia did not obey the rules of the rules-based globalist order, when Russia invaded Ukraine.

Iraq disobeyed the global rules-based order, by invading Kuwait, and Iraq got invaded, and lost its head, by the U. S. military.

Like any collectivist, centralized, non-democratic authoritarian regime, the Western Global Corporate Trading Alliance seeks absolute obedience to the rules-based order in order to maintain the privileges of directing the world's global income to itself.

Part of that absolute obedience to the rules-based order is forcing lower standards of living on U. S. middle and working class citizens in order to make the management of the New World Order easier for global corporations.

As we described in Chapter 3, on the destructive economic power of vertically integrated global value chains, the management of the globalist regime is easier if American citizens are forced to behave, and are forced to have the same lower standards of living, as other citizens in the world.

Instead of many different nations, with many different moral values and cultural norms, the New World Order seeks a one-world global government to impose authoritarian order on all citizens, in the Western Global Corporate Trading Alliance.

Obviously, the Houthis pawns in Yemen, and BRICs nations outside of the Western Global Corporate Trading Alliance, do not want to be ruled by the power of the U. S. military, acting in its role as policewoman of the world.

Those types of external threats are known and quantifiable, and subject to the application of monetary or military power by the Western Global Corporate Trading Alliance.

As long as the status quo of power in the Western Alliance rules-based international order is maintained, the flow of global income to the large corporations and the Western central bankers, is secure and stable.

The international rules-based order functions as the legal institutional framework for globalization of trade, by establishing the legal contracts of exchange for vertically integrated global value chains.

The rules-based order does double-duty by establishing the enforcement mechanism of political control, outside of sovereign national democratic processes, of the authoritarian application of U. S. military and central bank financial power over their foreign affiliates at the bottom of the Duke global value chain smile diagram.

The greatest vulnerability to the continued operation of the rules-based Western Trading Corporate Trading Alliance is the uncontrolled, and unquantifiable threat of radical technology innovation.

Radical technology innovation creates new products, which then create new future markets, which then create new flows of future income in those new markets.

New flows of future income, in new future markets, disrupt the status quo distribution of profits, in existing global markets, which large corporations direct to themselves, via their legal contracts in the vertically integrated global value chains.

Prior to 1992, radical technology innovation constituted an internal threat to the operation of the U. S. corporate vertically integrated global value chains, in the sense that the technology innovation occurred internally in 350 metro regions in the domestic U. S. economy, which had high rates of entrepreneurial new venture creation.

After 2002, when the U. S intermediate demand production chains were moved to China, the source of tacit knowledge creation in technology innovation in U. S. metro regions was eliminated.

After 2002, the rate of new technology venture creation in the domestic U. S. economy ground to a halt, as did job creation and authentic national economic growth.

The continued flow of pure profits to large corporations depends on maintaining the rules-based global order so that large corporations can control the pace and direction of technology innovation in order to keep their legacy technology products safe from the competition of new technology products.

Gideon Rachman, in his Financial Times, article, asks, "Is there such a thing as a rules-based international order? (April 20, 2023.).

Rachman answers his own question by citing Anthony Blinken, the current U. S. Secretary of State.

Blinken is quoted by Rachman,

"We must defend and reform the rules-based international order, the system of laws, agreements, principles and institutions that the world came together to build after two world wars to manage relations between states, to prevent conflict, to uphold the rights of all people. Its founding documents include the UN Charter and the Universal Declaration of Human Rights, which enshrine concepts like self-determination, sovereignty, the peaceful settlement of disputes. These are not western constructs. They are reflections of the world's shared aspirations."

The entire propaganda of the New World Order is revealed in the deceit of Blinken's description of the international rules-based order that they are not "western constructs," but instead reflections of the world's shared aspirations.

The Houthis rebels apparently do not share these western aspirations.

Rachman explains that the rules-based order is disintegrating, and states,

"Fractures appear in the postwar system that was designed to maintain global peace."

The rules-based order propaganda is based upon the deceit that it was designed, after World War II, to maintain global peace.

Bretton Woods, the U. S. dollar, as the world's reserve currency, and the division of the world into Western and Eastern blocs, was designed to maintain U. S. global corporate and banking power.

Rachman notes that,

"In Russia and China, American talk of a rules-based international order is usually dismissed as pure hypocrisy."

The origin of Russia's allegation of U. S. hypocrisy is that so-called Western liberal values originated in Madison's constitution of 1787.

Putin knows this historical difference and is aware that the American spirit of liberty originated in 1776, with George Mason and Jefferson's principles of liberty, not in Madison's framework of a centralized ruling class aristocracy. (Vass, Laurie Thomas, George Mason's America: The State Sovereignty Alternative to Madison's Centralized Ruling Class Aristocracy, Gabby Press, 2023.).

John Ikenberry, the Albert G. Milbank Professor of Politics and International Affairs at Princeton University was the guest on Rachman's podcast, and elaborated on the deceit that the rules-based order promotes global human rights and global environmental preservation.

Ikenberry states,

"It [international rules-based order] really initiates a process that in some sense liberal societies are inviting. And this is what I would say: liberal societies, not just the United States, but particularly the United States at its founding, [Mason's founding not Madison's founding] was built on a set of principles [Jefferson's] And so we have a kind of sense that we [royal We] are in a process, we're in a building mode. We always are."

The deceit and the pretending that Russia sees as American hypocrisy, is not that the United States is trying to build a just global society.

Russia correctly sees that the United States is attempting to maintain global power through the operation of the Western Global Corporate Alliance through the operation of its rules-based international order.

Ikenberry suggests that, "the liberal democratic world doesn't really have boundaries."

Ikenberry reveals the deception of the Western Trading Alliance by saying that the propaganda of global human rights and global environmental preservation must not be seen by pawns, like Yemen, for the lies and the deceit, that it is.

Ikenberry states,

"So if it looks [to Yeman or India] like it's more [U. S.] weaponised economic sanctions for more narrow interests, [pure corporate profits] that's a problem. [for maintenance of the rules-based order]. It [rules-based order] can't be [seen by Russia] asAmerica running the world."

Which is exactly what the rules-based international order is: American corporations running the world to direct global income to themselves.

In the absence of radical technology innovation, the rules-based global order is stable.

If the U. S. metro regions re-construct the entrepreneurial capitalist economies that existed, prior to 1992, the Western Trading Alliance is vulnerable to an internal threat of radical technology innovation that the large corporations cannot control.

Chris Buskirk characterizes the quest for total global control by the rules-based order as built on sand.

The framework of international political and economic control of the rules-based order is "brittle," according to Buskirk because it is built upon lies of global equal human prosperity and the "shock and awe" terror of the U. S. military.

Buskirk writes,

"The current complex of elite institutions that run the modern order and seem so powerful are, in fact, quite brittle. What looks like hegemonic political, economic, and cultural authority is, in reality, built on sand…Like all [authoritarian] tyrannies, they base their power on terror and intimidation because they lack both the legitimacy and the charisma to rule by acclamation. They [the global ruling class elites] are terrified someone [Trump] will find out and replace them." (Only Bold Proposals Can Displace Globalism, American Greatness, August 13, 2019.).

Radical technology innovation and the political decentralization of metro entrepreneurial capitalism provide the countervailing ideology to replace the ideology of globalism.

Buskirk continues his analysis of the ideology of globalism.

"Globalism is the ideology of the powerful. It is the ideology of transnational bureaucrats, elite media, respected academics, and global capital...One of the reasons for the [global technology] innovation slowdown is that the monopolists aren't interested in innovating...Globalism in practice insists on centralizing power in the hands of a supranational economic, cultural, and political vanguard... [and seeks to] supplant the nation state, representative government, national sovereignty, and all of the [democratic] institutions upon which our societies rely."

We agree with Theodore Roosevelt Malloch's characterization of rules-based globalism that it is in reality the application of a one-world Marxist tyranny by large corporations.

Malloch writes,

"Globalism" is one world government run on the basis of democratic socialism and world citizenship. Economic populism and its political cousin, political populism, are an antidote and a reality check to excessive globalization and globalist values and institutions." (Exposing the Roots of Globalism, American Greatness February 26, 2020.).

Our term for economic populism is entrepreneurial capitalism, and our term for political populism is decentralized state sovereignty, that is beyond the control of the rules-based international order.

Clayton Christensen has provided a useful theoretical distinction between sustaining innovation and radical technology innovation. (Christensen, Clayton M. The Innovator's Dilemma: When New Technologies Cause Great Firms to Fail, 1997. And The Innovator's Solution: Creating and Sustaining Successful Growth, with Raynor, Michael E., 2003.).

We apply Christensen's theoretical insights to our argument that radical metro regional technology innovation exploits the primary vulnerability of rules-based corporate globalism.

We argue that in the U. S. macrotechnology, that existed prior to 1992. the formerly open flows of tacit knowledge in metro regional economies were an important source of radical technology innovation.

Christensen writes from the perspective of what improves the welfare of large corporations, not in terms of how economic growth benefits the social welfare of citizens in the United States.

From Christensen's perspective, it is important for the large corporations to avoid having their internal proprietary technology slip off their plate onto the plate of a competitor, or into the hands of a potential entrepreneur.

Christensen called this potential loss of corporate proprietary technology a spillover.

The spillover of technology from the large corporation was dangerous to the future profits of the corporation because if the technology fell into the wrong hands, it could lead to radical technology innovation.

Radical technology innovation had the potential to "blow away" the large corporation because the large corporation would lose its markets for technologically obsolete products.

From the financial perspective of the large corporations, it was important to keep their legacy technology products in the market as long as possible by eliminating the threat of technology spillover that may possibly result in radical technology innovation.

Christensen's term for non-disruptive innovation is "sustaining innovation," because it is controlled within the corporate legal structure, and sustains the company's legacy technology.

Sustaining innovation within the large global corporations is primarily created by "codified" knowledge, which means the knowledge is in the form of proprietary written text, often in the form of a patent, which can only be shared with selected interested parties, outside the corporate structure.

Sustaining technology innovation is aimed at making an existing product more user-friendly by adding features which do not disrupt the legacy technology platform of the large corporation.

A sustaining innovation to an existing product is more likely to gain consumer acceptance because consumers have seen a slightly different version before, and can visualize and imagine how those new product features fit into the consumer's welfare function.

While a sustaining innovation is more likely to be accepted by consumers than a radical innovation, the sustaining innovation does not lead to new market emergence. It only redistributes the exiting flow of income within an existing market.

Generally, sustaining technology innovation leads to a future lower Nash equilibrium because sustaining innovations do not create new future flows of income in new future markets.

In our argument about the vulnerability of the international rules-based order, the U.S economy, and the Chinese economy are both on a trajectory to lower Nash equilibrium of economic growth, and consequently, causing a lower global rate of economic growth for all nations that are components of the Western Global Corporate Trading Alliance.

Radical technology innovation contains a logical market irony. The more radical the product innovation, less likely it is to gain market acceptance because consumers cannot figure out how it fits in their welfare function, when they first see it.

Chistensen calls "the unexpected results," of a radical new product a "radical" innovation, in contrast to the sustaining innovation, that is controlled by the corporation.

According to Christensen, radical innovation creates new future markets, which disrupt existing incumbent markets because the new future markets create entirely new intermediated demand production relationships, as visualized by the appearance of new coefficients in the economic input-output model of the economy.

In their review of the typology of radical economic innovation, entitled "When Is An Invention Really Radical? Defining and Operationalizing Technological Radicalness," Kristina Dahlin and Dean Behrens provide 3 useful criteria for defining a radical product innovation, (Research Policy, 2005.).

For them, a successful radical product innovation is:

(1) novel, [new to the world].
(2) unique, [contains new technological features].
(3) has an impact on future pace and direction of technology. [by creating new interindustry relationships which then cause more radical technology innovation.].

In their case, they emphasize the technological content of the new product as the key characteristic that defines radical technology innovation.

"We focus," state Dahlin and Behrens, "the definition of radicalness on an invention's technical content, thus avoiding the drawbacks of many commonly used definitions that often confound [the definition of] radicalness with its impact on an industry."

Dahlin and Behrens cite both Shane (2001) and Astebro & Dahlin (2005) who find that the more radical an innovation, the less likely it is to be commercialized.

The more radical the innovation, the less likely it is to become commercialized, but the greater the economic impact on the regional economy, if the innovation is eventually accepted by the market, because the new product creates entirely new intermediate demand production relationships, that did not exist in the prior economic industrial structure.

In other words, the degree of "radicalness" is the extent to which the product innovation causes a new market to emerge. (Vass, Laurie Thomas, How a New Market Emerges from a New Radical Product, SSRN, 2008.).

In the absence of radical technology product innovation, the macro economy settles into a Nash equilibrium of lower economic growth.

In the case of lower economic growth in the U. S. and China, the allegiance and commitment to maintaining the existing intermediate demand production structure, through the use of long term legal contracts, inhibits radical technology innovation.

The Nash equilibrium conditions are reached over a long period of time based upon allegiance to the status quo distribution of income.

After entering the trajectory towards the Nash equilibrium, it becomes impossible to reverse the trajectory to lower economic growth because the cause of economic growth is new capital investment in new technology products, which create new intermediated demand relationships.

As domestic national and global economic growth slows, income competition over the smaller economic pie becomes more intense, with the more powerful agents able to extract greater income from less powerful agents, as a result of political manipulation of the rules of reward

The large corporations in the Western Corporate Global Trading Alliance divert resources from productive capital investments to increasing expenditures to capture the police power of the state in order for them to preserve the status quo distribution of income.

This diversion of capital of using the police power of the state as it relates to innovation begins to address the vulnerability of global corporatism to radical technology innovation.

Placing political and legal authority to direct the pace and direction of technology innovation in the hands of the rules-based international agents leads to global political inbreeding and market decline, not market emergence.

It also leads to distributive injustice and corruption, as agents of government use the police power of the state to distribute incomes according to political values of Marxist ideology.

The political diversion of income to social class groups can only be accomplished by an authoritarian form of government.

Economically, this trajectory to a Nash equilibrium can be depicted in an input-output model as the loss of technological coefficients, over a 20-year period of time, in the intermediate demand A matrix.

In Chapter 3, we described how the appearance of a coefficient in the intermediate demand production matrix described a flow of tacit knowledge between two industries.

The loss of a coefficient in the A matrix, over time, means that the former flow of tacit knowledge no longer exists.

The loss of the coefficients is biologically equivalent to the loss of neurons in the human brain.

Once the economy loses it neuronal pathways of knowledge creation, there is no way for the economy to regenerate the neuronal connections of the technological coefficients of economic innovation that used to exist in the prior intermediate demand matrix.

While the coefficients in the intermediate demand matrix can describe the trajectory to a Nash equilibrium economic resting point, the input output matrix cannot describe how to get out of it because the tacit knowledge creation networks no longer exist.

We explain, in our theory of technological evolution, that under Schumpeter's entrepreneurial economic growth model, national interindustry relationships [supply chains] are the communication pathways of diffusing tacit technical knowledge. (Vass, Laurie Thomas, The Theory of Technology Evolution, Gabby Press, 2019.).

In contrast to regional entrepreneurial capitalism, the authoritarian rules-based new world order global macrotechnology features intermediate demand corporate supply chains tightly controlled by long term legal contracts, and centralized by large corporations in very few locations, such as the large metro regions of China.

We argue that the ultimate economic consequence of international rules-based new world corporatism is worldwide economic decline because there is insufficient technological innovation to allow the global economy to break free of the trend to a global Nash equilibrium.

The managed crony capitalist corporate global system allows the large corporations to gain political control over the pace of technological innovation by replacing metro regional tacit knowledge creation and diffusion with an autocratic, centralized NGO one-world-government.

We argue that the rules-based new world order of global corporate fascism is vulnerable to the re-emergence of radical technological innovation in each of the 350 U. S. metro regional economies.

Chapter 5. The New Evolutionary Economic Growth Theory of Entrepreneurial Capitalism.

Technology evolves.

Our criticism of the canonical neoclassical marginal theory of economic growth is that the theory no longer describes the real economy of the vertically integrated global value chain macro global economy.

The predictions of neoclassical theory are based upon a hypothesis that the economy is on a timeless, ahistorical trajectory to equilibrium, based upon the solution to a series of differential equations that describe how market prices bring supply and demand into equilibrium, in all markets, and in every single market, simultaneously.

The theory of general equilibrium was useful, prior to 1992, for describing the existing U. S. economy, in an existing defined time period, given existing unchanging production functions, in any three to five year period of time.

Beyond five years, a better, more accurate theory of economic growth, is based upon the concept of technological evolution.

The new evolutionary theory can describe a growth trajectory that can either be upwards, towards a bifurcation point, leading to more economic growth, or the trajectory can be moving to a lower equilibrium point, which describes an economy stuck in a Nash equilibrium.

As applied currently to vertically integrated global corporate value chains, the global economy is stuck in a global Nash equilibrium of declining economic growth.

The great benefit of the new Evolutionary Economic Growth Theory of Entrepreneurial Capitalism is that the theory provides a solution to disintegrate vertically integrated global value chains by describing how economic growth can be re-started by decentralizing the forces of technology innovation to 350 U. S. metro regional economies.

We begin with a brief analysis of the defects of conventional economic growth theory in order to contrast that theory with a better theory of economic growth..

Section 1 of Chapter 5. Defects of Existing Growth Theory: Breaking Away From Equilibrium.

As a point of reference, we begin our criticism with Robert Solow's two articles, "A Contribution to the Theory of Economic Growth, and "Technical Change and the Aggregate Production Function." (Solow, Robert M., A Contribution to the Theory of Economic Growth, The Quarterly Journal of Economics, 1956., and Technical Change and the Aggregate Production Function, The Review of Economics and Statistics, 1957.).

Solow concludes that,

"Over the 40-year period output per man hour approximately doubled. At the same time, according to Chart 2, the cumulative upward shift in the pro duction function was about 80 per cent. It is possible to argue that about one-eighth of the total increase is traceable to increased cap ital per man hour, and the remaining seven-eighths to technical change."

While Solow can identify technological innovation as the force that creates economic growth, as we also do, Solow's model of economic growth places the technological innovation outside of his general theory of economic growth.

In contrast to technology as an exogenous, hidden factor, we place technological innovation into the general entrepreneurial capitalist theory of Joseph Schumpeter.

Solow predicts that given only two factors of production, capital and labor, that the economy will achieve a steady-state rate of growth.

Solow states that all economic growth is caused by increased capital investment in new, more productive plant and equipment.

In contrast, we place economic growth into the theory of radical technology innovation in new products, not simply in new production technology.

In our new theory, the economy is either growing or it is dying. We deny the existence of an equilibrium steady-state of economic growth.

In our theory, radical technology innovation causes the economy to trace out an upward trajectory to a new bifurcation point, where the economy may rest for 3 to 5 years.

Or else, from any given equilibrium point, in the absence of technology innovation, the economy may trace out a trajectory to a lower point of economic growth, and become stuck in a Nash equilibrium.

Solow is silent on the topic of income competition between social classes because any reference to the institutional political framework is considered non-objective, from the neo-classical tradition.

In our new theory, at the new macro market bifurcation point, the prior income distributions change. After income distributions change, the economy will never return to the prior equilibrium, because that former market does not exist, anymore.

At the future bifurcation point, costs of production change, and consequently, prices on existing older goods decline at a faster rate than new products, and the profit calculation of venture capitalists change, as prices on older products change.

The Solow Growth Model assumes that the fixed, unchanging production functions in the ahistorical equilibrium time period, exhibit constant-returns-to-scale.

Under this initial unrealistic assumption, if the rate of capital equipment investment goes up, then the rate of output, or economic growth, also goes up at the constant rate.

In contrast to an increase in capital investment, our new theory suggests that capital investment in radical new technology may create new future economic growth, but that the realization of future economic growth is contingent, and uncertain, given the dynamics of the social/political institutional framework of the economy.

The Solow model predicts economic growth convergence between poor nations and rich nations, which means that an additional unit of capital investment in a poor nation may lead to a faster rate of economic growth than a comparable additional unit of capital in a rich nation.

In our new theory of entrepreneurial capitalism, the unit of analysis is no longer a sovereign nation, because in the vertically integrated global corporate value chains, sovereign nations no longer trade with each other.

The more accurate unit of analysis is trade among parent and subsidiary corporations in global value chains.

As the global macro production technology becomes standardized, the multinational corporations abandon the pursuit of new radical technology innovation, and seek out advantages associated with tax incentives and political support for legacy sustaining technology that complements the corporate core technology.

As the competition over global legacy income distribution in the dying global economy intensifies, the institutional political structure of the region undergoes a profound transformation from one characterized as a democratic representative republic to a society characterized by crony capitalism.

Solow's model cannot incorporate the concept of crony capitalism because neo-classical theory abstracts from social/political analysis.

The large corporations are engaged in political "rent-seeking" to replace the rates of profit they obtained before the older products entered the period of price declines in the mass global market.

The political manipulation of government agencies is aimed at controlling the flow of knowledge because uncontrolled tacit knowledge creation and diffusion jeopardizes their flow of legacy income from existing legacy technology.

In contrast to Solow's constant returns to scale, our new theory of entrepreneurial capitalism explains the 67% price markup over marginal costs in global value chains as an application of corporate monopoly pricing power.

In contrast, Solow begins with his canonical assumption of perfect competition, which is clearly not a realistic description of vertically integrated global value chains.

Our new theory of economic growth is not about price competition in a perfect competitive market.

Our model is about income competition between the ruling global corporate social classes, and the rest of society, based upon control over the pace and direction of technology innovation.

Section 2 of Chapter 5. Overview of Theory of Technology Evolution.

Our theory of economic growth applies the metaphor of biological evolution to technology evolution in order to show how technology evolves from the cross-breeding of the technology of two distinct product parents.

In the theory of technology evolution, each parent product passes on technological characteristics that it has acquired through production, and subsequent market selection by consumers.

Readers who are interested in reading more about this theoretical paradigm are directed to The Theory of Technology Evolution. (Vass, Laurie Thomas, Gabby Press, 2019.).

In this overview, we provide an abbreviated summary of the elements of the theory in order to describe how a new theory of economic growth can be used to guide the disintegration of vertically integrated global corporate value chains.

In its essence, the new theory begins with how consumers react when they first see a new radical technology innovation.

If consumers shift their buying preferences from old, existing products to new technology products, there is a possibility that a new future market may emerge.

If that potential new future market is created, it is possible for technology to continue to evolve based upon the shift in consumer preferences.

Given a certain type of prior social and political conditions in political power and cultural values, the economy could be predicted to take a certain type of trajectory.

Given another constellation of political power, the economy would maintain the status quo of legacy technology.

In terms of the evolutionary metaphor, the social and political conditions represent the "environment" within which the units of analysis adapt or modify their behavior.

The analytical framework for economic evolution is based upon an analysis of how the social structure affects the economic structure, as captured by the technological coefficients in the A matrix of input-output accounting models, as the coefficients change over time.

Consumer market final demand is providing the selection force, and, depending on what the consumer does the first time she sees a new product, the final demand market forces can have both positive and negative feedback mechanisms to both firms and products that tend to "direct" the future contingent pathways of technological evolution.

New products that inherit technology exclusively from old products, (sustaining innovation), do so through technology heredity and mutation, which leads to greater rates of market selection, because consumers had seen something like the new product before.

In other words, new sustaining technology products, which look and function like old or existing products, have a greater rate of market adoption by consumers, when they first see the new product.

On the other hand, the more that new products look like old products, the less likely the introduction of radical new products will lead to new future market emergence.

We describe sustaining technology evolution as Kimura's nearly neutral genetic evolution. (Kimura, Motoo, The Neutral Theory of Molecular Evolution, 1983.).

The paradoxical result is that new radical products with new technology, obtained through two-parent technology genetic crossover, have a lower initial rate of market selection, but have the greatest effect on new future market emergence.

Future economic growth is based upon the birth of new firms, who introduce technologically different products than existing products, and the production of the radically new products creates new exchange relationships in the intermediate demand market.

If, as a matter of contingent evolutionary process, these new technologically different products create new income flows, and if those new income flows modify the initial distribution of income in the economy, then future economic growth may occur.

It is not automatic, however, that economic growth will occur, even if income distribution changes.

We apply the classification scheme for initial biological populations provided by Austin Hughes, to our product classification scheme. (Adaptive Evolution of Genes and Genomes, 1999.).

The processes of product technological evolution would initially be placed within an analytical framework that had five of the Hughes classification features:

- Initially, there is a population of firms and products. The population is either growing or declining from one generation to the next.
- There is non-random, or "directional" asexual mating between products within existing technological industrial clusters.
- Firms and products have overlapping generations, and subsequent generations of products eliminate earlier products via a process of technological obsolescence.
- There are adaptive mutations of existing products, as owners of firms tinker with the outward appearance and inward technological features of the product, within the product's limited life-cycle of technological utility.
- The genotypes are the technological characteristics of products, and positive assortive mating between products that look alike or function alike technologically, and are called "industrial clusters."

The industrial clusters represent "groupings" of firms by product, and the industrial clusters can be represented in input output transactions tables that have been modified by factor analysis to show non-obvious technological similarities among product groups. (Vass, Laurie Thomas, Using Feser's Input-Output Model of Technological Affinities to Target Innovation Investments to Regional Industrial Value Chains, SSRN, 2008.).

The environmental conditions for breaking away from equilibrium, and for disintegrating global value chains, depends both on the supply of product genetic diversity, caused by firms seeking new sources of technological food, and environmental chance, in the form of initial technological conditions that allow for inter-species technology cross-product breeding.

Chapter 5 Diagram 1. Economy Breaking Away From Equilibrium In Time Period One to Potential Attractor Point in Time Period Two.

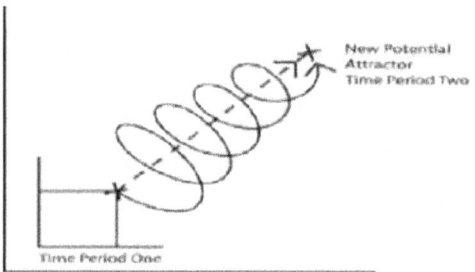

Vass, Laurie Thomas, The Theory of Technology Evolution, 2019.

On the upward spiral of economic growth, the center points of each oscillation could be determined and connected as a line through those center points.

Even though the amplitude of the oscillations are declining, the center points would be tracing out a logarithmic curve whose rate of change would be approaching zero at some future point in time.

As the economy breaks away from the old equilibrium, each initial increment of growth adds a large amount of transactions to the cycle of growth in the intermediate demand matrix.

Later increments of growth add to the cycle, but at a diminishing marginal rate.

The hypothesized future attractor point is where the marginal rate of change is close to zero, which represents the economy's next equilibrium point.

The economy reaches its future attractor point through a series of micro bifurcations in growth caused by consumer selection preferences.

The process of breaking away from equilibrium in time period one can also be described as a downward trajectory to a future attractor point of economic decline, characterized as Muller's Ratchet. (Muller, H. J.,The relation of recombination to mutational advance, Mutation Research. 1964.).

On the downward spiral of economic decline, the amplitudes of each cycle become smaller, representing the idea that the overall economic activity of exchange transactions in the intermediate demand matrix is diminishing.

The rate of growth in the economy is diminishing because the product genetic diversity is being used up in mutation through redundancy, without the addition of a new supply of genetic material from two product parent cross-breeding.

Once an economy loses the ability to generate new genetic diversity, it loses its neuronal pathways.

Losing technological genetic diversity for an economy is just like the human brain losing neuronal pathways. Once the neuronal pathways are destroyed, the brain loses its ability to imagine new futures.

If no new genetic material is added from 2-parent cross-breeding, the economy slowly drifts down through micro bifurcation points, through which a return to economic growth is very difficult because the supply of technological diversity is eroding over time..

Diagram 6 describes the rate of change in economic activity as a curved line that connects the midpoints of each oscillation.

At the future Nash Equilibrium, the economy can spin around and around the equilibrium, for decades at a time. The economy has ratcheted down to a low level of macro aggregate demand, and has adjusted to the lower rate of status quo technological diversity.

Chapter 5 Diagram 6. Economy Breaking Away From Equilibrium.

Diagram 6. Economy Breaking Away From Equilibrium In Time Period One to Potential Attractor Point of Economic Decline in Time Period Two.

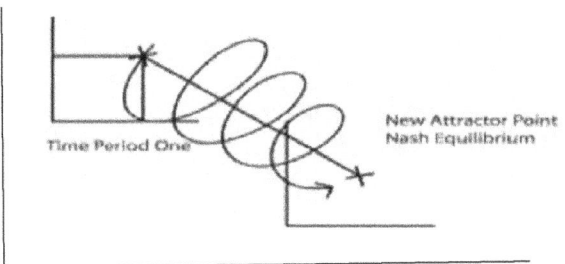

Future Potential Attractor Point of Economic Decline

Diagram 8 depicts the two possible pathways an economy can take from the equilibrium point in time period one.

Breaking away from equilibrium, in time period 1, to a future economic growth point in time period 2, would be rare, and dependent on just the right mix of events to push the technological evolutionary process to the strange attractor point that looked entirely different than the current state of equilibrium in time period one.

Chapter 6 Diagram 8. Two Possible Pathways.

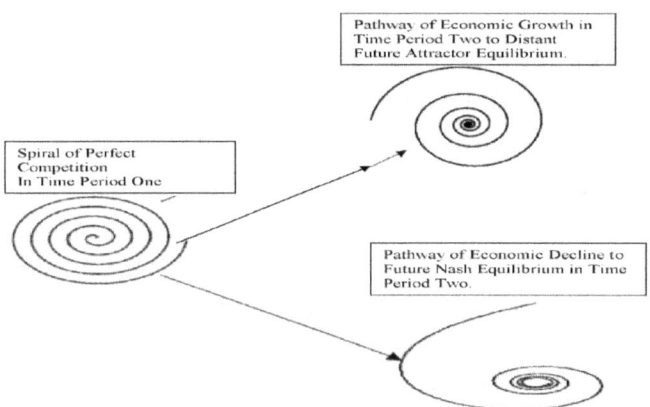

Diagram 8. Two Possible Pathways From Equilibrium In Time Period One to Future Equilibrium Points In Time Period Two.

The probability of a two-parent technology crossover leading to a bifurcation in market demand for a new product is contingent upon what consumers do when they first see the new radical product.

Under conditions where a product crossover in technology between two species occurs, if consumers select that new product, the probability for market bifurcation exists, where demand characteristics between the two market environments change.

Unlike the selection process in Darwin, the consumer selection process in technology evolution is influenced by political and financial interests who are committed to keeping the legacy technology alive, as long as possible.

Their allegiance to the status quo technology retards radical technological innovation in time period one, and consequently, retards macro economic aggregate demand in future time periods.

Existing firms producing an existing product, and existing commercial bankers who may have loaned money to those firms, have a motivation to control the direction of technology in order to maintain their incomes.

"Research and development is directed towards shaping and refining knowledge in very specific ways," states Peter Hall. (Innovation, Economics and Evolution: Theoretical Perspectives on Changing Technology in Economic Systems, 1994.).

The shaping of knowledge that Hall is describing is an allegiance to the sustaining innovation in an existing product. In other words, making the existing product more user friendly in order to extend the legacy technology of the product.

Hall explains that,

"Research and development is worth doing only if it generates a product or process of commercial value...which both fits with the firm's existing [technological] capabilities and meets market requirements (of existing consumers)."

The crony capitalist political manipulation of the regulatory rules and economic laws and tariffs, becomes more pronounced as income competition regarding maintenance of the status quo income distribution intensifies.

The sustaining innovation product selection of consumers leads to or "causes" variation in technology to decline as a result of consumers selecting existing products because they do not have radical new products to choose, as an alternative.

Consumers have no new products to choose, in time period 2, because of political manipulation of the rules that have the effect of eliminating the rate of investment in radical new products.

"Sustaining innovations," states Clayton Christensen, "are what move companies along established improvement trajectories. They are improvements to existing products on dimensions historically valued by customers." (Christensen, Clayton M., The Innovator's Dilemma, 2000.).

Christensen is describing a movement along a production possibilities frontier, in an existing state of equilibrium. Movements along the PPF merely change the existing distribution of income among social classes.

The creation of new flows of income occur as an outward shift of the PPF, as a result of new technology that causes economic growth.

"After a radical disruptive technology takes root in new markets," said Christensen, "and after new growth is created, disruption can invade the established market and destroy its leading firms."

As Christensen notes,

"The techniques that worked so extraordinarily well when applied to sustaining technologies, however, clearly failed badly when applied to markets or applications that did not yet exist."

Of the 172 companies studied by Christensen, 95% reached a point where their growth in sales stalled to rates at or below the rate of growth in the GNP. After the period of time that the growth rate stalled, "only 4% were able to successfully reignite their growth even to a rate of 1% above GNP growth."

Those 172 companies had entered Muller's Ratchet, and only 4% of them had been able to regenerate economic growth, after they had used up the initial supply of technological diversity of sustaining innovation.

The significance of Christensen's insight about technological features is that users who see the radical new product for the first time are engaged in a mental imagination process of trying out mentally how the new product may fit into their utility function.

If those potential consumers decide to buy the new product, they may contribute to the creation of an entirely new future market, which causes the PPF to shift outward.

Economic growth comes from the new flows of profit and incomes in new future markets. The new future markets are created by radical new technology products.

The theory of technology evolution predicts that if,

•A new two-parent product is imagined and visualized by an entrepreneur, and if,
•A new product phenotype prototype is created, and if,

- The new potential product can find capital to produce and market the product, and if,
- The new radical product can find a small consumer niche to buy the higher priced product, when the consumers first see it,
- Then, there is a slight possibility that the new product phenotype can survive, without being killed by the incumbent firms.

If the new product is commercialized, it may create new inter-industry intermediate demand relationships between the suppliers from both the product parents.

The increased exchange transactions in the intermediate demand relationships, in time period 2, create new flows of income, and the latent possibility of a second round of technological evolution of radical new products resulting from cross-breeding of technology from two distinct parent products.

The latent possibility of a second round of technological evolution, in time period 2, could possibly move the economy towards a new economic growth distant attractor point, in time period 3.

Section 3 of Chapter 5. Mental Utility Maps and Consumer's Brains.

The underlying fundamental human behavior being investigated in technology evolution is how the human brain processes information in the presence of a novel event.

Predicting the direction of technology depends on predicting what humans are going to do when they first see a new, radical product.

The brain, in this case, is aiming at individual sovereignty, or as biologists may interpret the behavior, individual control over the environment.

The same idea in economic theory is called welfare maximization.

In the existing equilibrium time period one, there are two different brain processes that are relevant to the theory of technology evolution.

One process is in the brain of the owner of the firm, the first time she sees, or gains knowledge, of a new product or new production technique.

The other brain process is the consumer, the first time she sees a radical new product for the first time, and tries to imagine how that product may fit into her welfare function.

Both human brains are acting, in a biological way, as the "searching/selection" mechanism for the product mutation/innovation process.

Products currently selected in the existing market are more "fit" than those not selected.

In order to separate the various brain processes under investigation, Melanie Mitchell, in An Introduction to Genetic Algorithms, (1998.), breaks the two processes into a "search space," and a "selection space."

The brain of the firm owner is sorting and shuffling thousands of mental images, searching for decisions about the solution to the new situation.

"When one hypothesis fails, notes John Holland, the brain [of the owner] comes up with "competing rules that are waiting in the wings to be tried." (Hidden Order: How Adaptation Builds Complexity, 1995.).

In the case of new conditions, Holland suggests that the owner of the firm "...combines tested rules to describe novel situations."

Holland describes how the brain decomposes the new situation [searching] into familiar parts in order to apply rules of decisions [selection] in the past that had been successful in similar situations.

The brain of the consumer goes through a similar searching and selection sorting and shuffling process.

Just like the guesses made by managers of firms about the best course of action, the consumer is also making guesses about the future.

The consumer guesses are based upon the notion of the "rational pursuit of self interest," as perceived in the brain of the individual making the decision.

The consumer's brain is filtering thousands of images, trying to come up with something that looks like the new product.

The internal images in the brain are comparing the old internal brain images with the new external images of the product, in order to come up with a strategy for how to respond to the new thing.

This guessing activity of consumers about novel events is in contrast to consumer behavior in existing markets, with older versions of the product.

With old products, the consumer brain has developed rules of thumb making selections, primarily based upon maximizing utility at the lowest cost.

With new products, the selection behavior of consumers is not a priced-based activity, it is an insight-imagination, mental-guess-based activity.

Much of what happens in the theory of technology evolution depends on what the consumer does when she first "sees" the new product.

When she first "sees" the new product, she "imagines" how the new product may "fit" with her expectations of the future.

The seeing and imaging part of the explanation is a biological function that occurs in the brains of each consumer, when they are confronted by a new thing.

In the sequence of events leading to technology evolution, the guesses being made by consumers influence the guesses made by both venture capitalists and potential entrepreneurs about what consumers are going to do when they first see the new product.

Section 4.of Chapter 5. Mental Imagination of Entrepreneurs About Future Market Emergence.

The entrepreneur is the agent of technical change that links the unknown future of consumer preferences to market possibilities that result from radical product innovation.

Entrepreneurs perform the economic function of creating the future markets by imagining how that market will work. They provide the guesses of prices and profits, and how technological change in production units will interact with, as yet unseen, consumer preferences.

Charles Kindleberger, in World Economic Primacy, noted how a certain set of cultural values tended to favor an attitude towards technical innovation.

He characterized this attitude as the,

"Capability and will of individuals, companies and governments to break free of existing habits, perceptions, institutions, and task allocations, in order to revise them in light of constantly changing circumstances and developments." (1996.).

In other words, consumers imagine how the radical new product may fit into their utility function, and entrepreneurs imagine how that future market may function.

According to Robert McAdams in Paths of Fire, the entrepreneurs have a "creative vision" in their capacity to "anticipate a new convergence of consumer preferences and technological possibilities." (Paths of Fire: An Anthropologist's Inquiry into Western Technology, 1996.).

In making the distinction between unknown costs and risks of the future, and the known costs and risks in the existing old production unit, McAdams hits upon the single greatest economic contribution that entrepreneurs make to technological evolution.

Entrepreneurs create the future market by imagining how technology in that market may function.

The reason that the latent entrepreneurial technological skills of engineers and scientists is so important is that "technology" is defined as a body of knowledge about how things work.

The short-term competition between firms is based upon price competition of existing products, in existing markets, primarily with fixed production technology in the exiting manufacturing plant.

The primary form of long-term market competition between existing firms and new entrepreneurial ventures is based upon competition for technological knowledge.

Entrepreneurs possess technological knowledge about how things work.

Pier Saviotti describes why the supply of entrepreneurs in a distinct economic region is so important to the process of technical change. (Technological Evolution, Variety and The Economy, 1996).

Generally, the entrepreneurs are drawn from the ranks and staff of existing large companies.

Prior to starting a new venture, the staff in the old firms meet with each other in their social business networks, and discuss how to solve technical problems.

Saviotti writes,

"The knowledge of engineers, scientists, managers, technicians, etc., involved in the implementation of the technology becomes specialized around the process, technical and service characteristics used."

In other words, within the existing regional economic social-business network of skilled individuals, there is a shared specialized knowledge about production processes and markets.

According to Saviotti, one reason an economy develops specialized technological knowledge is related to the,

"...specific institutional configurations and by the cumulative, local, and specific character of the knowledge that the institutions possess."

Saviotti notes that entrepreneurial innovative firms,

"...tend to cluster in those (areas) that were already innovating countries...this specificity cannot be explained by factor endowments, but is more likely to be caused by specific institutional configurations, and by the cumulative, local and specific character of the knowledge that the institutions possess."

The geographical closeness of the firms facilitates tacit knowledge creation and diffusion.

Peter Temin makes this same point in his article, "Entrepreneurs and Managers." (Temin, Peter, "Entrepreneurs and Managers," in Higonnet, P., Landes, D. Rosovsky, H., (Eds.), Favorites of Fortune, Harvard University Press, Cambridge, 1991.).

He states that,

"Entrepreneurs are the agents of change, ...(they) see new opportunities, invent new machines, discover new markets, ...(they) perform a different function from that of the manager, who works within a known technology, organization, and market."

In our New Evolutionary Economic Growth Theory of Entrepreneurial Capitalism, we conclude,

"Entrepreneurs have a mental map of the future market, consumers have a mental map of how a new product may fit into their utility maximization function, and investors have a mental map of how to make profits from an innovation investment opportunity." (The Theory of Technology Evolution, 2019.).

The data in the mental map of the entrepreneur, of technology knowledge, is linked to the economic concept of "the emergence of the future market."

In other words, in most neo-classical marginal economic theory, the theory just assumes from the beginning that innovation opportunities exist, and that the 2 actors in the market, named capital and labor, will automatically discover the opportunities that exist, and then exploit them.

In our new theory, entrepreneurs use their mental maps of technological knowledge to "see" economic relationships that, at first glance, do not seem obvious.

Levenhagen, et al., presented evidence from research on how 13 software entrepreneurs first noticed, or discovered their new obscure investment opportunity. (Levenhagen, M.J.,

Thomas, H. & Porac, J., The formation of emergent markets: Strategic investigations in the software industry, 1993.).

They found that the entrepreneurs relied on internally created conceptualizations to visualize how cross-breeding technology could create a new radical product.

In other words, entrepreneurs tend to connect unrelated technological events, and then use their mental maps to visualize how the technical change from cross-breeding two parent products, could be applied in a future market that they intend to create.

Section 5 of Chapter 5 Regional Intermediate Demand Production Relationships as the Source of Technological Knowledge.

The accumulation of technological knowledge, and the pace of technical change, are contingent outcomes of the social and political institutional structure of a regional economy.

Technological knowledge is created and diffused when two products are located close to each other, and share some technology characteristics, both in the intermediate demand production processes and in the final market of consumer preferences.

The professional executives, scientific staff, engineering staff, sales staff and plant floor supervisors meet each other in professional meetings or other social business networks in the regional social environment.

Mostly, they talk about how to solve the problems they are having in production and marketing.

From a theoretical perspective, what they are doing is sharing and diffusing technological knowledge about how things work.

When these staff from these social/business network events return from the meetings, our evolutionary theory calls them "boundary-crossers," because they cross industry and product boundaries to bring back technological knowledge to their firm.

In our biological metaphor, these boundary-crossers look just like honey bees who return to the hive with nectar.

In most cases, the boundary-crossers contribute to sustaining innovation in existing products by making small adjustments in production and technological features for their existing firm.

In very rare cases, the boundary-crossers may collaborate with staff from other firms on the creation of entirely "new-to-the-world" products.

Feser's work on modifying regional input-output models with factor analysis provides the analytical framework for investigating the region's knowledge creation and diffusion of new knowledge. (Feser, Edward, National Industry Cluster Templates: A Framework For Applied Regional Analysis, 2000, and A Test For the Coincident Economic and Spatial Clustering of Business Enterprises, 2002.).

Feser's basic hypothesis is that co-located businesses that are in the same production chain, share similarities in intermediate input consumption, technology or worker skill mix and are related through other intermediary institutions or informal means.

The intermediate demand structure serves a double duty of describing both the production technology of the economy, and the institutional social class structure of market relationships.

In our theoretical application of Feser's method, each technical coefficient in the regional A matrix describes a knowledge flow between two industrial sectors.

In our application, technological knowledge is a factor endowment, or asset, of the economy, which can grow or can erode over time.

Feser's analytical framework of an input-output model, modified by factor analysis, describes how both the feed forward and the feedback of how new knowledge affects technological evolution.

The coeffcients in Feser's interindustry matrix, as thy changes over time, is a reflection of how new knowledge is created, diffused and, contingently, commercialized in the form of a new radical product.

Each time a new coefficient shows up in the A matrix from product crossbreeding, the coefficient is describing the creation of new knowledge.

Each time a coefficient disappears from the A matrix, the regional economy has suffered a loss of neuronal pathways.

As Feser explains,

"...it is not just the size of the district alone, but social, cultural, and political factors, including trust, business customs, social ties, and other institutional considerations."

Feser notes that,

"The clusters represent distinct technological groupings of sectors or product chains...Although the conduits of interdependence between firms extend well beyond supplier linkages, input-output flows provide the single best uniform means of identifying which firms and industries are most likely to interact through a myriad of interrelated formal and informal channels."

In other words, applying the biological metaphor, Feser's method predicts which product parents, who share technological affinities, are most likely to cross breed to create a new radical product.

It is not obvious, or immediately apparent, which parent products share technological affinities. Some of the combinations between products, such as cell phones and digital cameras, could not be analyzed, without Feser's method.

As Feser explains,

"By grouping those firms that are most likely to interact with each other, both directly and indirectly, the clusters reveal relative specializations in the economy in terms of extended product chains (buyer-supplier, import replacement, and entrepreneurship based strategies) as well as technology deployment and cross firm networking initiatives."

The technology clusters that are uncovered by Feser's method are surrogates for the environmental social networks which allow new knowledge to flow within the economy.

The higher the density of technological affinities in the matrix, the faster the rate of knowledge contagion, as the disease of new knowledge rapidly infects those knowledge-bearing units closest to the outbreak of new knowledge.

In other words, the intermediate demand matrix diffuses knowledge back through all the firms who supply intermediate inputs in the intermediate demand matrix.

We provide a diagram to describe how this potential new radical product may emerge from knowledge flows between two parent firms in the regional economy.

Diagram 10 shows that hypothetical A-B yellow-green parents created a blue AB offspring product.

Chapter 5 Diagram 10. Hypothetical A-B Yellow-Green Parents Created a Blue AB Offspring Product.

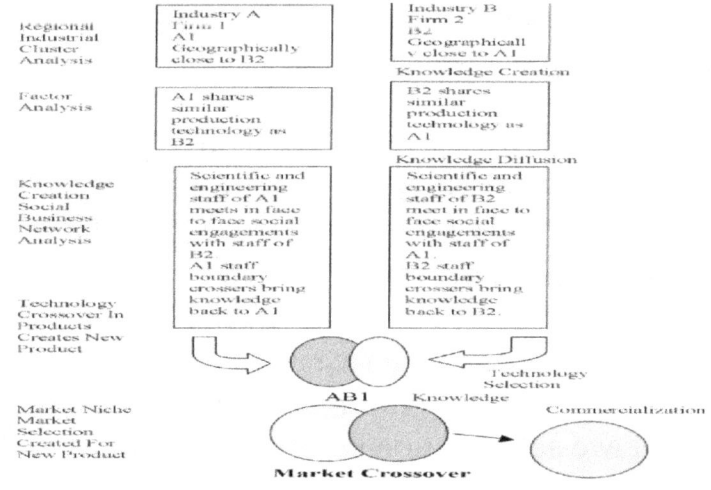

Chapter 6. Creating the New Institutional Infrastructure to Support Regional Technology Innovation and Product Commercialization.

The vulnerability of vertically integrated global value chains arises from uncontrolled tacit knowledge creation and diffusion, and the subsequent possible emergence of new radical products which disrupt the status quo global distribution of income.

Elected representatives in each U. S. metro region will need to implement an economic growth administrative and management system to support regional technology innovation in order to exploit the weaknesses of the vertically integrated global value chains.

The goal of the regional entrepreneurial capitalist growth model is to replace the existing corrupt crony corporatist global business model with a new model of regional decentralized economic growth.

Achieving that goal for elected representatives means adopting an ideology of allegiance and loyalty to the citizens of their region that is strong enough to withstand the political counter-attack that will be coming from the proponents of the New World Order agenda. (Vass, Laurie Thomas, The Importance of Regional Allegiance and Territorial Loyalty For Elected Representatives In Implementing Economic Development and Job Creation Policies: Economic Policy Advice For Local and State Elected Representatives Who Oppose the New World Order Crony Corporate Fascism. SSRN, 2023.)

The first step towards creating the institutional management framework for elected and business leaders in each region is to visualize economic growth in their regional economy as if the regional economy was a business venture whose main product is the creation of new technological small business ventures.

Chapter 6 Section 1. Replacing Global Crony Capitalism With The Rule of Law in An Entrepreneurial Capitalist Economy.

The U. S. domestic economy collapsed, after 2008, when it became apparent that the Rule of Law did not apply to the most powerful elites in the nation, undermining a very easy to understand legal principle about equality before the law.

In the corrupt global crony capitalist model, the law does not apply equally to everyone.

Some elites operate beyond the reach of the law, and other elites have subjugated the allegiance to obey the law to their own ends. (Vass, Laurie Thomas, The American Rule of Law and the Collapse of the American Economy, SSRN, 2008.

The American entrepreneurial capitalist economy only works when a veil of trust and honesty under lays the enormous quantity of transactions that occur between strangers in the market every second.

Legal philosophers sometimes call this cloud of trust, the Rule of Law, to distinguish the concept from real legislative laws and court decisions.

The Rule of Law means that Americans can trust other Americans not to take advantage of them in financial and economic transactions.

More importantly, the Rule of Law states that Americans can trust other citizens not do something that undermines the sovereign national commonwealth provided by the original endowment of individual liberty, in Jefferson's 1776 Declaration of Independence.

Part of the fraud perpetrated on American citizens by ruling class elites, before China was admitted to the WTO, was that global values of trust and honesty in other countries were just like those moral values in America.

The other part of the fraud was that free trade in goods is no different than freely trading away America's initial factor endowments of individualism and innovation.

Moving American innovation technology and R&D to India and China is perfectly legal, economically rational, and absolutely immoral individual behavior because it violated the heritage of American moral values not to harm other citizens.

Trading away America's ability to innovate undermines the basic promise citizens make to each other not to destroy America's heritage in order to gain personal financial advantage.

Under the Rule of Law, before 1992, American citizens had some reasonable expectation that elected representatives, corporate executives, and agents of government, would protect the commonwealth.

That prior expectation no longer exists, and the framework for the Rule of Law must be reconstructed in each metro region.

The new institutional framework to administer the regional entrepreneurial capitalist system begins with the reconstruction of trust in economic and political exchange.

Corinne Grenier et al., in their article, The Process of Creation and Capitalization of Knowledge Within Distributed Organizations: The Case of Clusters, (SSRN, 2008.) identifies the moral value of trust as an essential component of economic exchange.

As they note,

"Trust is usually one important characteristic of clusters (Belussi, 2005) which eases the exchange of tacit knowledge (Gottardi, 2003) facilitated by informal relationships (Abecassis-Moedas and Grenier, 2007). Proximity and trust facilitate, rather than prevent both competition and cooperation among their members which are dual strategic and relational modes of acting within clusters strongly useful for firm and technology development."

The moral quality of trust exists within a 50-mile metro economic envelope characterized by in-person, face-to-face, relationships. This 50-mile envelope is the same distance used by economists to define the daily commuting distance to jobs.

In The Reason of Rules, (1985), Brennan and Buchanan explain that the minimal social and political conditions for allegiance to obey the rule of law begins with premise that citizens will follow fair constitutional rules that they give to themselves, in the pre-constitutional setting.

Buchanan's rules aim at creating a society based upon mutual reciprocity of fairness and trust.

The issue of trust involves the reliance of a citizen that another party to a financial exchange will reciprocate in the future on keeping promises that involve a future payment.

In the institutional context of radical technology innovation, both the entrepreneur and the investor must trust each other to obtain a future payment.

In The Rule of Law, Freedom, and Prosperity Todd J. Zywicki, extends the concept of trust to the institutional framework of an entrepreneurial capitalist economy. (SSRN, 2002.).

Zywicki writes,

"Economists have increasingly come to realize the importance of political and legal institutions, especially the presence of the rule of law, in providing the foundation of freedom and prosperity. The rule of law constrains arbitrary action by political actors that is not taken pursuant to established rules and procedures announced prior to the action. Government under the rule of law preserves individual freedom; government without the rule of law is tyranny, in that it leaves individuals subject to the arbitrary will of rules…The rule of law enhances individual freedom by permitting individuals to choose and pursue their own ends in life, without improper influence from the state. Because the law speaks only to the means that individuals can use to achieve their personal aspirations, the purpose-independent rules of the rule of law permits a maximum flourishing of individual choice...The link between the rule of law and economic growth derives from the micro-level incentives created by the conditions sustained by the rule of law. By constraining arbitrary governmental activity, the rule of law provides an institutional framework conducive to investment, entrepreneurship, and long-term capital development."

Buchanan states that economic growth and social prosperity arise from the economic market institutions that allow for voluntary exchange to take place, in the post-constitutional setting. (Vass, Laurie Thomas, Buchanan's Fair Constitutional Rules as the Foundation of the Entrepreneurial Economy, SSRN, 2009.).

The lynchpin that binds citizen allegiance to obey the rule of law is future economic growth, in which all citizens have an equal opportunity to benefit.

Peter J. Boettke and Christopher J. Coyne describe the relative importance between the function of economic growth, and constitutionally protected individual liberty.

They state,

"The connection [Buchanan sees between free market exchange and individual liberty] begins with his individualistic approach to economics. Individuals have their own goals and desires, and the purpose of economic activity is to enable them to cooperate with each other so they can further those goals. As economists depict it, individuals have "utility functions" and they make choices that enable them to maximize their utility [wealth]. What this means in more common language is that individuals have their own goals, which each individual understands better than does anyone else. And the subject of economics, as Buchanan saw it, is to analyze how individuals interact for their mutual benefit in furtherance of those goals…The distribution of product among social classes [welfare redistribution] is clearly secondary to production…[economic growth]. [Economic growth occurs] by the removal of government constraints on individual liberty." (Boettke, Peter J. and Coyne, Christopher J., Methodological Individualism, Spontaneous Order and the Research Program of the Workshop in Political Theory and Policy Analysis, George Mason University, Department of Economics, 2004.).

In the individualist entrepreneurial capitalist society, fairness constitutes the ability of the individual to appropriate the income that they produce through free market exchange.

The only unambiguous goal of public economic policy is private sector economic growth, caused by private capital market investments.

Progress towards that goal entails reconstructing economic and political institutions, in each metro region, based upon trust and the Rule of Law.

In the current corrupt crony corporate institutional setting, no public or private entity aims at the public purpose of future growth or technological innovation.

That future obligation of reconstructing the institutional framework rests with elected representatives in each metro region who have allegiance and loyalty to the sovereignty of individuals who live in their region.

Chapter 6 Section 2, Citizen Economic Sovereignty and Constitutional Individual Liberty.

Voluntary allegiance to obey the rule of law, in an entrepreneurial capitalist economy, results from the fact that all citizens have an equal opportunity for upward mobility and individual prosperity.

As Buchanan points out, voluntary allegiance to obey the rule of law results from the realization that it is in one's best interest for his or her life's mission to be consistent with the public purpose of the rule of law.

Buchanan argues that there is only one constitutional configuration that produces maximum economic growth, based upon maximum rates of knowledge creation and diffusion.

That unique constitutional configuration of rules creates the free enterprise innovation entrepreneurial capitalist economy.

That single constitutional configuration creates the maximum level of trust among citizens, so that citizens can trust each other to obey the rule of law.

Coincidentally, that same constitutional configuration also creates the maximum rates of knowledge creation and diffusion among citizens.

Maximum rates of knowledge creation create the social conditions for maximum rates of technology innovation.

Buchanan's fair constitutional rules link the individual choice, in the free market system, to individual choice in the political system because economic individualism is linked to equal political natural rights.

No other constitutional configuration starts out with this set of equal natural rights.

Equal natural rights create maximum economic growth, which, in turn, creates maximum social welfare.

The relationship between constitutional individual freedom and metro regional economic growth is through the ability of individuals to create new technology ventures that commercialize new technology products.

Generally, in the absence of fair constitutional rules that point to the goal of open competition for income, the reward structure associated collectivist rules about income distribution are manipulated to the benefit of the most powerful set of elites, who obtain crony corporate power over setting the rules and the laws.

Buchanan's constitutional rules would severely limit the central government's range of power so that citizen free choice in subsequent market and political institutions would allow a stable social order to emerge.

Buchanan's constitutional rules aim at the creation of rules, in the pre-constitutional setting, that limit the power of government to solely and exclusively providing the functions of protecting individual liberty, property-rights protection and public-goods provision, without overstepping its limits into civil rights predation or wealth redistribution.

Buchanan writes,

"These [pre-constitutional] rules provide the framework within which [the post-constitutional institutional] patterns of distributional end states emerge from the interaction of persons who play various complex functional [market and political] roles."

In the post-constitutional setting, institutions, such as banks and judicial institutions, are created that are bound to obey the fair constitutional rules

We agree with Buchanan that a stable social order would emerge from the operation and transactions that occur in a free market entrepreneurial capitalist society, including the free market determination of rates of interest.

Buchanan states that economic growth and social prosperity arise from the economic market institutions that allow for voluntary exchange to take place, in the post-constitutional setting.

In other words, a fair distribution of income and wealth, under Buchanan's fair rules, is obtained through just rules of financial and economic exchange, which is based upon voluntary allegiance to obey the Rule of Law. (Vass, Laurie Thomas, Justice and the Rule of Law, SSRN, 2019.).

Implementing this type of constitutional framework in each metro region is an essential step for elected representatives to take in creating the regional entrepreneurial capitalist economy that aims at maximum rates of economic growth.

Chapter 6 Section 3. Managing The Metro Regional New Venture Innovation Pipeline.

Regional elected representatives need to visualize their regional economy as an economic growth machine, whose output is a great number of small new technological ventures, or enterprises.

Their job is to manage and administer the regional economic growth machine as if it was a business enterprise.

We provide a diagram of the logical sequence of events that occur in a regional economy that depicts the economy as if it were a small business deal creation pipeline. (Vass, Laurie Thomas, Doing More Deals: Re-Envisioning the Use of Industrial Clusters to Target Regional Innovation Investments, SSRN, 2008.).

Chapter 6 Diagram 1. The Small Business Deal Creation Pipeline.

The Small Business Deal Creation Pipeline™

Deal Mapping	Deal Creation	Deal Funding	Deal Exits
To convert knowledge and ideas into small business ventures and new products	To prepare new ventures or product ideas to enter the market	To find capital to fund commercial ventures	To manage the reinvestment of profit from the first generati of ideas into the next generation of innovation

At the very top of the regional deal creation pipeline is deal mapping, which is the easiest component of the regional economic growth business model for elected representatives to manage.

This part of the business management model consists of providing social business networking events in the region, on a periodic time frame.

These social/business networking events look just like the current model of technology innovation in the Research Triangle Park, N. C., administered by the Council for Entrepreneurial Development (CED).

The CED states its mission on its website as,

"CED acts as the connective center for all of this (technology new venture creation) to happen. Through high-touch support, education, access to capital, and crucial connections, we bring entrepreneurs together with the optimal resources needed to turn a new company into a success story. Programs like Connect to Capital have enabled entrepreneurs to connect with potential investors via formal introductions–with more than 600 made since 2014."

The purpose of the networking events is to allow the scientific staff, engineers and salespeople in the regions industrial clusters to meet each other and discuss doing deals by sharing and diffusing tacit knowledge.

The CED website mentions many other organizations and support associations that assist in the process of tacit knowledge creation and diffusion.

These other business and political organizations were first identified in 1982 N. C. Department of Labor research document as important to the North Carolina initiative to create new technology ventures to stimulate regional economic growth. (Vass, Laurie Thomas, Industrial Recruitment and the Path of North Carolina's Economic

Development to the Year 2000: A Public Discussion Paper for North Carolina's Project 2000 - Advocating the Creation of the NC Council for Entrepreneurial Development (CED), North Carolina Department of Labor, Raleigh, NC, 1982. SSRN.).

All of these regional support organizations need to have representatives who operate within the regional management framework in order for the mission of the business model to have a unified mental image of their regional economy as a business venture, whose purpose is to create many new high technology ventures.

Edward M. Bergman and Edward J. Feser call this idea of visualizing the regional economy as "seeing the regional economy whole."

They write,

"In large measure, industry cluster analyses and policies may be viewed as applications of a set of well-worn but rejuvenated theories of how geography helps drive economic growth and the greatest value in the industry cluster concept is its capacity to help both the analyst and policymaker "see the regional economy whole."…Industry cluster analysis can help exploit the growing wealth of regional economic data, provide a means of thinking effectively about industrial interdependence, and generate unique pictures of a regional economy that reveal more effective policy options." (Industrial and Regional Clusters: Concepts and Comparative Applications, 2nd ed., West Virginia University Regional Research Institute, 2020.).

Chapter 6 Diagram 2. Graphic from NC Department of Labor, 1982.

Organizational roles and relationships

Local chambers of commerce (existent)
Identify market opportunites. Have a dialogue with the local economic planning board about future growth and industrial recruitment. Would supply the needs of newly recruited industry through their affiliation with the entrepreneurs association.

North Carolina Department of Commerce (existent)
Identifies market opportunites that result from newly recruited industry. Would communicate with the Rural and Community Ventures Corporation about industries moving to North Carolina and about plant closings.

Center for New Business Executives (non-existent)
Would train local business people. Would refer clients to the Venture Finance Corporation. Would receive client referrals from the Rural and Community Ventures Corporation. Would be a statewide, privately funded organization.

Entrepreneurs association (non-existent)
Would serve as a community focal point for people who want to go into business for themselves. Would be a locally based, private, nonprofit organization. Would receive projections about the local economy and information about the types and numbers of jobs that employers need to fill from the local economic planning board. Would also receive information about newly recruited industry from the local chamber of commerce. Would exchange information with the Rural and Community Ventures Corporation about new ventures.

Rural and Community Ventures Corporation (non-existent)
Would provide guidance to local communities about development projects. Would be a statewide, nonprofit organization. Would receive information about industries moving into North Carolina and about plant closings from the North Carolina Department of Commerce. Would refer clients to the Center for New Business Executives and to the Venture Finance Corporation. Would exchange information with the entrepreneurs association about ideas for venture capital investment.

Venture Finance Corporation (non-existent)
Would package capital investment programs. Would receive client referrals from the Rural and Community Venture Corporation, the Center for New Business Executives, and the Service Corps of Retired Executives/Active Corps of Executives (SCORE/ACE). Would assist clients referred by SCORE/ACE in obtaining venture capital.

Local economic planning boards (non-existent)
Would estimate basic needs for jobs in local communities. Would make projections about the local economics. Would be public agencies, and would receive assistance from county planning staffs. Would send information about local economic projections to the entrepreneurs association. Would exchange information with the local community and technical colleges and technical institutes about: (1) the number of students in training; (2) occupational outlooks; and (3) career guidance. Would also exchange information about the

60

We operationalize their idea of "seeing the regional economy whole," by placing it into an economic growth policy management framework that regional elected leaders could administer. (Vass, Laurie Thomas, Placing the Concept of the RTP Startup Ecosystem into a Regional Innovation Policy Framework, SSRN, 2015.).

Feser and Bergman use the same type of input-output value chain analysis of regional interindustry intermediate demand networks that also describe vertically integrated value chains in the global economy.

In our earlier criticism of globalism, we identified these former U. S. regional intermediate demand networks as the metro regional networks that were moved to China and India, after 2002.

Moving the regional intermediate demand networks to China destroyed the ability of U. S. metro regions to promote tacit knowledge creation and diffusion, which consequently reduced U. S. job and economic growth.

The economic growth strategy of entrepreneurial capitalism is to re-construct these value chains in the regional administrative and management policy system of creating new technology ventures by regenerating the forces of technological innovation.

Feser writes that his approach to regional value chain analysis,

"shifts the policy objective from building clusters per se to increasing rates of innovation by implementing development strategies in ways that leverage inter firm synergies and connections to non market institutions, even when firms are not part of concentrated regional agglomerations."

We place the Feser-Begman input-output methodology into our theoretical paradigm of how technology evolves to show how technological cross-over between two industrial parent members of a regional value chain create the potential for radical product innovation. (Vass, Laurie Thomas, The Theory of Technology Evolution, Gabby Press, 2019.).

The Feser-Bergman methodology uses very sophisticated statistical factor analysis of interindustry relationships in the regional A matrix to uncover technological relationships among member firms that are not obvious.

They provide Exhibit 2.1 to describe how firms in a regional industrial cluster interact with each other.

As we explained earlier, in our theoretical paradigm, each transaction technical coefficient in the modified input-output A matrix describes a flow of tacit knowledge that is exchanged based upon a price-based exchange between members of the regional cluster.

Chapter 6 Exhibit 2.1 Regional Industrial Clusters.

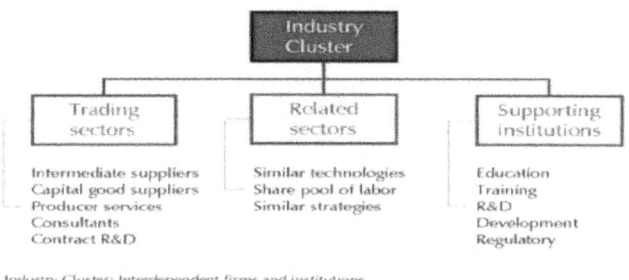

Exhibit 2.1 from Industrial and Regional Clusters: Concepts and Comparative Applications, 2nd ed., 2020.

In Exhibit 3.10, below, they describe the linkages between firms in the North Carolina motor vehicle manufacturing industrial cluster, identified by Standard Industrial Classification (SIC) code 308, after the application of their factor analysis to uncover hidden technological relationships among member firms.

The arrows in Exhibit 3.10 describe significant trading partners among member firms in the regional intermediate demand networks.

The direction of an arrow between a firm in sectors i and a firm in sector j indicates that sector j purchases a significant share of its inputs from industry i, where "significant" is defined as exceeding a threshold based on the distribution of linkages between all sectors in the cluster.

Chapter 6 Exhibit 3.10. Industrial Cluster Purchasing Patterns Vehicle Manufacturing.

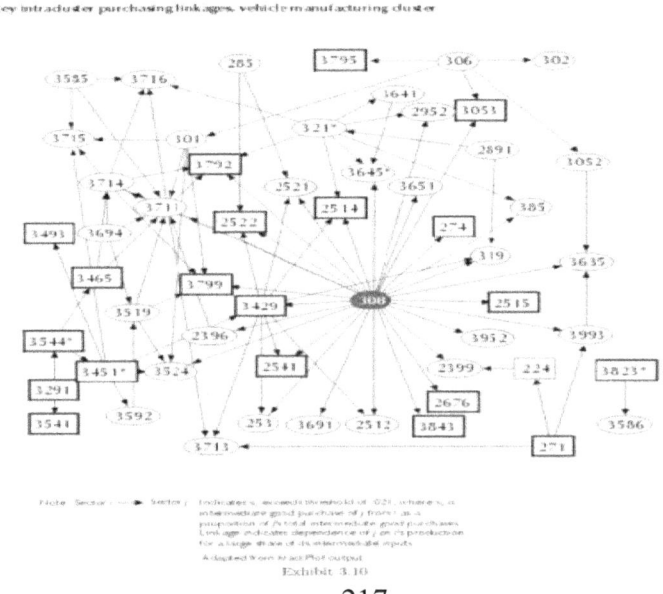

Exhibit 3.10

Exhibit 3.10 from Industrial and Regional Clusters: Concepts and Comparative Applications, 2nd ed., 2020.

As applied to just a single N. C. economic region, the Research Triangle, they show the relationships in member firms of this regional cluster in Exhibit 4.9.

Chapter 6 Exhibit 4.9. Research Triangle, N. C. Industrial Linkages.

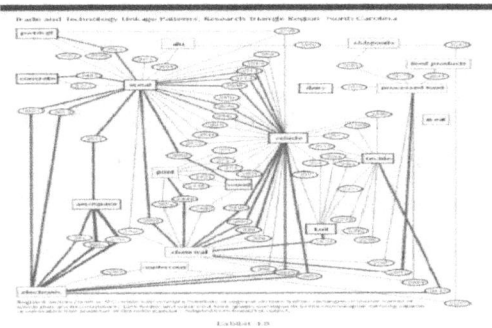

Exhibit 4.9 from Industrial and Regional Clusters: Concepts and Comparative Applications, 2nd ed., 2020.

The arrows and linkages in the diagrams reveal potential flows of tacit knowledge between member firms in the modified regional input output econometric model.

The managers and administrators of the regional economic growth business model are searching for potential relationships among member firms, in this case, among member firms in the RTP motor vehicles industrial cluster. (Vass, Laurie Thomas, Searching for Investments in the Nine High Technology Clusters, SSRN, 2008.).

The managers and administrators would use the Feser-Bergman econometric model to identify and invite representatives of these firms to the social/business networking events in hopes of facilitating a two parent technological product cross breeding from different firms.

The evidence and potential for radical new product creation is very slight, and very hard to discover because the potential new firms are very small, and sometimes only exist as ideas in the minds of the scientific staff who share tacit knowledge.

In their recent research, "Firms in Scottish High Technology Clusters," Gavin Reid and Vandanna Ujjual describe five Scottish high tech clusters: software, life sciences, microelectronics, optoelectronics and digital media. (Semantic Scholar, 2008.).

They write,

"The average time it took a small firm to go from the generation of a new idea to launching a new product or process was 1.25 years...the creation of new (product) possibilities (occurred) through the 'collision' of existing technologies... The average employment size (of the new venture) was four in 2002 and six (estimate) in 2003... The average (occupational structure) number of full-time employees were: three technical/scientific staff, and one managerial staff. Many of these high technology firms did not employ manual and clerical staff. Without fail, all scientific, technical and managerial employees had university degrees. In other words, these firms were high skill, high-human capital and knowledge intensive in character."

The technical and scientific staff identified by Reid and Ujjual constitue the target market of attendees in the regional social/business networking events managed by regional managers and administrators.

As we mentioned above, there are political and financial special interests in each region which are opposed to the creation and operation of these types of regional social business networking events because these events create and diffuse tacit knowledge, which may disrupt the status quo distribution of power and income in each region.

The political opposition is primarily from large global corporations who may have located a branch plant, or a product distribution center in the region, as a component of their vertically integrated global value chain strategy.

Drucker and Feser term this political opposition as "regional industrial dominance" of large global corporations in a region.

They write,

"An environment of small, independent establishments is more supportive of entrepreneurial networks, group learning, and other entrepreneurial activities than a setting dominated by a small number of large firms (Porter 1990; Malecki 1994; Acs 1996; Carree and Thurik 1999; Enright 2000; Gordon and McCann 2000; Helmsing 2001). Regional social organizations and culture help to determine support for business risk-taking, and are shaped partly by the presence of or degree of corporate dominance within regional industries (Norton 1992; Rosenfeld 1996). (Drucker, Joshua M., Feser, Edward, Regional Industrial Dominance, Agglomeration Economies, and Manufacturing Plant

Productivity. US Census Bureau Center for Economic Studies Paper No. CES-07-31. SSRN. 2008.).

At the very top of the small business innovation pipeline, in addition to managing the social/business network events, there are two primary management tools required by regional innovation managers and administrators in order to promote new technology venture creation:

1. Ongoing, periodic analysis of the region's technological clusters using the Feser Technological Affinities Model. (Vass, Laurie Thomas, Using Feser's Input-Output Model of Technological Affinities to Target Innovation Investments to Regional Industrial Value Chains, SSRN, 2008.).

2. Analysis of the regions social and business networks using social network analysis (SNA) computer software. (Vass, Laurie Thomas, Income Distribution and Technological Evolution. SSRN, 2019. **And** (Vass, Laurie Thomas, Where Were They and What Were They Doing Before They Became Entrepreneurs? SSRN, 2008.).

We advise regional elected representatives to place these two management tools into a computer blockchain economic policy framework to track and evaluate the effectiveness of the regional entrepreneurial capitalist growth model.

Chapter 6. Section 4. Administering the New Venture Creation Block Chain Institutional Framework.

Diagram 5. below, describes the sequence of events in radical product innovation, as seen from the perspective of large corporations as a threat to the vertically integrated corporate global value chains. (Vass, Laurie Thomas,

Updating Schumpeter's Gales of Creative Destruction: Exploiting the Vulnerability of New World Order Corporate Globalism With Regional Blockchain Entrepreneurial Economic Growth, Gabby Press, 2022.).

The existential threat to the large global corporations comes in the last block of profit reinvestment because that ongoing reinvestment of profits signals the emergence of a new market bifurcation which permanently disrupts the existing status quo of global product markets.

Chapter 6 Diagram 5. Chronological Sequence of Events of a Radical Innovation Leading to A Potential Market Disruption.

Appearance of novel radical product from two-parent technology crossover.	Emergence of small niche market, as consumers select the new product.	Displacement of old product by new radical product. Product market micro bifurcation.	Creation of intermediate demand markets to support production and distribution of product.	Creation of new income flows where none had previously existed.	Profit reinvestment from capital "exit" events into technology trajectory created by new radical product.

Joseph Schumpeter explained the significance of profit reinvestment in terms of how the capitalist society reproduced itself. (The Theory of Economic Development, 1961.).

His insight was that the source of capital for a new firm was not derived from price-based exchanges in the sphere of production in an existing economic time period.

As Schumpeter stated,

"By far, the greater part of it (capital) does not come from thrift in the strict sense, that is from abstaining from the consumption of part of one's regular income, but it consists of funds which are themselves the result of successful innovation, and in which we shall see later (and) recognize as entrepreneurial profit."

The profits from the earlier investments are re-invested in the second time period, according to Schumpeter, and the effect of the investment in time period two, is to create new income and wealth in time period three.

The investment of profits from exit events in new firms created new income in the future, which Schumpeter called "purchasing power." The investment in new firms eliminated existing firms, through the gales of creative destruction.

Schumpeter's term for radical product innovation was "new thing."

Schumpeter wrote,

"It (entrepreneurial profit) attaches to the creation of new things, to the realization of the future value system...Without (entrepreneurial) development, there is no (entrepreneurial) profit, and without profit, no (economic) development...without (entrepreneurial) profit there would be no accumulation of wealth."

According to Schumpeter, the "new thing," created by the entrepreneur is based upon the entrepreneur's application of technology, and comes into the market alongside of the "old thing."

He stated,

"...the new enterprises either completely eliminate old businesses or else force them to restrict their operations."

Schumpeter wrote,

"The new enterprise...does not grow out of the old, (enterprise) but appears alongside of it, and eliminates it (the old enterprise) competitively, so as to change all the conditions that a special process of adaptation becomes necessary." (Schumpeter quoted in Vass, Laurie Thomas, The Contribution of Schumpeter to the Theory of Technology Evolution, SSRN, 2019.).

We place Schumpeter's sequence of radical product innovation, described above in Diagram 5, into a policy framework that can be managed and administered by elected regional leaders to promote regional entrepreneurial growth. (Vass, Laurie Thomas, Updating Schumpeter's Entrepreneurial Economic Growth Model as the Economic Alternative to the Corporate New World Order. SSRN, 2022.).

The regional policy framework consists of placing the sequence of entrepreneurial events into a computer blockchain business model of the regional economy, which is administered by regional economic development managers.

We describe this regional policy framework below, in Diagram 2.1.

At each step in the blockchain administrative model, events and communications are tracked and monitored by regional economic development managers.

Chapter 6 Diagram 2.1 Regional Blockchain New Technology Venture Creation.

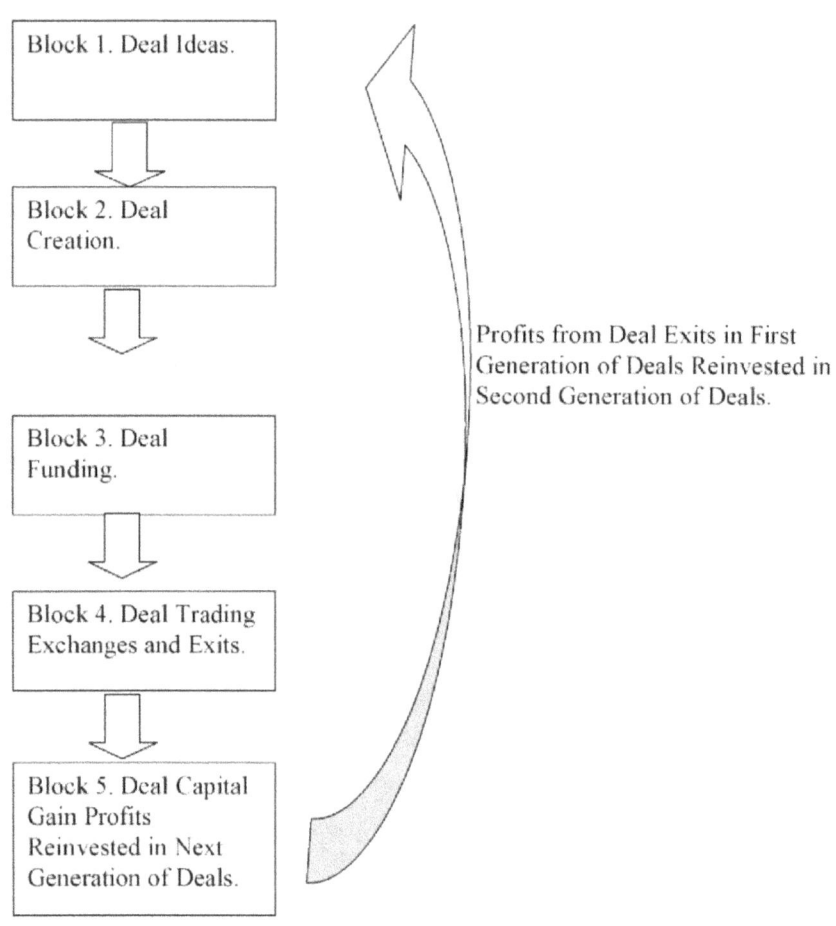

Diagram 2. Regional Blockchain New Technology Venture Creation Model.

Clayton Christensen et al., cited the new blockchain computer technology as a tool to help manage economic growth, and we extend and modify his idea to include regional blockchains that replicate the economic development process from entrepreneurial idea creation to private securities exchanges for capital market exit transactions, in regional stock exchanges. (Christensen, Clayton, et.al., The Third Answer: How Market-Creating Innovation Drives Economic Growth and Development. SSRN, 2018.).

The entire process of regional technological innovation can be visualized and facilitated by Christensen's concept of using blockchain as a management tool to promote economic growth.

Christensen writes,

"Blockchain is a public, decentralized, distributed digital ledger that is used to record electronic transactions. Each "block" in a blockchain contains specific information that cannot be altered, due to the distributed nature of the technology. In a blockchain-based economy, the market-creating innovation [new venture investment] and the institutions governing it [social-business networks] are fundamentally intertwined."

All of the engineers, scientists, mid-level managers and sales staff, in the regional technology clusters who meet in the social/business network events communicate with each other about new venture ideas, and when they leave to create their own new entrepreneurial venture, the blockchain management tool manages the entrepreneurial process, as if it were a business venture.

The end goal of the blockchain management tool aims at creating new future regional intermediate demand markets and networks.

As Chistensen notes,

""Market-creating innovations do exactly what the term implies: they create new markets. But these are not just any new markets; they are new markets that serve people for whom either no products existed or existing products were not accessible for a variety of reasons, including cost or a lack of the expertise required to use them... the ideas (or recipes) that are critical to market-creating innovation, and that actually propel growth and development, are overwhelmingly uncodified, context dependent, and transferable only at significant cost, which is to say that tacit knowledge dominates, information asymmetries are the norm, and transaction costs are significant."

The tacit knowledge creation that Christensen references occurs in business social networks among citizens who are deeply engaged in contributing prosperity to their community.

We connect Christensen's concept of the management of blockchain innovation to the concept of the Feser-Bergman analysis of nine regional high technology clusters, within which technology innovation occurs at the regional geographical level.

Blockchain computer technology drives metro economic development by enabling market-creating innovations, primarily in geographically specific regions because the diffusion of tacit knowledge that is personal, and done mostly in face-to-face communications, can be visualized and ideas and intellectual property can be made explicit and protected with the blockchain technology.

The intent and purpose of the regional blockchain model of knowledge creation and diffusion is to increase the rate of new technology venture creation in the particular metro region.

The blockchain technology business model allows the entire process of regional new venture creation to be replicated via internet collaboration.

At the very top of the blockchain are the tacit knowledge face-to-face meetings between scientific and engineering citizens who live in the region, and bear knowledge that potentially leads to the creation of a new radical product.

Chapter 6 Section 5. Visualizing Metro Regional Entrepreneurial Capitalist Growth As A Business Model.

Product development professionals have a term of art that they apply to the length of time it takes an entrepreneur from idea to new venture launch.

Their term for this period of time is "the fuzzy front end."

Alan S. Gutterman, in his research article, Product Development for Small Businesses and Startups, discusses the length of time potential entrepreneurs spend wandering around in the fuzzy front end. (SSRN, 2023.).

Gutterman writes,

"For example, one study found that the average development time for a start-up company's initial product was about 15 months; however, the actual time for companies within the study ranged from as quickly as nine months to as long as 24 months."

Gutterman concludes his article with this observation:

"Wouldn't it be nice if an entrepreneur could quickly execute a new idea by summoning an entire organization with just a click?"

Our concept of having regional elected representatives visualize the metro regional entrepreneurial capitalist growth as a business model is based upon placing all of the region's resources to support entrepreneurial new venture creation into the blockchain policy framework.

The jobs created by any single entrepreneurial venture are very small, generally only 4 or 5 jobs in the first five years.

Almost all of the new technology ventures die in the first five years. If the new venture can survive to year eight, the rate of job growth is exponential.

In years 5 and 6, the new venture needs a slug of growth capital to continue to survive.

Yet, in a paradox of job creation, it is small technology ventures that create almost 100% of the nation's new jobs.

In their research on new venture job creation, Michael Horrell and Robert Litan write,

"Prior research has established the essential role of startups in new job creation and employment growth in the American economy. Kane (2010) states, "Startups aren't everything when it comes to job growth. They're the only thing," and he shows through an analysis of the Business Dynamics Statistics (BDS) dataset that, "without startups, there would be no net job growth in the U.S. economy." (After Inception:

How Enduring is Job Creation by Startups? Ewing Marion Kauffman Foundation, July 2010.).

In other words, it takes an incredibly high rate of new technology venture creation just to run in place in job creation.

Figure 3, below, from the Kaufmann Foundation, describes that about 60% of all job creation is due to firms less than 5 years old.

Chapter 6 Figure 3. Young Firm Job Creation.

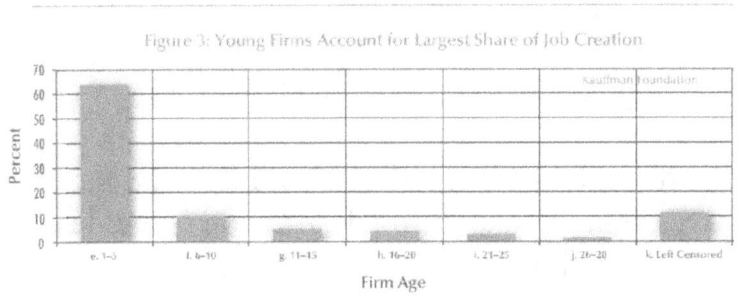

Research by John Haltiwanger shows the dynamics of job creation and job loss in U. S. new high tech ventures from 1978 to 2011, in Figure 1, below.

Chapter 6 Figure 4. Gross Job Creation and Destruction Rates.

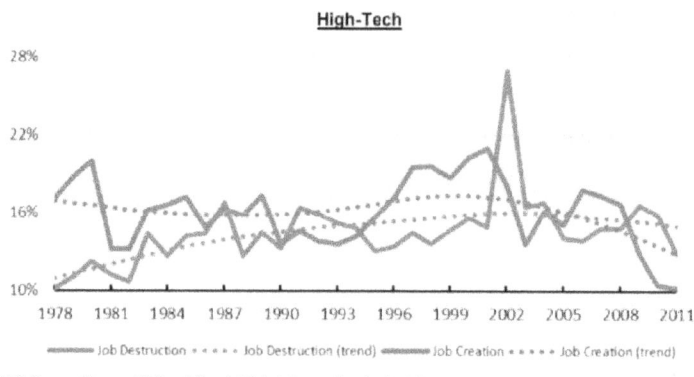

Fig. 1: Gross Job Creation and Destruction Rates in High-Tech Sector (1978–2011)

Source: U.S. Census Bureau, BDS and Special Tabulation; authors' calculations
Note: Trends are calculated by applying a Hodrick-Prescott filter with a multiplier of 400

The dramatic decline in job creation after 2002, and the dramatic increase in the rate of job destruction coincides with the implementation of the vertically integrated corporate global value chain business model.

Haltiwanger writes,

"Start-ups are small; more than 90% have less than 20 employees, and small start-ups account for about half of all start-up employment (see Figure 3). Approximately 90% of start-up employment is accounted for by firms with less than 250 employees." (Job Creation, Job Destruction, and Productivity Growth: The Role of Young Businesses, The Annual Review of Economics, 2015.).

The ultimate economic goal for elected representatives of seeing the region as a business venture is to create self-sustaining, self-renewing economic growth from profit reinvestment back into the second generation of new ventures that were created in the first generation of new ventures.

In our theoretical paradigm of technology evolution, that second generation of new technology ventures would indicate the approach to a new bifurcation point of upward economic growth, where the income and employment multipliers in the regional intermediate demand networks were becoming stronger.

That goal of profit reinvestment will only occur in the 350 metro regional economies if the regional intermediate demand networks are reconstructed, which allow for tacit knowledge creation and diffusion among latent entrepreneurs..

It is a long-term economic strategy that requires patience, and allegiance and loyalty to the citizens who live in the metro regions.

Chapter 7. Knowledge Creation and Diffusion in U. S. Metro Regional High Technology Industrial Clusters.

New tacit knowledge is created in a mental "insight-imagination" process when the brain encounters a novel circumstance.

This mental process is commonly called "imagination."

The future that is imagined is tried out mentally, thousands of times a second in an individual's brain as it sorts and searches for what may happen if a sequence of events occurs.

As the mental image of the novel condition is filtered and processed by hundreds and thousands of neural synapse firings, the brain is searching and sorting for the right fit between the new external image and the brain's internal model of the image.

The main goal of the sorting and searching, from a biological perspective, is quantum coherence in a course of action or behavior to either seek advantage or seek survival.

The brain is calling upon memory circuits of something that looked like the novel circumstance, and combining those memories with new internal images to come up with the right fit and the right course of action.

The new knowledge takes the form of new mental constructs and neural connections in the brain.

New knowledge is created as a result of the coherence of beliefs associated with an individual's internal and external images lining up together.

The knowledge creates a permanent construct in the brain, so that the individual will "know" what to do if the novel event occurs again.

As the thousands of images are sorted, the neural networks tend to line up and fire in sequence, which is a condition called "making up your mind."

Humans are confronted with novel circumstances primarily in their dealings with other humans.

Evolution of the brain has allowed humans to anticipate the response of other humans, and imagine what the other humans may do in the future, as if it had, in fact, already occurred.

Applied to economic behavior, humans in a market are continually imagining what other humans are going to do, and hypothesizing about the future.

When the brains of other humans "see" the same novel event, and change their own internal mental images and insights, then the reality of the new knowledge is confirmed as "real," by the humans who are imagining the same future.

Scientists call this confirmation of realty between different humans as the "intersubjective" verification of reality.

Humans, in a regional technological community, interact with each other every day, by exchanging technical information on production and markets, based upon their store of knowledge and memories.

In our biological theoretical paradigm, new knowledge in technological evolution seems analogous to food, or energy, which gets "eaten" in the Lotka-Volterra biological setting.

In the biological metaphor, the boundary-spanners of scientific staff, in regional firms, are seeking food in the form of market and technical knowledge in their environment.

Translating to the biological metaphor, if the boundary-spanner gets back to her firm, and if the firm "imitates" the best production practices of other firms, the firm is "adapting" to the new knowledge in the environment.

The creation of new technical knowledge is a social phenomenon caused by the interaction of humans engaged in social/business relationships.

Tacit knowledge creation is a social, cultural process and takes place in the institutional social networks defined by the regional intermediate demand production networks.

The scientific and technical staff in the firms communicate with individuals in other firms, at continuing education seminars, professional trade meetings and social/business networking events, such as the events managed by the N. C. Council for Entrepreneurial Development.

Tacit knowledge, in its economic context, is created, and is diffused among a distinct economic population, generally within a 50-mile envelope surrounding the metro region.

In this evolutionary biological depiction of tacit knowledge creation, the scientists, engineers, sales staff and service repair technicians are the agents who "bear" knowledge, and cross boundaries.

These agents consume knowledge, and their pursuit of knowledge becomes an important activity in understanding the evolution of technology.

Rinaldo Evangelista, explains, in Knowledge and Investment: The Sources of Innovation In Industry, (1999),

"The general process of technological change can be conceptualized as a process of
generation of new technological knowledge as distinct from the process which leads to its actual use in production...in the form of new or improved machines, technical devices and operating systems."

In our Structural Evolutionary Regional Economic Theory (SERET), new products, created by new tacit knowledge, represent, in the Darwinian context, a new species, that are mutations of old genetic technology. (Vass, Laurie Thomas, The Theory of Technology Evolution, Gabby Press, 2019.).

To the extent that the scientific and technical staff in a firm can imagine a new product, there is a slight possibility that new tacit knowledge will be created.

The units of analysis in the measurement of knowledge creation are the knowledge-bearing humans, who carry knowledge around in their heads.

Tacit knowledge, in the theory of technology evolution, builds upon what exists in the memories of humans, and knowledge is cumulative, in the sense that it builds upon existing memories.

The social intermediate demand networks that exist within the regional economy serve as the institutional framework for both knowledge creation and knowledge diffusion.

Tacit knowledge, unlike autonomous price-based transactions in neoclassical tradition, does not start over from scratch with each new encounter between boundary crossers.

New tacit knowledge is diffused within the social networks when the boundary crossers meet each other, in face-to-face encounters. The reason that face-to-face engagements are so important to the theory of technology evolution (SERET), relates to how humans interpret and anticipate each other's behavior.

It is the very subtle change in voice inflection and tone, the slight change in the eyes, and facial expression that convey much of the exchange in the new tacit knowledge.

The diffusion of knowledge is not random, but Lamarkian, in the sense that the search for knowledge is purposeful and results in behavior adaptations that affects technological genetics.

"When people meet, they communicate," wrote Ilya Prigogine, and "when they leave the meeting, they keep the memory of their encounter. When they meet other people, this communication is propagated to an ever-increasing number of participants." (Exploring Complexity: An Introduction, 1989.).

In Theoretical Welfare Economics, (1957), Jan de Van Graaff made this same point about the social process of diffusing knowledge.

Graaff states that:

"The ultimate repositories of technical knowledge in any society are the men (humans) comprising it, and it is just this knowledge which is effectively summarized in the form of a transformation function…new knowledge, created with perhaps one purpose in mind, [increased production efficiency] but is in fact valuable in a very different context."

Rikard Stankiewicz, in Technological Systems and Economic Performance: The Case of Factory Automation, (1995), notes that:

"Every engineer is embedded in a particular technological tradition characterizing his profession, the company he works for, and the team he is a part of- the technological community…The accumulation and transmission of knowledge occurs in, and through, the formation of technological communities, and is strongly affected by their structure and dynamics."

What the engineer does with his knowledge, and how the knowledge is diffused within the technical community, become important elements of the theory of technology evolution.

Tacit knowledge diffusion, in the regional intermediate demand networks, looks like the spread of a disease or infection throughout a population.

Epidemiologists call this diffusion of a disease a contagion, and speculate that the density of the humans in the human's habitat influences the rate of contagion, or knowledge diffusion, within the region.

Some regional economies have social networks that share norms and culturally-based systems of interpretation, where the deliberate behavior of knowledge creation occurs.

If knowledge can be defined as an economic asset, or a pool of knowledge, then that pool or asset must be measurable, and additions to new knowledge must be distinct from the old knowledge.

Unlike natural resources, however, like a region's deposits of iron ore, the resource of tacit knowledge can either grow, or can also decline.

In this case, at the beginning of the time period one, a regional economy could be characterized as having a "stock" of knowledge, based upon the number of agents in the economy who are engaged in searching for the food of knowledge.

An initial stock of regional knowledge could either "flow" into a greater base of knowledge, in time period two, or in the case of loss of genetic diversity, the stock of knowledge may "leak" out of the economy.

Sometimes, this phenomenon of knowledge leakage is called "brain drain," to refer to the idea that the agents who bear knowledge have left the region.

In our criticism of vertically integrated global value chains, 350 U. S. metro regions experienced "brain drain" when the regional intermediate demand networks were moved to China and India.

The genetic diversity of the knowledge grows when knowledge-bearing workers from one high technology cluster of add to knowledge in another cluster of technology.

In SERET, the increase in technological genetic diversity is called two parent genetic cross-over, which causes radical product innovation.

The intersubjective verification of the reality of new knowledge would be represented by a new production coefficient in the intermediate demand A matrix, signaling the entry of a new interindustry relationship for the new product.

The appearance of a new coefficient in the regional A matrix is, biologically, just like the appearance of a new neural synapse in the brain resulting from an insight/imagination that became new tacit knowledge.

The new coefficient shows linkages between the two product parent firms that describe knowledge transfers and exchanges that did not exist in the prior time period.

In other words, the priced-based transaction coefficients in a conventional input output A matrix are also describing a nonpriced knowledge transaction.

Feser's input output transaction table, modified by factor analysis, with the newly added correlation coefficients in the intermediate demand sales matrix, allows for the emergence of this market to be tracked and investigated.

Biologically, tacit knowledge created and diffused by the scientific staff boundary-spanners in regional economics would look like bees pollinating flowers in nature.

In contrast to tacit knowledge, codified knowledge is in the form of books, and manuals, or other documents, such as patents, where the knowledge has been written down, or "codified."

Codified knowledge does not create new coefficients in the transaction matrix, it only modifies the size of existing coefficients, based upon the fixed production functions of existing products.

The codified knowledge is easier for large global corporations to control than tacit knowledge because the corporate executives can control who has access to the codified knowledge.

The exclusive reliance in vertically integrated global value chains on codified knowledge, inside the global value chain, acts to limit the creation of new technology, even if a boundary-spanner, or some other source of knowledge, happened to find its way back into the regional firm.

Regional reliance on codified knowledge leads to regional economic "path dependence" because the application of codified knowledge constrains the choices of technology and the choices of people to imagine new opportunities.

A regional economy becomes "locked" into a pathway because the old ways of doing things become entrenched, and new knowledge, new ideas, new ways of doing things are limited by the reliance and corporate control on codified knowledge.

From the biological evolutionary perspective of SERET, the reliance on codified knowledge in the region is contributing to the creation of conditions of neural sclerosis and homogeneity in genetic production technology, as a result of this allegiance to the technological specialization.

The creation and diffusion of tacit knowledge, as a regional asset, cannot easily be subjected to U. S. crony capitalist political manipulation and political control, in the absence of the application of the police power of the state, such as exists in Communist China.

Rather than deploying the police power of the state, in the U. S. domestic economy, in 2002, the large U. S. corporations moved the regional intermediate demand networks in 350 metro regions, to China, thus eliminating the threat of new tacit knowledge creation and diffusion in the domestic U. S. economy.

When the U. S. regions lost their intermediate demand knowledge worker networks, they also lost the ability to create new ventures, and new technology ventures create most of the new jobs in each metro region.

The loss of so-called U. S. "business dynamism" is linked to the decline of new venture creation in small high technology firms in the 350 metro regions.

We cite research by Akcigit and Ates on the critical economic importance of knowledge creation and diffusion for stimulating economic growth. (What Happened to US. Business Dynamism? NBER Working Paper No. w25756. SSRN. 2023.).

"The knowledge diffusion channel accounts for more than 70 percent of most symptoms of declining business dynamism and at least 50 percent of all considered trends. In the past several decades, the US. economy has witnessed a number of striking trends that indicate a rising market concentration [of large global corporations] and a slowdown in business dynamism. . . Our results highlight thedominant role of a decline in the intensity of knowledge diffusion from the frontier firms [large corporations] to the laggard ones [the U. S. firms left behind in the New World Order offshoring] in explaining the observed shifts. We conclude by presenting new evidence that corroborates a declining knowledge diffusion in the economy. . . The entry rate of new businesses, the job reallocation rate, and the labor share have all been decreasing, yet the profit share, market concentration, and markups have all been rising."

They continue,

"With knowledge diffusion slowing down, [in metro regions] the direct effect is that market leaders [large global corporations] are protected from being imitated [with technology innovation from new ventures]. As a result, the technology gaps [between large corporations and metro regional new venture creation] start widening, presenting market leaders a stronger market power. [global monopoly power] Market concentration and markups rise on average. Profit share of GDP increases, [for the American ruling class] and labor share decreases. [for middle and working class citizens]. Larger gaps also discourage the followers, [entrepreneurs in the U. S] causing the productivity gap between them and the leaders to open up. The strengthening of leaders [large corporations] also discourages forward-looking entrants; hence, firm entry and the employment share of young firms go down. [in U. S. metro regions]. Discouraged followers [small firms left behind] and entrants exert smaller competitive pressure on market leaders; as a result, market leaders relax, and they experiment less. Hence, overall [technology innovation and commercialization] dynamism and experimentation decrease in the economy."

The U. S. Department of Labor identified 10 high technology clusters, in the Information and Technology (ICT), macro cluster, based upon the concentration of technology workers in each cluster.

The BLS also identified 4 other smaller technology clusters

Their graphic of the ten high technology clusters is reproduced below, as Table 2.

Chapter 7 Table 2. High Technology Industries.

Table 2: High-Technology Industries

NAICS Code	Industry
Information and Communications Technology (ICT) High-Tech	
3341	Computer and peripheral equipment manufacturing
3342	Communications equipment manufacturing
3344	Semiconductor and other electronic component manufacturing
3345	Navigational, measuring, electromedical, and control instruments manufacturing
5112	Software publishers
5161	Internet publishing and broadcasting
5179	Other telecommunications
5181	Internet service providers and Web search portals
5182	Data processing, hosting, and related services
5415	Computer systems design and related services
Miscellaneous High-Tech	
3254	Pharmaceutical and medicine manufacturing
3364	Aerospace product and parts manufacturing
5413	Architectural, engineering, and related services
5417	Scientific research-and-development services

Source: Bureau of Labor Statistics

Prior to 1992, each of the 350 U. S. metro regions had some components of each of these industrial clusters, where scientific staff shared tacit knowledge.

Any single metro region did not have all components of each technology cluster, but all metro regions had some representation of most of the clusters.

After 2002, the rate of creation of technology firms in each metro region began to decline as a result of off-shoring the intermediate demand industrial sectors of the high technology industries.

The scientists and engineers who were employed in these metro regions were "knowledge workers," who lost their jobs, and no longer created or diffused tacit knowlwedge.

After the large corporations relocated their intermediate supply chains to China and India, the knowledge creation and knowledge diffusion process in each U. S. metro region declined, to the point where net new job creation in new ventures is too low to employ surplus U. S. middle and working class workers.

Feser's work, (National Industry Cluster Templates: A Framework For Applied Regional Analysis, 2000, and A Test For the Coincident Economic and Spatial Clustering of Business Enterprises, 2002.), modified and extended the analysis of the BLS high tech clusters.

Chapter 7 Table 3. General Benchmark Clusters.

General Benchmark Clusters, U.S.

Clusters	Employment			Payroll			
	1997 (000's)	% Private Sector 1997	Annual % Change '89-'97	1997 (millions)	% Private Sector 1997	Annual % Change '89-'97	Average Wage 1997
Printing and publishing	8,948.9	8.76	2.09	355,541.2	11.57	9.03	39,730
Hospitals, labs, specialized medical services	6,646.5	6.51	3.71	252,558.2	8.22	12.16	37,999
Metalworking and industrial machinery	5,155.3	5.05	0.41	194,332.2	6.33	4.78	37,696
Information technology and instruments	3,935.6	3.85	1.13	208,092.1	6.77	8.63	52,875
Banking and advertising	3,316.7	3.25	0.37	163,189.0	5.38	9.22	49,805
Construction materials	3,266.8	3.20	0.48	121,870.8	3.97	5.32	37,308
Transportation, shipping and logistics	3,110.4	3.04	2.88	102,872.7	3.35	6.64	33,074
Motor vehicle manufacturing	2,881.8	2.82	1.16	113,422.5	3.69	5.71	39,358
Chemicals and plastics	2,771.6	2.71	1.87	106,967.7	3.48	6.80	38,594
Securities and insurance	1,681.0	1.65	1.81	71,585.0	2.33	9.12	42,584
Packaged food products	1,640.9	1.61	0.37	50,290.6	1.64	4.24	30,647
Fabricated textiles	1,320.2	1.29	-2.42	32,016.2	1.04	1.86	24,251
Apparel	1,286.9	1.26	-2.98	30,816.2	1.00	0.75	23,945
Wood products (incl. furniture)	1,000.0	0.98	0.27	31,018.5	1.01	4.02	31,017
Legal services	948.5	0.93	0.76	48,113.4	1.57	5.38	50,725
Aerospace	785.9	0.77	-4.75	42,343.6	1.38	-1.37	53,881
Primary nonferrous metals	579.9	0.57	1.05	20,426.6	0.66	5.42	35,222
Stone and clay products	303.7	0.30	0.97	14,904.8	0.49	1.26	49,076
Pharmaceuticals	269.8	0.26	2.08	17,040.2	0.55	10.53	63,162
Canned and bottled beverages	200.8	0.20	1.19	9,108.9	0.30	3.59	45,375
Boat building	198.5	0.19	-1.79	8,021.3	0.26	1.93	40,407
Aluminum	196.3	0.19	-1.87	9,426.1	0.31	1.24	48,022
Petroleum products	141.9	0.14	-1.44	8,453.7	0.28	4.76	59,557
Platemaking and typesetting	89.2	0.09	-1.89	3,973.9	0.13	2.52	44,554
Leather goods	80.1	0.08	4.62	1,928.4	0.06	0.99	24,047
Jewelry	60.6	0.07	-2.26	2,137.3	0.07	1.26	31,178
Tobacco products	41.2	0.04	-2.54	2,301.7	0.07	1.57	55,820
Food oil mills	32.5	0.03	0.32	1,244.5	0.04	5.01	38,286
Total Private Sector Employment	102,175.1		1.73	3,071,807.3		6.71	30,064

Source: Minnesota IMPLAN Group, Inc. ES-202 files and authors' calculations. Clusters are not mutually exclusive.

(National Industry Cluster Templates: A Framework For Applied Regional Analysis, 2000).

Feser applied his national technology cluster template methodology to North Carolina's 7 regions to describe how each N. C. region had some components of the national technology clusters. (Feser Edward J., and Renski, Henry, High-Tech Clusters in North Carolina, North Carolina Board of Science and Technology, 2000.).

Chapter 7 Table 4. North Carolina Industry Clusters.

Table 3
North Carolina Industry Clusters

Clusters	Employment 1998	Annual % Change '89-'98	Location Quotient 1998	Average Wage
Existing general industry clusters				
Apparel	207,698	-3.3	4.46	25,057
Fabricated textiles	128,893	3.8	2.70	23,538
Wood products (incl. furniture)	77,549	0.0	2.15	26,445
Pharmaceuticals	17,783	3.0	1.82	48,538
Tobacco products	16,151	-3.8	10.84	47,151
Stone and clay products	13,838	5.8	1.26	40,161
Emerging general industry clusters				
Printing and publishing	279,849	4.9	0.87	35,621
Hospitals, labs, specialized medical services	226,117	6.1	0.94	34,657
Transportation, shipping and logistics	118,989	2.6	1.06	32,918
Construction materials	118,390	2.2	1.00	31,990
Information technology and instruments	105,796	4.4	0.74	47,378
Chemicals and plastics	104,367	3.9	1.04	36,070
Banking and advertising	95,259	5.3	0.79	40,978
U.S. technology clusters, presence in the state				
Information technology and instruments	104,420	4.5	0.86	47,363
Communications services and software	63,660	10.0	0.66	48,241
Chemicals and plastics	53,923	4.1	1.12	38,106
Motor vehicle manufacturing	44,277	4.1	0.82	35,169
Pharmaceuticals and medical technologies	34,629	1.7	1.01	41,915
Industrial machinery	21,464	1.3	1.06	35,870
Aerospace	5,545	5.8	0.19	41,168
Household appliances	1,139	n.a.	0.36	23,492

Source: NC Employment Security Commission and Minnesota IMPLAN Group, Inc. (ES-202 files). Clusters are not mutually exclusive.

Feser's basic hypothesis is that,

"co-located businesses that are in the same production chain, share similarities in intermediate input consumption, technology or worker skill mix and are related through other intermediary institutions or informal means." (Feser, Edward J., Agglomeration, Enterprise Size, And Productivity, CES Working Paper, U.S. Bureau of the Census, 2004.).

His analytical framework of an input-output model, modified by factor analysis, describes how both the feed forward and the feedback forces of new knowledge affect technological evolution.
Feser's interindustry matrix, as it changes over time, is a reflection of how new knowledge is created, diffused and, contingently, commercialized in the form of a new radical product.

As Feser explains,

"...it is not just the size of the district alone, but social, cultural, and political factors, including trust, business customs, social ties, and other institutional considerations."

Feser notes,

"the clusters represent distinct technological groupings of sectors or product chains...Although the conduits of interdependence between firms extend well beyond supplier linkages, input-output flows provide the single best uniform means of identifying which firms and industries are most likely to interact through a myriad of interrelated formal and informal channels."

In other words, applying the SERET biological metaphor, Feser's method predicts which regional product parents, who share technological affinities, are most likely to cross breed to create a new radical product.

As Feser explains,

By grouping those firms that are most likely to interact with each other, both directly and indirectly, the clusters reveal relative specializations in the economy in terms of extended product chains (buyer-supplier, import replacement, and entrepreneurship based strategies) as well as technology deployment and cross firm networking initiatives.

The technology clusters that are uncovered by Feser's method are surrogate indicators for the business/social networks, such as those managed by the N. C. Council for Entrepreneurial Development, which allow new tacit knowledge to flow within the regional economy, and potentially create a new radical product from two product parent cross breeding of technology.

Feser compared two different manufacturing industries to demonstrate how the higher technology industry obtained greater benefits from tacit knowledge creation and diffusion. (A Flexible Test For Agglomeration Economies In Two U.S. Manufacturing Industries, CES Working Paper 04-14, , U. S. Bureau of Census, 2004.).

Feser concluded,

"Thus, we might expect technology- or knowledge-intensive industries that utilize highly specialized equipment, expertise, and knowledge to benefit more from proximity to other enterprises in their same industry (localization effects) than low to moderate technology sectors would, other things equal. Lower technology industries producing less knowledge-intensive goods may, by contrast, benefit relatively more from general advantages in large urban environments (urbanization effects) since such industries typically require workers of less specialized skill, as well as technology and equipment of more common application."

As we noted above in our chapter on the blockchain business model methodology, Clayton Christensen has also made a distinction between tacit knowledge and codified knowledge, and suggested that large global corporations in vertically integrated globalvalue chains want to avoid open flows of tacit knowledge to protect the corporation's core technology. (Christensen, Clayton, et al., How Market-Creating Innovation Drives Economic Growth and Development, Innovations /Blockchain for Global Development, 2019].

Christensen writes,

"The ideas (or recipes) that are critical to market-creating innovation, and that actually propel growth and development, are overwhelmingly uncodified, context dependent, and transferable only at significant cost which is to say that tacit knowledge dominates, information asymmetries [and] are the norm, [in new market creation] when transaction costs are significant."

Christensen notes that tacit knowledge cannot be easily be controlled by large global corporations, which is why corporations seek eliminate the sources of tacit knowledge.

We argue that the key to disintegrating vertically integrated global corporate value chains is the reconstruction of new tacit knowledge networks in each of the 350 U. S. metro regions, which may lead to the creation of new radical products, and new flows of income in future markets that would disrupt the new world order status quo distribution of income and profits.

Chapter 8. The Metro Regional Business Professional Support Network for New Venture Creation.

Chapter 8 Section 1. Professional Navigation of The Fuzzy Front End.

One of the reasons latent entrepreneurs wander around in the "fuzzy front end" for months at a time is because they cannot find the full range of professional advice that they need to help them launch their new ventures.

The fuzzy front end is a very confusing time for most technology entrepreneurs, and the most recent data from the Panel Studies of Entrepreneurial Dynamics (P SED) indicates that up to 35% of all entrepreneurial ventures get stuck in the fuzzy front end for up to four years, trying to launch their venture.

Most entrepreneurs do not know what kind of professional advice that they need, at each stage of the new venture creation pipeline.

In Product Development for Small Businesses and Startups, Alan S. Gutterman discusses the complexity and costs associated with getting a product idea out of the fuzzy front end to a venture launch. (SSRN, 2023.).

He writes,

"In fact, the National Research Council has estimated that approximately 70% of the costs associated with a product's development, manufacture and use (i.e., its life cycle) are determined in the initial design stage. [fuzzy front end]. Among other things, product developers and designers play a leading role with respect to specification of raw materials, energy inputs, purchasing specifications, hazardous materials generated, recycling and worker health and safety."

The product design and developers are an essential professional advisory component of the new venture creation business community that we identify in our small business creation business pipeline.

As Gutterman suggests, this professional advisory component of the new venture creation business model tends to see the complexity of the entire new venture project, or as Feser and Bergman suggest, they see the venture as a part of the "whole economy."

Gutterman writes,

"Innovation is a term that is increasingly being used to define the process of bringing a concept for a new product or service through development and into commercialization, which takes the form of active marketing and sales of the finished product or service in the target marketplace…What ancillary products or services will (or should) the company be offering in connection with its core products and services? For example, does the company expect to take on any warranty or service obligations with respect to its products? What intellectual property rights are involved with the company's products or services? If intellectual property rights are essential to the company's business, what steps have been (or can be) taken to protect the company's position? What are the critical stages of developing and selling the company's products and services? Are there any processes in this cycle that have not yet been completed? If so, is there a clear strategy for getting the job done, including raising sufficient capital and recruiting the necessary personnel or business partners?"

Part of the reason that entrepreneurs cannot identify professional help is because the new venture professional advisors in a region do not have group self-awareness of their collective identity to support new venture creation.

In other words, the professional advisors in a metro region do not share a common mental map of the new venture creation pipeline, or the economic importance of new venture creation to the future prosperity of their region.

Obviously, a great social benefit could be provided by the community of professional advisors and regional economic developers in managing the deal flow pipeline if they would just rescue the poor entrepreneurs from wandering around for four years in the fuzzy front end.

All of the professional advisors in a metro region would want to contribute to a coherent professional business network that efficiently converted technology ideas into ventures.

Part of the entrepreneurial confusion in new venture creation is that the existing venture capital model is the wrong mental map for promoting long-term regional prosperity.

Because there is not a viable technology innovation economic development model, such as the Small Business Innovation Pipeline, securities attorneys and intellectual property attorneys simply send their entrepreneurial clients into the jaws of the venture capitalists, which does not serve the economic development goals of the metro region. (Vass,

Laurie Thomas, Will More Venture Capital Spur Regional Innovation? SSRN, 2008.).

We agree with Brian Kingsley Krumm that "Shark Tank Shouldn't be the Model," for technology new venture creation. (Fostering Innovation and Entrepreneurship: Shark Tank Shouldn't be the Model, Arkansas Law Review, SSRN, 2017.).

Krumm points out,

"The reality is that most start-ups do not qualify for venture capital and likely never will. Most venture capitalists invest only in fast growing ventures that have a proven record of accomplishment."

On the other hand, new technology ventures have a great potential for creating future prosperity, and the financial goals of the venture capitalists are incompatible with the goals of technology innovation caused by new venture creation.

Krumm addresses the capital investment requirements of technology startups, and writes,

"The price of professional services to complete the required documents [for raising capital] and assist in compliance, can be costly. The SEC estimates that raising $100,000 may cost up to $39,810, and as much as $151,660 for a $1 million dollar raise. If, during the course of advertising, an issuer [new technology company] "makes an[y] untrue statement of material fact or omits to state a material fact" [the omission] creates liability against the issuer. [entrepreneur]."

Krumm suggests that an association of business professional advisors would greatly facilitate the creation of new technology ventures.

Krumm

"proposes the creation of a business association specifically designed to help entrepreneurs secure the necessary capital and to assist them in the management of their businesses."

We extend and modify Krumm's proposal of a professional business association to help entrepreneurs to include a more complete set of tasks that confront an entrepreneur, beyond raising capital.

Diagram 2, below, begins to place the small business creation pipeline model into the blockchain management tool for regional new venture creation.

In our extended model, we break the stages of metro regional new venture creation into deal mapping, deal creation, deal funding, and deal exits.

Chapter 8 Diagram 2. Set of Small Business Analytical Tools.

Diagram 2. The Set of Small Business Analytical Tools For Small Business Innovation Systems

Deal Mapping Tools:	Deal Creation Tools:	Deal Funding Tools:	Deal Exit Tools:
The Feser Technological Affinities Model to find latent or hidden innovation investment opportunities in the region's technology value chains.	The New Business Sales and Marketing Social Network Mapping Tool to see how potential investments may create new regional value chain relationships.	The Private Capital Market Assessment Social Network Analysis Tool to see all the private market transactions required to fund both new ventures commercializing radical innovations, and existing small manufacturing firms involved in sustaining innovations.	The Investment Banking Resource Assessment Social Network Analysis Tool to see regional resources that can offer M&A services.
The Regional Knowledge Creation and Diffusion Social Network Analysis Mapping Tool to see latent or hidden knowledge flows in the region.	The Regional Product Development Assessment of Engineering Consulting Firms.		The Political Elite Influence Analysis Tool to see which political elites would support tax credit policies for reinvestment of capital gains into the next generation of innovation investments.
The Regional Innovation Competitive Assessment Social Network Mapping Tool to see which existing business and social networks would potentially support innovation in the region.	The Regional/Global Supply Chain Network Mapping Tool to describe relationships between small regional firms and MNCs that would provide the marketing portal to the global markets.		

Chapter 8 Section 2. Organizing the Community of Third Party Professionals.

We cited Feser's work in modifying the conventional A matrix in a regional input output model with factor analysis to uncover obscure relationships between regional technological clusters. (Vass, Laurie Thomas, Using Feser's Input-Output Model of Technological Affinities to Target Innovation Investments to Regional Industrial Value Chains, SSRN, 2008.).

In his work boiling down the 463 national industrial sectors into nine high technology value chains, Feser was continually coming across unusual clusters that did not appear to be like other industrial clusters.

Feser initially had a hard time figuring out how to categorize their value-added contribution to innovation.

As he noted,

"While the [unusual] clusters appear to correspond to basic industry categories, many are comprised of sectors that fall into multiple industries, or two and three digit NAICS codes. For example, the chemicals based products cluster includes paper and paperboard bills (NAICS 3221), phosphatic fertilizers (NAICS 3253), and carbon and graphite products (NAICS 3359), among others." (Feser, Edward, National Industry Cluster Templates: A Framework For Applied Regional Analysis, 2000, and A Test For the Coincident Economic and Spatial Clustering of Business Enterprises, 2002.).

Eventually, Feser categorized the unusual clusters as "knowledge clusters." (Vass, Laurie Thomas, The Role of Professional Third Party Service Providers in the Regional Innovation Economics Process, SSRN, 2008.).

As Feser noted,

"The largest technology-based clusters are technical and research services (4.3 million employees in IIQ 2004) and architectural and engineering services (3.5 million workers). There is, however, considerable overlap between those two clusters."

Feser's method was uncovering the obscure contribution made by hundreds and hundreds of small engineering and professional advisory consulting firms who provide services to small firms in the nine tech clusters in a defined geographic region.

All in all, Feser lists over 50 categories of professional service providers who form the small business consulting backbone of most regional economies.

In the input-output factor analysis method that Feser deploys, these knowledge consulting firms would be located in the regional intermediate demand market.

The consulting firms create and diffuse knowledge, and they also connect innovative firms that buy and sell goods to each other, and sometimes, the goods that they are buying are the most radical new products that fit into the regional value chains.

In other words, way beyond the role these consulting firms play in the knowledge creation and diffusion process, their network relationships provide a built-in regional market demand for the most risky, radical new products, by connecting the new products to buyers, when the radical products first appear in the market.

In our theory of technological evolution (SERET), these regional consulting firms are creating the new future market by helping new technology ventures find buyers for the radical new products.

Feser's input output method tended to show that technology innovation occurs in nine high tech clusters, and that each cluster has its own unique set of third party professional advisors, who provide consulting advice if an investment occurs anywhere in the regional intermediate demand cluster, either in upstream suppliers, or downstream clients and customers.

In one of his economic development applications of his method, for the State of Kentucky, Feser called this 10th cluster the Knowledge Cluster of Engineering, Technical & Research Services." (Feser, Edward, and Koo, Jun, Kentucky Clusters: Industrial Interdependence and Economic Competitiveness, Innovation Management and Policy, 2001.).

The Feser knowledge cluster in Kentucky was comprised of the following occupational titles:

- Environmental & other technical consulting services
- Architectural & engineering services
- Management consulting services
- Scientific research & development services

- Specialized design services
- Other ambulatory health care services
- Custom computer programming services
- Other communications equipment manufacturing
- Information services

By calling the Kentucky consulting network a knowledge cluster, Feser was highlighting the importance that the flow of tacit knowledge plays in stimulating regional technology innovation.

In our application of the Regional Innovation Pipeline, described above in Diagram 2, we modify and extend Feser's work by adding other third party professional advisors, and place them into the blockchain management tool, in the Association of New Venture Professionals, at the top of the regional blockchain tool, as described below in Diagram 1.

The other third party professional advisors that we add to the blockchain management tool, in addition to the consulting firms identified by Feser are:

- Law firms who provide general business law, securities law, and intellectual property law.
- CPA firms who provide accounting and tax advice to new ventures and small technology ventures.
- Product design and developer firms who provide technical advice on new products.
- Commercial real estate firms who provide advice on geographical cluster location of both industrial recruitment targets and new technology firms and structure rental agreements for firms in regional technology clusters.

Of particular concern for most regions is the inadequate supply of attorneys who specialize in helping new ventures issue securities in order to raise capital. (Vass, Laurie Thomas, The Case for Increasing the Supply of Private Placement Securities Lawyers in North Carolina: The Law of Supply and Demand for Securities Lawyers, SSRN, 2015.).

Two internet websites that provide directories of securities attorneys in North Carolina (FindLaw and Justia) indicate that there are only about 100 lawyers in North Carolina who practice in the area of securities law.

A review of the law firm websites indicates that many of the firms are involved in securities fraud litigation and broker/dealer defense representation, not securities private placements.

In other words, in the 9th most populated state in the Union, there are probably less than 100 lawyers who can provide private placement legal services to private firms who need to raise capital to grow their firms.

From a regional economic growth perspective, the supply of private placement attorneys in a region can be seen as a factor of production. Regions that possess more of this factor endowment of securities lawyers have an economic competitive advantage over regions that have less of that factor endowment.

Chapter 8 Diagram 1. Regional Blockchain New Venture Creation.

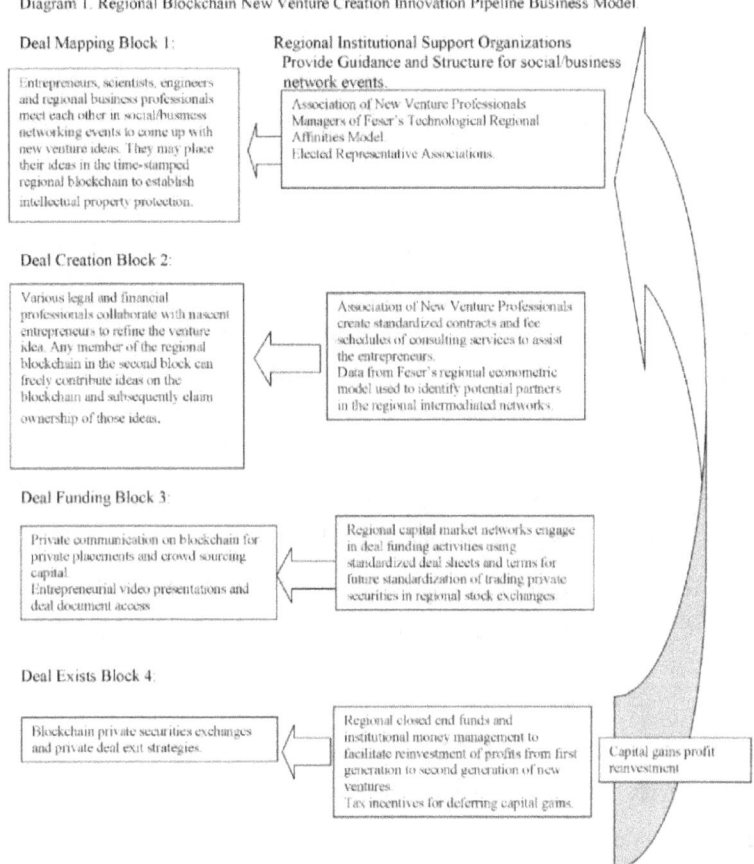

Diagram 1. Regional Blockchain New Venture Creation Innovation Pipeline Business Model

Those regions with a competitive advantage also have a competitive advantage over large corporations in the vertically integrated global value chains because the new ventures that securities lawyers help get organized create radical new products which disrupt the global corporate distribution of income.

The blockchain management tool provides the professional advisors with a shared mental image of how technology innovation contributes to their metro region's economic prosperity. (Vass, Laurie Thomas, The Crowd Funding Business Bonanza for Lawyers, Accountants and Consultants: Professional Business Advisors about to Surf a Financial Tsunami of New Crowd Funding Business, SSRN, 2013.).

The proposed Association of New Venture Professionals, in each metro region would operate as a voluntary membership non-profit, similar in concept and function to the existing Chamber of Commerce, but with a mission focus on new technology venture creation.

The members of the Association of New Venture Professionals would be members of the regional blockchain management group, and participate in the deal mapping social/business networking events, as event sponsors and speakers.

The second block in upper right corner of the above Diagram 1, describes how existing regional economic developers, who already have an existing professional organization, can share tasks in a professional division of labor between consulting and advisory professionals and the economic developer community. (Vass, Laurie Thomas, The Nexus of Financial and Political Interests between Crowd Funders and Regional Economic Development Professionals: The New-New Innovation Economics, SSRN, 2013.).

In other words, in the division of labor involving third party professional advisors and economic developers, the most important job of the economic developers is to manage the Feser Technological Affinities model and distribute the results of the model to all of the third party professional advisors.

Managing and administering the Feser model is not a revenue-generating activity, so no private sector entity is going to conduct this function. But, the results of the model would be very valuable information for the entire new venture ecosystem, and the existing non-profit economic development agencies are in the best position to manage this tool.

The added potential benefit of having the regional economic developers manage the Feser Technological Affinities model is that the data results of the model provide an intellectual framework for economic developers to link their existing industrial recruitment tasks to the recruitment of firms which strengthen the regional inter industrial demand networks, in the emerging regional technological clusters. (Vass, Laurie Thomas, How Economic Developers Can Manage the Regional Deal Flow Pipeline, SSRN, 2013.).

These potential new emerging technological clusters would be topics for discussion at the periodic Deal Mapping social/business events, such as those managed by the N. C. Council for Entrepreneurial Development.

As described in Diagram 1, regional new venture creation, using blockchain computer technology, is intended to be an on-going process of profit reinvestment that creates self-sustaining, self-renewing regional economic growth.

In other words, one of the goals of regional new venture creation of disintegrating global value chains is to create an on-going capital gains reinvestment process from deal exits, so that profits from one generation of technology ventures can stay in the regional economy and can be re-invested in the next generation of innovation.

In order to be an effective economic development alternative to vertically integrated global value chains, the blockchain management tool must become a permanent part of the region's new venture creation pipeline institutional framework for third party professional advisers and regional economic developers.

It takes about three years from deal mapping ideas to new venture launch. (Vass, Laurie Thomas, The Three Year Time Lag Between Innovation Collaboration and New Product Introduction, SSRN, 2008.).

In their research on collaboration events, "R&D Collaborations and Product Innovation," Un et al., studied 781 manufacturing firms over a five year period of time to find out more about the effects of collaboration between different types of firms. (Journal of Product Innovation Management, May 2008.).

They characterized the inter-firm collaboration in terms of informal social exchanges.

Most collaborations were,

"temporary exchanges of researchers, conference attendance, graduate student internships, and a variety of other creative mechanisms allow universities and companies to connect and exchange knowledge in a mutually profitable relationship…The main mechanism of collaboration was in the industrial value chains, by which knowledge is accessed and transferred between suppliers and buyers/assemblers is personnel exchange in the new product."

From the moment of collaboration to product introduction, they found a range of events over a five year period. Some ideas hatched in one year, more events hatched in two years, but the highest rate of hatchings, [new venture creation] about 96%, took place in year three.

The regional blockchain management tool is intended to achieve long-term economic development and regional prosperity that is designed to match the three year time lag of new venture creation, with a capital gain reinvestment exit event around year 10.

Chapter 8 Section 3. Placing the Technology Innovation Pipeline Into the Regional Blockchain Management Tool.

The blockchain technology reduces the confusion and uncertainty that entrepreneurs face in the initial deal creation phase of new venture creation.

The intent and purpose of the regional blockchain model of knowledge creation and diffusion is to increase the rate of new technology venture creation in the particular metro region.

A blockchain is, in the simplest of terms, a time-stamped series of immutable computer records of data that is managed by a cluster of computers that are not owned, or controlled, by a centralized organization, or by a state or federal government agency.

The idea that the blockchain data cannot be owned, or controlled, by global corporations, or the government, is one of the key strengths of the blockchain economic growth model.

Each of these blocks of data (i.e. block) is secured and bound to another block of data using cryptographic principles (i.e. chain).

Each "block" in a blockchain contains specific information that cannot be altered, due to the peer-to-peer distributed nature of the technology.

As a result, the blockchain technology has the potential to reduce uncertainty around ownership of new venture ideas and intellectual property rights and other property claims, by providing verified records, and thereby strengthening private capital market institutions.

The blockchain technology allows the entire process of regional new venture creation to be moved from physical interactions to internet collaboration.

The new venture creation process envisioned by the block chain model can be described as a series of "if-then" contingent statements, where any citizen in the region with an interest in economic growth could participate in the first two blocks of the regional blockchain computer network.

As described in Diagram 1, the entire process of new venture creation is envisioned to take place in a blockchain network of computers, geographically located within 50 miles of the metro region.

The regional new venture creation blockchain is maintained by a peer-to-peer social network of people in the region who have an interest in new venture creation and regional economic growth.

Ideas that gain community traction among participants in the first block of deal mapping are gated through to the second block for further processing into more definitive new venture ideas.

The communication in the second block brings in the set of professional advisors and other interested parties to view the progress of a potential new venture transaction.

In a process similar to current new venture angel capital networking events, potential investors also have unlimited access to the shared data about a venture in the second block.

This process is commonly called "deal creation," where various legal and financial professionals collaborate with nascent entrepreneurs to refine the venture idea.

Any computer on the blockchain network, in the second block, can freely contribute ideas and subsequently claim ownership of those ideas.

The nature of information exchanges in block 3 is more like a private password protected set of computers on the blockchain network.

The members with access to the third block would be potential private capital investors and third party professional advisors to the new venture.

The new venture team would prepare a private placement memo to place online in the third block, and conduct both online and in-person forums for all interested investors, in order to present the venture concept and answer questions.

Part of the social benefit of the Association of New Venture Professionals in any metro region is the development of standardized contacts and terms and conditions for private offerings that facilitate future private securities transactions.

(Vass, Laurie Thomas, Establishing The Capital Market Transition From Private Capital To Public Capital, SSRN, 2008.).

In the current venture capital model, the venture capitalists dictate the unfavorable terms and conditions for new ventures, which sentence many promising new ventures to oblivion because the ventures could not perform to the unrealistic financial goals of the VC offering contracts.

The Association of New Venture Professions would collaborate on a set of standardized offering documents for regional new ventures which would more favorable to the survival of promising new ventures and facilitate the exchange of securities in regional private stock exchanges. (Vass, Laurie Thomas, Favorable Terms and Conditions for a Small Business Private Offering: Taking Full Advantage of the Direct Corporate Private Offering, SSRN, 2012.).

At the third stage of raising private placement capital for a new venture, the likelihood of corruption, misunderstanding, and administrative errors is significantly reduced when a transparent, distributed, and immutable system of communication is used to manage the transfer of information assets from one party to another in the blockchain network.

After the funding has taken place, only members who contributed private capital to the venture would be allowed access to on-going financial performance reporting on the progress of the ventures, in block four.

This periodic performance reporting would be somewhat like the 10-Q of listed public companies, but with less stringent auditing standards.

In the fifth, and final block, private investors could place bid and ask prices for the venture and transact secondary market exchanges, in private online stock exchanges to facilitate deal exits and market liquidity.

If, and when, there was some type of exit event, the existing investors would be eligible to participate in the event by re-investing their capital gains, and could defer capital gains taxes by investing in subsequent regional new ventures. (Vass. Laurie Thomas, Why Exits Matter For Future Innovation Investments, SSRN, 2008.).

In the case where there is no exit event, the new venture would continue to grow into a large private company, like SAS, in the RTP, and the investors would continue to monitor the performance of the venture, and continue to trade their ownership interests, in the closed, private regional stock exchange, much like they currently do in the pink sheets.

SAS was started in the late 1970's by 3 people connected to N. C. State University, and is now the biggest private company in the world, and, by some accounts, the single best private company in the world for corporate employee benefits.

The secret sauce of SAS success was continual innovation in statistical software. (Vass, Laurie Thomas, Placing the Concept of the RTP Startup Ecosystem into a Regional Innovation Policy Framework, SSRN. 2015.).

Chapter 8 Section 4. Political Allies and Enemies of the New Venture Creation Pipeline.

In the current special interest driven political system of global crony capitalism, the organized political forces of the status quo compete with the unorganized political interests of domestic entrepreneurs.

Generally, the organized global special interests will win this competition, which is one of the reasons why economic growth occurs in some regions and not others. (Vass, Laurie Thomas, Do Cities Still Matter? The Economic Strength of Cities and the Economic Failure of Globalism in Promoting Regional Technological Innovation and Economic Prosperity, SSRN, 2013.).

In his review of technical change in Sweden, Bo Carlsson described how a business-social network opposed to technical change could influence a much wider social network of organizations.

He described the case where,

"...there may be a certain self-reinforcing mechanism at work...A vicious circle, in which (existing) industry chooses not to become involved in an expanding technology, influencing universities and government policy makers to make the same choice." (Carllson, Bo, "Technological Systems and Economic Development Potential: Four Swedish Case Studies," in Innovations In Technology, Industries and Institutions, 1994, and Technological Systems and Economic Performance: The Case of Factory Automation, Springer-Verlag, 1995.).

The type of self-reinforcing business-social network at the regional level, described by Carlsson often is connected to a much larger network at the national and international level.

The monopoly corporations studied by Schumpeter (Capitalism, Socialism and Democracy, 1942), have evolved to become a much larger global corporatist network that has a political and financial interest in controlling uncertain future markets created by uncontrolled technological innovation.

This political and financial linkage between local groups and global groups is the essence of the term "globalism."

Globalism is based upon the needs of global corporations to obtain profits in a global market, which requires political and monetary stability across national borders.

As we mentioned in the earlier chapters, the globalist corporations have a coherent social class awareness of their own financial interests, and have established extensive lobbying and political influence networks to promote their own selfish interests.

In contrast, the new venture professional advisors in a region do not have group self-awareness of their collective identity to support new venture creation.

While the global corporations need the cooperation of sympathetic elected representatives in states and metro regions to promote stability, cities do not matter as long as all states and cities look and act the same in the vertically integrated global value chains.

Generally, the regional/multi-national network is facilitated through regional organizations like the Chamber of Commerce, or local industrial recruitment groups.

These regional groups are predisposed politically to protecting the status quo, and will often recruit branch manufacturing plants of multi-nationals if those corporations will contribute to the political stability of the status quo political power arrangement at the regional level.

In other words, the local political elites seek alliances with the global corporations when that arrangement does not upset the status quo of power relationships at the local regional level.

The senior managers of the global corporations seek out regions which promote the stability they need across national and metro regional political boundaries.

To summarize, the business-social network of entrepreneurs and venture capitalists in a region compete with the business-social network comprised of old production units, commercial bankers, institutional money managers, and senior management of branch plants of multi-national corporations.

One social network acts to facilitate technical change, but is often not organized as a special political interest group.

The other network has financial interests in maintaining the status quo because uncertainty upsets the flow of benefits that they achieve from the status quo arrangement of power.

The reason one metro region develops a macrotechnology that supports new venture creation, as opposed to any other region is related to the,

"...specific institutional configurations and by the cumulative, local, and specific character of the knowledge that the institutions possess." Saviotti, Pier Paolo, Technological Evolution, Variety, and The Economy, 1996.),

In the first conflict between regional new venture creation and globalism, elected leaders, acting as fiduciaries, would want the most open flows of tacit knowledge regarding technical change and product innovation.

Corporations would want private/proprietary flows in order to absorb, internally, as much benefit from the spillovers in technology as possible.

In the second conflict of interest between regional new venture creation and globalism, the corporations want to protect the 67% rate of profits gained by price markups over marginal costs, in the vertically integrated global value chains, and direct those profits to the current global distribution of income.

These conflicts between regional new venture creation interests and globalist corporate interests involve a conflict over information flows between industrial sectors, the openness of inter-corporate career transfers of scientific personnel between existing firms or potential new ventures, and the conflict over the path of technical change in the region.

We also identify a major ideological conflict over the cultural/political values regarding global/collectivist values and the values of individual freedom and reward based upon individual merit in an entrepreneurial capitalist system. (Vass, Laurie Thomas, America's Final Revolution: Reconstructing Jefferson's American Dream of An Entrepreneurial Capitalist Society, Gabby Press, 2022.).

We argue that the only economic force capable of dislodging the global corporatist monopoly pricing power is free market competition in technology innovation in metro regional intermediate demand markets.

Disintegrating global corporate value chains requires an institutional market mechanism at the regional level to re-invest capital gains from new venture exit events in the second and third generation of new technology ventures.

The pace of technological innovation depends on a cumulative feedback mechanism that influences the path of economic development in the region, via what Rostow has called the "plowback of profits for plant and equipment." (Rostow, W. W., The Stages of Economic Growth: A Non-Communist Manifesto, 1960.).

In the case of regional technological innovation,, it is not plowback from net positive cash flow from operations, but profits generated from either capital gains on venture capital investments, or as a result of the merger and acquisition of the new ventures by other corporations.

The organized political and financial interests in metro regions that would oppose innovation economics and the plowback of profits into new ventures are the status quo industrial recruitment interests, local chambers of commerce, globalist organizations, like the Brookings Institute and, interestingly, the status quo members of the angel and venture capital community, who enjoy a monopsony over directing private capital to their handpicked selection of entrepreneurial companies. (Vass, Laurie Thomas, The Nexus of Financial and Political Interests between Crowd Funders and Regional Economic Development

Professionals: The New-New Innovation Economics, SSRN, 2013.).

In order to be an effective countervailing power to the globalist interests, the third party professional advisors in the regional innovation blockchain model must be integrated into the entire sequence of capital market transactions that support regional technological innovation.

The Association of New Venture Professionals and the professional economic developer community must begin to see themselves as a self-aware collective
political advocacy support team to advance the financial interests of the region in order to compete with the globalist forces that desire to maintain the status quo distribution of income derived from the vertically integrated global corporate value chains.

Chapter 8 Section 5. Why Exits Matter for Future Regional Innovation.

In our theory of technological evolution (SERET), the network of third party professional advisors are creating the new future market by helping new technology ventures find buyers for the radical new products.

That activity supports stronger inter industry multiplier effects in income and employment, within the regional economy in an existing 3 – 5 year period of time.

Beyond the regional economic benefits of stronger income and employment multipliers, the third party professional advisors who promote the re-investment of capital from deal exits back into the regional technology business pipeline are moving the regional economy to the next economic bifurcation point of growth.

Diagram 5, described earlier, describes an economy breaking away from the equilibrium conditions in a 3 – 5 year time, in period one, to a potential new attractor point of increased economic growth in time period 2.

Diagram 5. Economy Breaking Away From Equilibrium In Time Period One to Potential Attractor Point in Time Period Two.

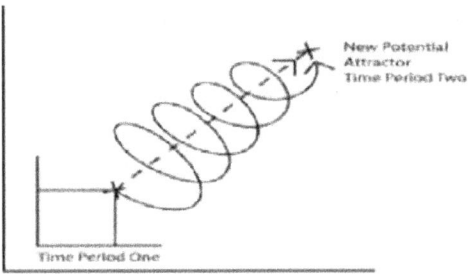

In our theory of Structural Evolutionary Regional Economic Growth (SERET), the movement of the economy to the new attractor point is caused by capital investment in technological innovation in time period one.

At the top of the blockchain deal flow pipeline, professional third party advisors and professional economic developers would facilitate capital investments into the first generation of small technology firms, in time period one, in block 3 of the blockchain business model.

Those first generation new technology ventures will require small additional capital investments at around years, 3, 6, and 10.

The blockchain business model, in block 4, facilitates capital investment in these later years.

Those later rounds of capital can be managed more easily if the initial terms and conditions of the first capital raise are standardized so that the early rounds can be exchanged in the private capital market transactions in block 4.

Generally, the time horizon for a deal exit of a new technology venture is 10 years.

If the terms and conditions of the prior rounds are consistent, the capital gains from the deal exit can be more easily re-invested back into the regional technology innovation economic growth model.

If the small private technology companies can survive to age 10, and get small amounts of growth capital during their growth phase, their rate of job creation will be exponential and regional economic growth will lead the trajectory of economic growth to the next future attractor point.

Those job creation benefits and economic growth benefits depend on the creation of new institutional capital market mechanisms, that do not currently exist, but could easily be created by a network of third party professional advisors who had regional allegiance and territorial loyalty to the welfare of citizens in their metro region. (Vass, Laurie Thomas, The Importance of Regional Allegiance and Territorial Loyalty For Elected Representatives In Implementing Economic Development and Job Creation Policies, SSRN. 2023,

Chapter 9. The Regional Capital Market Institutional Support Structure For Regional New Venture Creation.

Section 1 Chapter 9. A Comprehensive Regional Capital Market Support Structure For New Venture Creation Economic Growth

In the previous chapters, we made use of a simple diagram that describes the chronology of events in new venture creation called the Small Business Deal Creation Pipeline.

The Small Business Deal Creation Pipeline™

Deal Mapping	Deal Creation	Deal Funding	Deal Exits
To convert knowledge and ideas into small business ventures and new products	To prepare new ventures or product ideas to enter the market	To find capital to fund commercial ventures	To manage the reinvestment of profit from the first generation of ideas into the next generation of innovation

The entire sequence of events in the deal creation pipeline can be visualized as taking place in a regional blockchain business management model, whose purpose is to increase the rate of new venture creation in a metro region.

In the blockchain management model, the first two blocks of deal mapping and deal creation, involve scientific and technical professionals, potential entrepreneurs and third party professional advisors meeting each other, both online and in person, at social/business networking events, such as those managed by the N. C. Council for Entrepreneurial Development (CED).

The last two blocks in the pipeline describe activities that take place in a private, pass-word protected blockchain internet portal intended to facilitate capital market transactions related to both funding new ventures and providing additional capital to the existing ventures, during their growth cycle.

The single most important component of the deal creation pipeline is not simply funding the new venture, in block 3.

In order to disintegrate vertically integrated global corporate value chains, the most important activity takes place in block 4, on the blockchain model, about 7 – 10 years after a new venture obtains its initial round of funding.

Block 4 is called deal exits because what happens to capital gains and profits from deal exits determines whether the regional economy will continue to grow towards a distant future economic growth attractor point, or slip into a lower level of economic growth, called a Nash equilibrium.

According to Wassily Leontief, it is not the effect of "capital accumulation" from operating revenues, by itself, that contributes to economic growth, it is capital investment, and then, most importantly, the subsequent round of investments made from the capital gain profits from the first round of investments in innovation.

Leontief was raising this issue about the role of on-going capital investment in technological innovation in one of his last published papers in 1989, Input-Output Data Base For Analysis of Technological Change. (Economic Systems Research.).

He said,

"Thus, the introduction of a new method of production in one sector cannot be adequately assessed without knowledge of changes taking place in the input-output structure of the other sectors."

Leontief referred the subsequent rounds of capital investment as the tapestry of the economy as it was being woven through time.

Leontief described how the earlier rounds of investments in capital equipment become obsolete and less valuable when the subsequent rounds of investments are made in both new and existing technology ventures.

We use this same idea of technological obsolescence in both production technology and product markets for goods, in our explanation of the theory of technological evolution. (SERET).

We explain that unless the capital gains and profits from exit events are reinvested back into the regional intermediate demand networks, technological innovation in the region will end, and the regional economy will slip into a Nash equilibrium.

The regional capital market institutional framework for new venture creation requires a long-term time frame, where units of capital are invested in new ventures in their 5th and 7th years, leading to an exit event in year 10.

It also requires new institutions to facilitate capital market transactions that aim at regional economic growth through new venture creation, which is a different perspective than the current short-term perspective of the venture capital business model.

The private capital market infrastructure is not simply about getting business angels and venture capitalists to look at investment opportunities.

It is a full service small capital exchange market that involves the issuance of initial capital and also secondary market transactions of both small units of debt and equity for both existing small manufacturing firms and new technology startups.

While the initial seed stage investing in startup firms is important, the most important form of capital market investments in the regional small business innovation system needs to be targeted to firms in the 5th and 7th year of existence.

Those small firms create the most net new jobs in the regional economy, but it takes the company about 8 years before the job growth occurs.

Generally, the small firm needs the capital in the form of debt, and generally the capital required is less than $500,000. Generally, this type of investment never makes it onto the financial radar screen of most angels or venture capitalists.

We modify and extend the small business deal creation pipeline to include a more comprehensive business model of a regional small business innovation system, below, in Diagram 3.

Diagram 3 begins the process of combining the regional economic growth policy framework, in the top of the blockchain management model, with the new, as-yet-created institutional market mechanisms to facilitate future capital market investments in new ventures.

In the top portion of Diagram 3, the Association of New Venture Professionals work with potential entrepreneurs to create and refine ideas into new ventures.

In the bottom portion of Diagram 3, a second type of social/business networks, composed of all commercial banking and investment banking professionals in the regional economy work with ventures to raise capital throughout the life cycle of the new venture, ending in either a deal exit or the transition of the firm to a much larger successful private company, like SAS, of Cary, N. C.

The secret sauce of the SAS success was continual innovation in statistical software over an extended period of years. The success of SAS would not have occurred under the VC business funding model because the VCs would have sold off the company and cannibalized their intellectual property.(Vass, Laurie Thomas, Placing the Concept of the RTP Startup Ecosystem into a Regional Innovation Policy Framework, SSRN, 2015).

Section 2 Chapter 9. The Flaws In the Venture Capital/Angel Capital Business Model For Promoting Regional Economic Growth.

Brian Kingsley Krumm, in his article, Fostering Innovation and Entrepreneurship: Shark Tank Shouldn't be the Model, begins by describing the legal structure of a limited partnership for most venture capital (VC) companies.

The limited partnership legal structure is designed to provide maximum capital gains to both the VC firm and the limited partner investors who provide capital to the VC firm to invest.

The legal structure of the VC firm is the first flaw for applying the VC model to the promotion of regional economic growth.

Chapter 9 Diagram 3. Planning and Implementation of a Regional Small Business Innovation System.

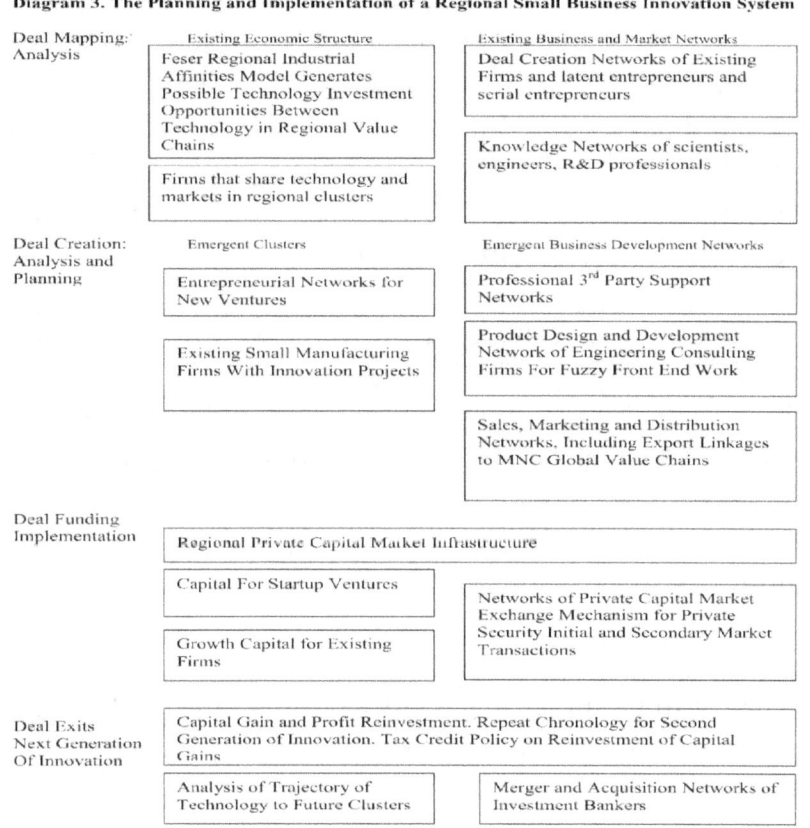

Krumm writes,

"The ultimate objective of venture capital funds is to invest in start-up companies and obtain a high rate of return in the shortest time frame possible…Under the typical venture capital model the investors are limited partners who supply

99% of the fund's capital. The general partners [the VCs] supply 1% of the capital and receive an annual management fee of 2% of the value of the fund. The general partners decide which start-ups to invest in and when such investments should be liquidated. The most common profit-sharing arrangement is an 80/20 split, [called 2 and 20] where after returning all the original investment to the limited partners, the general partner [VCs] keeps 20% of the fund's profit and distributes 80% to the limited partners. This compensation structure, known as Carried Interest, is taxed at the reduced rate applicable to the capital gain rate and is the incentive that makes private equity so enticing for investment professionals… investment rounds are typically in the $1 million to $5 million range."

Krumm explains the second flaw in the VC model related to the form of equity that the VCs use to invest capital, called the terms and conditions. The terms and conditions are stacked in favor of the VC firm and against the interests of the entrepreneur to grow a successful company.

Krumm explains,

"For example, the general partners will structure the investment in the portfolio company by taking preferred shares "with significant liquidation preferences and redemption rights, [which] 'puts them in a superior position to common stockholders'—i.e. the founder [entrepreneur] in liquidation or acquisition."

Krumm notes that the VCs generally only invest in 1 out of 10 deals they investigate, and upwards of 40% of those deals are terminated by the VCs within the first three years.

Our term for describing the VC termination of new ventures, after 3 years, is the "Dr. Kervorkian VC Assisted Suicide" model of new venture creation. (Vass, Laurie Thomas, Will More Venture Capital Spur Regional Innovation? SSRN, 2008.).

We ask,

"If the new venture is killed by the VCs in the first 3 years, who is left to re-start the next generation of firms in the innovation pipeline? In other words, if regional economic growth from innovation is the goal, then increasing the supply of venture capital [VC] may not be the greatest strategy because the goal of the business model of venture capital is inconsistent with the goals of regional economic development."

The firms that enter Dr. Kervorkian's VC graveyard are not killed because their technology was bad, or because the markets for the new products were bad. They are killed because their rate of profit in the VC model does not meet the target rate of profit in the VC model.

The VC exit model does not work well for either regional innovation economic development or for the community of entrepreneurs who start the new ventures.

In his research on exits, Innovation and Venture Capital Exits, (Economic Journal, 2007), Armin Schwienbacher explains this apparent conflict of financial interests.

"This paper analyzes how startups financed by venture capital choose their innovation strategy based on the investor's (VC) exit preferences, and thereby form different outcomes in the product market. It considers innovation choices and venture capital exits (IPO vs trade sale) in a setting in which entrepreneurs derive private benefits from staying independent, which is better guaranteed under an IPO."

We explain that what comes next in the regional innovation pipeline innovation pipeline depends on who gets there first.

If the regional economic goal is successful new firms that continue to thrive and grow, then the IPO exit is better for both the region and the entrepreneur.

An IPO exit for small innovative regional manufacturing firms, however, requires a new type of regional private capital stock market exchange, not simply more venture capital at the front end of the innovation pipeline.

In a type of type of dinosaur extinction model of innovation, if the VCs do not kill the firm first, then, in the VC model, the firm gets sold, by the VCs, to a bigger player, who pays a premium to kill the innovation so that the bigger firm does not have to compete with the innovation.

"In principle," notes Schwienbacher,

"the established company may want to acquire the newcomer whenever entry erodes its own profits, [New World Order globalism] but the question again is whether it is ready to pay a premium over what the newcomer is worth as a stand-alone firm. This depends on what is likely to be gained by avoiding the entry of the newcomer."

If the new venture is not killed in the first 3 years, by the VCs, and if the new venture is not sold to a bigger global corporation, who subsequently obtains the intellectual property of the new venture, and then kills the new venture, to avoid technological competition, then the last defect of the VC model for regional economic growth is how the VCs dispose of the profits from the exit event.

Generally, the exit success rate for VC firms is around 1 in 10 deals, which is not a problem for the VC model because the rate of profit for the few successful deals vastly outweighs all the losses on all the other deals.

The target rate of profits on VC deals is around 800%, capital gain, after a holding period of three years.

Those VC capital gain profits are not available, in the VC model, to be re-invested back into the regional interindustry intermediate demand networks to promote regional economic growth because 100% of the profits go to the VC firm and the limited partner investors.

In his research on the venture capital business, Boom and Bust in the Venture Capital Industry and the Impact on Innovation, Josh Lerner describes the typical outcome for the VC profits. (Negotiation, Organizations and Markets, Research Papers, Harvard NOM Research Paper No. 03- 13, 2004.).

As Lerner noted,

"Another contributing factor is self-liquidating nature of venture funds. When venture funds exit investments, they do not reinvest the funds, but rather return the capital to their investors. These distributions are typically either in the form of stock in firms that have recently gone public or cash. The pace of distributions varies with the rate at which venture capitalists are liquidating their holdings."

In Krumm's criticism of the Shark Tank VC business model, he suggests that an alternative capital market mechanism would be beneficial to both regional economic growth and to technology entrepreneurs who create new ventures. (Fostering Innovation and Entrepreneurship: Shark Tank Shouldn't be the Model, Arkansas Law Review, SSRN, 2017).

Krumm writes,

"It appears that a "Venture Development Company" (VDC) may be the next step in the evolution of innovation finance. VDCs could provide an effective, local mechanism to work with innovative small businesses to access these new federal funding opportunities. [Reg D 506-C]. They have the potential of filling the gaps that exist nationally in the provision of venture capital financial resources and guidance. Additionally, they can provide a mechanism to promote regional and economic development, since start-ups will no longer need to relocate to Silicon Valley or other areas of venture-capital density to receive funding."

We agree with Krumm's idea and modify and extend it to incorporate a more comprehensive range of capital market services to metro regions and potential technology entrepreneurs.

Krumm outlines the potential benefits of this as-yet-created institutional capital market mechanism.

"VDC agreements can offer more equitable terms. [to the entrepreneurs]. Because the VDC is not trying to protect the [VCs] members' personal financial investment, only the [entrepreneurs] company's potential investment opportunity, there is no need for such one-sided contract provisions.

Because the VDC will be an equity holder in the business, its interests will be aligned with those of the founders. The venture development relationship proves to be most successful when all of the parties' interests are aligned."

We add that the proposed VDC model protects intellectual property of the new venture through blockchain protected time-stamped information exchanges.

As Krumm notes,

"A VDC can play a critical role in this process by validating the information provided to investors and evaluating the selection of the financial intermediary to facilitate the offering. Since the VDC will have a financial stake in the company through the ownership of shares, they are accountable, along with the founders, for any untrue statement or omission of material fact that misleads the investors."

We add to Krumm's idea of the VDC by noting that,

"The entire innovation process in a metro region would be enhanced if the pathway from the private capital markets [at the top of the blockchain business model] to the public markets [at the bottom of the blockchanin model] was logically coherent and more transparent. The private capital markets are primarily local, and capital for most new ventures and for existing small manufacturing enterprises that need capital to finance innovation raise their money within 50 miles of where they are located." (Vass, Laurie Thomas, Creating the Private Capital Market Infrastructure for Sustainable Innovation Economics, SSRN, 2013.).

Section 3 Chapter 9. The Institutional and Administrative Components of a Regional Capital Market.

We argue that each metro region needs to create a comprehensive private capital stock market exchange, that includes:
1. New Asset Backed Packages of Investment Securities to accommodate the innovation process of small firms during their growth cycle
2. New Regional Closed End Mutual Funds to supplement the very fragmented private placement regulatory framework in each metro region in order to promote the continual capital reinvestment process when the M&A exit event occurs.
3. A new regional investment bank that facilitates capital investment in both new and existing forms of equity and debt in regional new ventures.

We place this concept of a comprehensive private capital market stock exchange into our blockchain business model in Diagram 4, below.

Diagram 4 emphasizes the role and responsibility of the executives of the new venture in raising capital, using the new regional institutional framework provided by the regional blockchain business model.

Much of the executive's job of raising private capital for the new venture has been made easier by the recent SEC regulatory changes on using the internet to solicit private placement investors.

Chapter 9 Diagram 4. The New Web-Based Business Model.

The New Web-Based Business Model For Solving the Small Capital Raise of a High Tech Company

The Company's Own Website Contains New Software Coding to Manage Capital Raise Communications	The Main Metro Regional Capital Marketplace Website Combines Many Functions Under One Website Roof Ex: The Atlanta Capital Marketplace	Outside Websites and Networking Groups Use Their Own Business Social Networks to Communicate Among Members And to Tweet News
The Company Uses The Technology of The Internet To Explain Its Growth Strategy to Interested Viewers Using Tools Like The Company Quick Deal Overview (QDO)	Customer Relationship Module Organizes and Manages Membership In the Local Capital Marketplace	LinkedIn Group Members Join Their Local Capital Marketplace LinkedIn Groups
The Company Website Connects To The Local Capital Marketplace to Make A Company Presentation at A Monthly Capital Marketplace Event	Event Management Module Allows For Easy Event Registration and Online Payment	MeetUp Groups In Each City Related to Capital Markets Use Grops To Communicate and Collaborate on Upcoming Events
Pass Word Protected Portals on Company Website Store Sensitive Documents and Presentations, Like Content For National Webinars	Online Media And Journal Module Allows Easy Article Uploads and Calendars Ex: The Atlanta Capital Marketplace Journal	Web-based Capital Market Resources like Angel Matching Websites and Software Vendors Like AngelSoft Link To Local Capital Marketplace Websites
	Online Directories of Professional Organizations Makes Finding Clients and Deals Easy	Capital Marketplace Directory Profile Pages Link to Professional Service Provider Websites
	Capital Marketplace E-Commerce Functionality Makes Online Selling Easy	
	Online Webinar Functionality Makes Hosting and Managing National Company Presentations Easy	

We describe this new internet-based model of raising capital in Diagram 5, below:

Chapter 9 Diagram 5. The New Internet-Based Model of Raising Capital.

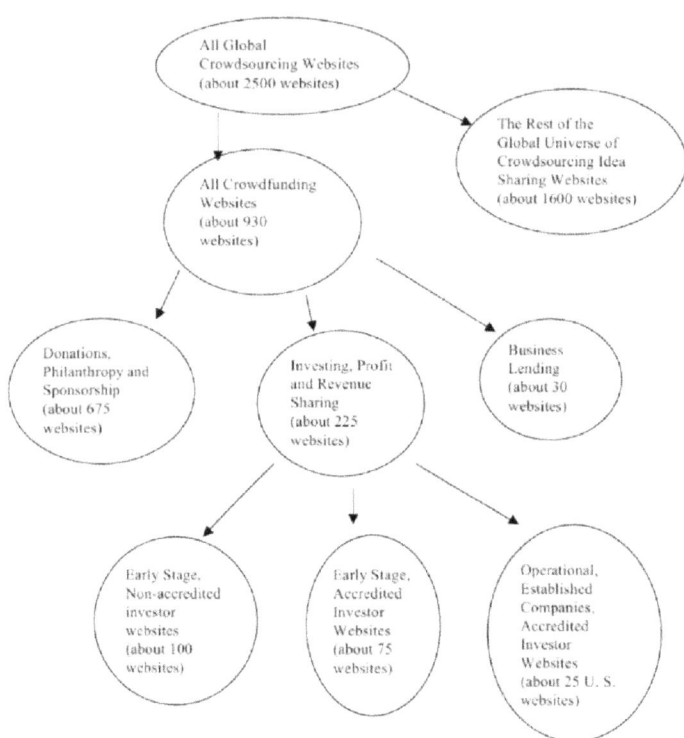

We used the Atlanta regional economy as an example of how a new type of closed end mutual fund could be administered by the network regional capital market professionals to target capital investments to both new and existing small technology ventures. (Vass, Laurie Thomas, Exploring the Idea of the Atlanta Capital Growth Fund:

Equity Crowdfunding as One Component of the New Atlanta Private Securities Exchange, SSRN, 2015.).

The operation and management of the proposed mutual fund would occur under the authority of a modified version of Krumm's model of the Venture Development Corporation (VDC), which we have re-named as the Regional Development Investment Bank.

The goal of the Atlanta Capital Growth Fund is to create a new private sector capital market mechanism that focuses on making the initial rounds of capital investments in Atlanta's new technology firms.

And, then, 10 years later, acting as the mechanism to reinvest the first round profits in subsequent rounds of investments in regional technological innovation.

The establishment and operation of the Atlanta Capital Growth Fund would act like a new intellectual asset of the region, and become a part of the regional blockchain innovation infrastructure.

The big difference in technological innovation that the operation of the Fund would make in Atlanta is related to diffusion of knowledge.

Knowledge creation and diffusion in the private sector capital markets is primarily based on face-to-face tacit knowledge communication.

Because tacit knowledge is based upon personal human interaction, it tends occur in distinct geographical areas, about 50 miles in diameter, leading to the creation of distinct regional technological knowledge. (Vass, Laurie Thomas,

Exploiting Knowledge: The Importance of Regional Allegiance and Territorial Loyalty in Implementing a Regional Small Business Innovation System, SSRN, 2009.).

This 50 mile envelope is the same distance used by the Bureau of Labor Statistics to identify job commuting distances around metro regions, and it is the same geographical distance that we identify for the establishment of trust relationships in new venture capital market investments.

The operation of the Fund would tend to create more territorial loyalty among the two major social/business networks that support small technology firms in Atlanta.

The existing crowdfunding policies and legislation in Georgia are too heavily tied to the promotion of the existing Atlanta venture capital firms [VC] financial interests. (Vass, Laurie Thomas, A Critical Analysis of the Recent Georgia Initiatives to Promote Intrastate Crowdfunding, SSRN, 2013.).

The Invest Georgia Fund is "return based," meaning that a portion of the profits from capital that is invested by private venture capital firms will be returned to the State of Georgia, which is a step in the right direction.

But, the over-emphasis of the VC financial interests, in the Georgia Fund for the first round of investment acts as a detriment of the re-investment of profits from the Fund back in to the Georgia economy.

A better approach is to de-emphasize political influence associated with the Invest Georgia Fund and to increase reliance on the private free-market principles associated with the operation of the Atlanta Capital Growth Fund.

Most private sector jobs are created by companies that are 8 years old, which need about $1.5 million in capital in order to continue to grow.

If these companies obtain the capital that they need, their job creation goes from about 20 jobs, in year 5, to about 40 jobs, per company, in year 9.

If the technology ventures continue to age 10, their rate of job growth is exponential.

The amounts of capital and types of financing needed by the small technology venture during the growth cycle are very small. The amounts are so small that most other capital market suppliers are not interested in making the funding available.

This is especially true of small manufacturing firms that have been in operation for more than five years, and need about $750,000 to finance the next generation of a product.

The existing commercial asset based banks do not want to lend the company funds because new technology companies do not own real estate.

Any type of debt or equity in the young venture is probably too risky for the commercial bank to finance on a non-secured basis.

The venture capitalists will not fund the company because it is so small, and there is not a fast exit path for investing in this type of an established operational company.

Some economists have called this the "small ticket problem."

For example, in his research on small high tech firms in Canada, Stephan Rousseau examined how the internet could substitute as an alternative to asset based lenders and VCs to overcome the "small ticket" problem of biotech firms. (Internet-Based Securities Offerings By Small and Medium-Sized Enterprises: Attractions and Challenges," Canadian Business Law Journal, 2001.).

In his article, describes how the banks and VCs routinely and systematically underprice the small offerings of small firms.

As he noted,

"The results showed clearly that the degree of underpricing varies negatively with the size of the issue. Thus, issues of $1-9.9 millions were underpriced by 23% on average. Issues of $10- 49.9 millions experienced underpricing of 10%, on average, while those of $50-99.9 millions of 15.6%. The largest issues of the sample ($100-199.9 millions) were underpriced by as mere 4.2% on average."

The term "underpricing" is also called, in the language of Wall Street, a "haircut," meaning that the banks and VCs take a portion of the legitimate market value of the company, simply because the size of the offering is so small.

We argue that a new type of regional closed end fund, in operation with a regional investment bank, would solve part of the problem of capital market exploitation of small companies, simply because the firms do not fit the business model of banks and VCs.

The proposed Atlanta Capital Growth Fund is one component of the bigger blockchain business model of the Atlanta Private Securities Exchange. (Vass, Laurie Thomas, Creating the Private Capital Market Infrastructure for Sustainable Innovation Economics, SSRN, 2008.).

The Atlanta Private Securities Exchange would include membership from the FDIC commercial bankers, asset based lenders, insurance companies, FINRA broker dealers, lawyers, accountants, rating services, and investment professionals who packaged both debt and equity investments into attractive investment products.

The Atlanta Private Securities Exchange is the business/social network that complements the work of the Association of New Venture Professionals, that provides services in the upper two blocks of the blockchain business model.

Private capital market companies would join the Atlanta Private Securities Exchange, just like they join the Atlanta Chamber of Commerce.

The Atlanta Private Securities Exchange would hope to become an SEC-approved Alternative Trading System, (ATS), for trading private securities, in the lower two blocks of the blockchain business model.

Most of the capital for investing in Atlanta innovation in the Atlanta Capital Growth Fund will come from local crowdfunding, within the 50-mile envelope surrounding the Atlanta metro region.

The most important function of the Atlanta Private Securities Exchange, however, is not in providing access to the initial investment in a single firm.

The most important function of the regional stock exchange is that the new private exchange provides the sympathetic environment for funding the full range of services required by technology companies, providing liquidity for investors of private securities and providing a pathway for profits from the exit events to be reinvested in the regional innovation economy, in a type of Bayesian economic success model. (Vass, Laurie Thomas, Adding a Geographical Component to an Equity Crowdfunding Project, SSRN, 2013.).

This local capital used to fund local investments is one approach to "bootstrapping" Atlanta's self sustaining, self-renewing technological innovation economic growth.

Section 4 Chapter 9. The Self Regulatory Organizational Framework for Regional Capital Markets.

The proposed new network of capital market member firms in the Atlanta Private Securities Exchange would function as a self regulatory organization, just like member firms of NYSE or NASDAQ.

The enforcement of capital market rules for the Atlanta exchange would be administered by professional staff, just like those in FINRA, (Financial Industry Regulatory

Association, formerly the NASD (National Association of Security Dealers).

The Atlanta Stock Exchange would seek legislative authority to operate from the General Assembly of Georgia. The legislation would create a uniform state regulatory framework for all Georgia metro regions, such as Savannah or any other metro region that wanted to have its own private securities exchange.

The regulatory framework for targeting capital investments to Atlanta firms begins with the understanding that any private company can issue its own securities directly to investors, bypassing venture capital firms and FINRA broker dealers.

The company can issue securities directly to investors in either a Reg D Rule 506c offering, or the new Reg A offering.

Under Rule 506c, a company can raise as much capital as it wants and have as many accredited investors as it wants. The company can set all the terms and conditions of the securities, and issue any form of securities that it desires.

The Atlanta Capital Growth Fund could buy the 506c shares issued by an Atlanta company, and the member firms of the Atlanta Growth Fund could assist the company by preparing standardized and uniform securities templates that the company would use to issue its securities.

There is nothing that prohibits a private company from selling its shares both to the Growth Fund and to any accredited investor outside of the Fund.

This would include all the regional venture capital firms and angel partnerships in Atlanta who may desire to invest directly in the company, and not make an investment through the Fund.

Just like a private company can issue securities under 506c, the Atlanta Capital Growth Fund can also issue securities, under Reg A, to investors who would like to invest in a portfolio of Atlanta companies, rather than investing in a single company.

The potential investors in Atlanta would come from the crowdfunding efforts of the Fund, and from the public presentations made by company executives in networking events sponsored by the Atlanta Association of New Venture Professionals.

Unlike the older model of raising capital, now called Rule 506b, both Reg D and Reg A allow public marketing and promotion of private securities.

In other words, both the Atlanta Capital Growth Fund, and each private Atlanta company can now engage in public promotion to sell their private securities.

The Atlanta Capital Growth Fund would offer investors diversification and professional management of capital investments targeted to Atlanta's technology firms.

The Atlanta Fund would be legally organized and taxed as a pass-through entity under the Internal Revenue Code.

As long as the Growth Fund meets certain income, investment diversity, and distribution requirements, the Fund, as a corporate entity, would pay little or no corporate income tax.

As is the case with the existing Invest Georgia Fund, the Atlanta Growth Fund could also seek tax exemptions, as a pass-through entity, from Georgia income taxes.

The Fund would deduct the operating expenses, and investment advisory fees from gross revenues, before making distributions to the shareholders of the Fund.

The Atlanta Growth Fund would have a small three person staff, and an outside investment advisor.

- A regional managing director.
- A regional fund administrator.
- A regional economist.

The staff of the Fund would perform three important functions as a precursor activity to making investments in Atlanta technology firms:

- The staff would coordinate the results of the Feser econometric model of the region and use the results of the model to conduct Bayesian statistical analysis to guess at the future trajectory of technology in Atlanta.

- The staff would conduct social network analysis to guess at latent social and economic relationships between firms in the Atlanta technology clusters who may have an interest in cross breeding technology.

Social network analysis [SNA] is the mapping and measuring of relationships and flows between people, groups, organizations, computers, URLs, and other connected information/knowledge entities.

The SNA activities occurs at the top two blocks of the blockchain business model, and the persons and entities identified in the SNA would be invited to join the Atlanta blockchain business model to view potential new ventures.

The nodes in the blockchain network are the people and groups while the links show relationships or flows between the nodes.

- The staff would sponsor and manage regional business networking and capital market events that aimed at bringing entrepreneurs and scientific staff together, who may have latent entrepreneurial interests, in the top two blocks of the blockchain business model.

The investment portfolio of firms inside the Atlanta Growth Fund would be managed by an outside professional manager called an "investment adviser." The portfolio of new ventures would not be managed by the VC firms in Atlanta, as is the case with the Invest Georgia Fund.

The investment advisor is retained by the Fund's board of directors. The advisor targets investments to the most promising firms in the 9 most promising high technology networks, as identified by the Fund's regional economist.

The Fund managing director would outsource the investor account administration to an outside fund administrator company for online services that include:

- Assistance with regulatory and fund authorization.
- Liaison with professional investment firms.
- Review of all relevant agreements between the fund and portfolio companies.
- Compliance and anti-money laundering checks on Senior company executives.
- Accredited Investor Verification required by Reg D offerings.
- Management of investor account formats and reports to meet investor requirements.
- Provision of information for tax reporting.
- Fund Accounting and financial records and calculating and paying all distributions.
- Custody and escrow services for investors who invest in the Fund.

Section 5 Chapter 9. Favorable Terms and Conditions for a Small Business Private Offering.

We mentioned above that one of the benefits of the Association of New Venture Professionals in any metro region is the ability to create standardized uniform offering documents for both the initial round of capital, and subsequent rounds, including the potential exit in year 10.

One of the advantages in issuing securities under the new SEC guidelines is the company's ability to control the terms and conditions of the offering.

By using standardized documents related to the offering in advance of the offering period, the company avoids the costs and time lost in frustrating negotiations with multiple sources of capital, all of who may want to impose their own terms and conditions.

The benefits of the company controlling the terms and conditions must be tempered by two key considerations.

First, the terms and conditions must be attractive to a wide range of investors based upon the merits of the investment itself.

In other words, the terms must be fair to the investors so that they may enjoy the benefits associated with making the investment. (Vass, Laurie Thomas, Favorable Terms and Conditions for a Small Business Private Offering: Taking Full Advantage of the Direct Corporate Private Offering, SSRN, 2012.).

Second, the terms and conditions for an early round of capital must be compatible with future rounds. This means that a logical sequence of terms and conditions must flow through all of the eventual rounds of capital raising.

An additional benefit for investors and the company in a direct corporate private offering (DCPO), is that standardization across many different new ventures in a metro region, all of whom issued stock with common terms and conditions, would eventually lead to easier transactions in the future via private metro securities exchanges.

Common terms and conditions regional securities markets would lead to greater liquidity in the private capital marketplace because less time and expense would be involved in determining how one security's rights and features differed from another security, at a future exit event.

The new venture company would create the offering documents, and the proposed regional growth fund would buy the company securities, and then issue its own mutual fund securities that had common terms and conditions to the company securities.

Both the company and the proposed regional growth fund could issue many different forms of securities, including:

- Preferred Stock and Convertible Preferred Stock.
- Convertible Debt.
- A Loan agreement and related security agreement.
- Revenue participation securities.

The initial legal fees in any metro region to create the standardized offering documents to do this set of tasks will be about $100,000, unless the Association of New Venture Professionals decided to do this legal work for free.

Both the new venture company and the proposed mutual fund would have on-going legal fees for regulatory compliance that would be about $20,000 per year.

The workhorse security for both the company and the growth fund will probably be in the form of convertible preferred stock.

As the name suggests, convertible preferred stock can convert into common stock at either the holder's option or at the option of the company.

Usually, there is some form of coerced or mandatory conversion feature for all investors if the company becomes involved in an Initial Public Offering (IPO), or company buy-out, where all the private stock is converted to publicly-traded stock, in a regional securities exchange.

The benefit of preferred stock over common stock is the additional protective provisions that protect both the company and the investor's financial interests. These protective provisions, or preferences, include:

• A majority vote of the outstanding preferred stock holders to make any amendment or changes to the rights, preferences, privileges, or powers of, or the restrictions provided for the benefit of, the preferred stock.
• A majority vote of the outstanding preferred stock holders to authorize any increases or decreases in the authorized number of shares of Common or Preferred stock;
• A majority vote of the outstanding preferred stock holders any action that authorizes, creates, or issues shares of any class of stock having senior rights or preferences over existing shareholders;
• The broadest possible information rights and inspection rights possible with greater rights attached to owners of at least 15% of the total outstanding preferred stock.

Documents such as audited annual and unaudited quarterly financial statements, annual budgets and monthly financial statements, minutes of the meetings of the Board could be made available to members of the regional blockchain, in pass word protected areas of the company's investor relations web page, in Block 3 of the blockchain business model.

An important provision of the standardized offering documents for the regional securities exchanges was described by Ronald Gilson, in Contracting for Innovation: Vertical Disintegration and Interfirm Collaboration (Columbia Law and Economics Working Paper No. 340, 2009.).

His proposed provision is based upon his analysis of a vertically integrated global value chain contract, which he describes as the "Warner-Lambert-Ligand" contract.

The contract provides for an option of either party to opt out of the contract because of the uncertainty of investing in radical new technology.

The contract also provides for a type of mediation and arbitration clause to mediate conflicts, which, in the case of the Regional Capital Market Professional Network, in blocks 3 and 4 of the blockchain model, would look like the current arbitration process between investors and broker/dealers in the FINRA SRO model.

Gilson writes,

[In] the Warner-Lambert - Ligand agreement, the contract contemplates a joint effort to develop pharmaceutical products having specified capabilities, with Ligand [the small biotech company] playing the leading role in the research and development stage and Warner-Lambert playing the primary role in the commercialization of the compounds – clinical trials, FDA approval and the like. The problem is that once the compound is developed, once the collaborative effort has been completed, Warner-Lambert seems to be in a position to take advantage of the sequential structure of the arrangement…The Warner-Lambert-Ligand contract creates an explicit nested options mechanism that prevents opportunistic renegotiation at the end stage. If Warner-Lambert does not extend, then the rights to compounds developed by Ligand employees remain with Ligand"

We propose that this on-going collaboration, and the nested provisions to opt out, are important features of the blockchain business model, throughout all four blocks of the collaboration between investors and investors.

Section 6 Chapter 9. Raising Local Capital for Regional New Venture Economic Growth

Raising local capital for local new ventures located in a metro regional economy is not a new idea. (Vass, Laurie Thomas, The Origins of Southern Equity Crowdfunding: The Rise of the Textile, Tobacco, and Furniture Industries in North Carolina after the Civil War, SSRN, 2013.).

W. J. Cash explains that North Carolina's textile and tobacco industries were funded, in the period after the Civil War, by local capital, in an early historical version of crowdfunding.

Cash wrote,

"The impulse leaps from community to community, as an electric current leaps across a series of galvanic poles—sweeping the citizens into mass assembly. . . . It actually sets yeoman farmers, too poor as individuals to provide even so much as a single share of capital, to combining into groups of a dozen or more for the purpose; it sets laborers to forming pools into which each man pays as little as twenty-five cents per week." (Cash, W. J., The Mind of the South, New York: Alfred A. Knopf, 1941).

As Dwight Billings described the early crowdfunding of new ventures in North Carolina, after the Civil War,

"A relationship grew up between the communities and their mills that was and has remained unique in an industrial region. *The communities built the mills, and the mills saved the communities. The mills 'belonged' to the communities.*" (Billings, Dwight B., Planters and the Making of a "New South": Class, Politics, and Development in North Carolina, 1865-1900, Chapel Hill, N.C.: University of North Carolina Press, 1979).

In a historical parallel to the development of vertically integrated global value chains today, after around 1910, the capital gain profits from the North Carolina industries were not re-invested back into the North Carolina economy, but were re-invested in other parts of the nation, or other parts of the world.

As Billings noted,

"By 1910. . . the [southern] barons and the stockholders of the mills were exhibiting a tendency to turn a smaller proportion of the total profits back to the building of more mills or the expansion of industry and business in general, and to take more for their own personal purposes."

As Cash correctly pointed out, after 1900, a group of ruling class business leaders in North Carolina,

"seized control of the mills."

The creation and implementation of the Regional Capital Market Institutional Support Structure For Regional New Venture Creation is an attempt to avoid making the same historical mistake again, by creating a pathway for local profits to be re-invested back into metro regional intermediate demand networks.

Our logic of the strategy of new venture regional economic growth is that local equity crowdfunding of capital results in local profit reinvestment, given the right institutional support structure.

New world order corporatism, and venture capital investments, do not result in local profit reinvestment.

Most initial capital investments in radical innovation depend on a high degree of trust in a 50-mile radius of the participants in the capital markets.

The new securities would be most successful when they were embedded in vibrant regional capital markets that are characterized by business social networks built upon a high level of trust within the regional economy.

We used the model of the Toronto Venture Exchange (initially TSVX, now TSX), as an example of what the 350 U. S. metro regional stock exchanges would look like, in the progression of new ventures from the local private placement capital to a metro regional public equity market. (Vass, Laurie Thomas, The New Financial Factory for Innovation Economic Development, The Journal of Financial Transformation, August 2009.).

The goal of the TSX is to promote the ongoing survival and commercial viability of regional firms, based upon the principle of the 50-mile rule of trust, by providing an internet based trading platform, as we envision in our blockchain business model.

The TSX provides liquidity for small stocks in Canada, and the higher success rate of firms when they graduate to the senior Toronto Exchange means that firms achieve a higher rate of commercial viability.

All trading through the TSX Exchange is done electronically, so the Exchange does not have a "trading floor".

As of November 2010, the TSX Venture Exchange had 2,364 listed companies with a combined market capitalization of $60,811,203,235.

Generally, about 20% of private capital deals in the TSX "graduate" to the public markets, either in the form of an IPO, or in the form of a reverse merger, when a private company backs into the empty shell of a defunct public company.

The new metro regional capital market blockchain model that we propose would probably look much like the TSX, but would be local in each metro region, harkening back to the days when America had many smaller regional stock exchanges. (Vass, Laurie Thomas, North Carolina's New Nexus of Innovation: Where Local Capital in N. C. Cities Funds Local Investment Opportunities in Technology Commercialization, SSRN, 2012.).

A recent revision to the 1933 Securities Act allows small companies to raise small amounts of capital using the internet to attract potential investors.

Section 4 of the Securities Act of 1933 (15 U.S.C. 77d) was amended to allow companies to solicit investors via internet social media.

Under the original provisions of the new law, private companies could raise up to $1 million a year, with the provision of nonaudited financial statements.

Companies in the original law could raise up to $2 million if they provided audited financial statements to potential investors.

Those original restrictive provisions have subsequently been revised and broadened.

What the new law did, however, was to create a new way for local knowledge to be shared in a local geographical setting, which is called local social capital.

In our blockchain business model, we identify 3 distinct regional social business networks of social capital: The Association of New Venture Professionals, The Regional Private Securities Exchange, and the existing network of professional regional economic developers.

In our proposed blockchain business model, these 3 networks of social capital combine with investment capital, in organizations like the regional capital growth mutual fund, to create the conditions of local technological innovation.

In his research article, "A Primer on Exempt Offerings: Capital Access for Small and Emerging Businesses, David Krause, provides evidence on the nature of raising small amounts of capital. (SSRN. 2023.).

According to Krause, the median issuer had been incorporated for approximately two years and employed around three people.

Most issuers had minimal assets, with a median value of about $30,000, and no revenues. Additionally, around 59% of issuers had some form of debt prior to the offering.

The average amount raised per offering in 2020 was $342,000, with equity deals being more prevalent, accounting for 48% of offerings compared to debt and SAFE structures.

In 2021, the Reg A Tier 2 funding cap was raised to $75 million. The most recent proposed revisions to Reg A is to raise the funding cap to $150 million.

Reg A operates as a partial public offering, but without the expenses of an IPO, which would fit well into our blockchain business model of regional stock market exchanges in block 4 of the model.

Regulation A allows companies to raise capital from both accredited and non-accredited investors, while the recent SEC provisions on crowdfunding impose investment limitations on individual investors and requires offerings to take place on registered broker/dealer internet funding portals.

The new SEC crowdfunding provisions, called Reg CF, allows businesses to raise up to $5 million from a large number of investors, including non-accredited investors. It requires utilizing an online platform registered with the SEC for the offering and imposes certain disclosure and reporting obligations.

Reg D Rule 504 permits businesses to raise up to $10 million from both accredited and non-accredited investors. Under certain provisions of Rule 504, issuers relying on Rule 504 may not use general solicitation or general advertising to market the securities, and securities are restricted from future trading, which makes Reg d Rule 506 a more attractive option for the small company.

Our major point of emphasis about the value of regional capital markets to raise local capital for small technology companies lies in the small amounts of capital required for most companies.

According to SEC data on Reg D private offerings, between 2009 and 2013 were for established, operational companies, with top line revenues in a range of around $1 million.

The median size of the Reg D offering was $1.5 million in 2012.

The July 10, 2013, SEC report continues,

"Offerings conducted in reliance on Rule 506 account for 99% of the capital reported as being raised under Regulation D from 2009 to 2012, and represent approximately 94% of the number of Regulation D offerings.

The significance of Rule 506 offerings is underscored by the comparison to public market registered offerings. In 2012, the estimated amount of capital reported as being raised in Rule 506 offerings (including both equity and debt) was $898 billion, compared to $1.2 trillion raised in registered offerings.

Of this $898 billion, operating companies (issuers that are not pooled investment funds) reported raising $173 billion, while pooled investment funds reported raising $725 billion.

As the SEC report states,

"An analysis of all Form D filings submitted between 2009 to 2012 shows that approximately 11% of all new Regulation D offerings reported sales commissions of greater than zero because the issuers used a broker intermediary. The average commission paid to these intermediaries was 5.9% of the offering size, with the median commission being approximately 5%. Accordingly, for a $5 million offering, which was the median size of a Regulation D offering with a commission during this period, an issuer could potentially) save up to $250,000 if it solicits investors directly rather than through an intermediary."

According to the data in the SEC report on solicitation, about 234,000 accredited investors made Reg D investments in 2012. As the SEC report states,

"In 2012, approximately 153,000 investors participated in offerings by operating companies, while approximately 81,000 investors invested in offerings by pooled investment funds [VC limited partnerships]."

The 153,000 investors who made direct investments in operating companies, in 2012, are called "lone wolf" investors.

The 81,000 other investors are commonly called "Angels."

The primary target investor population for regional blockchain social/business networking events in each metro region are the lone wolf investors.

The SEC estimates that there are about 5 million American households that would fit the SEC definition of accredited investors.

The new Reg D rules allow for both accredited and non-accredited investors to make capital investment in small technology companies.

In 2012, 95 percent of Reg D offerings involved less than 30 investors per deal and involved very small amounts of capital, invested in very small companies,

The goal of the Comprehensive Regional Capital Market Support Structure For New Venture Creation Economic Growth is to provide a market mechanism to connect both lone wolf and angel investors to local small tech companies to raise small amounts of capital.

Chapter 10. Ending The Predatory Global Corporate War on the American Middle Class and Restoring the American Dream of Upward Social Mobility.

Our intent in writing this book is to, first, describe the massive, global, corrupt system of vertically integrated global value chains, and then to take the further step of describing a solution to ending the predatory global corporate war on the American middle class.

The contents and layout of our book consists of three topic sections.

First, we describe what the vertically integrated global value chains are, and how they function to extract plunder from American middle class citizens.

Second, we spent a great deal of time and effort to describe the extensive damage this global corporate system does to the welfare and lives of ordinary, common American middle class citizens.

Finally, in the last part of our book, we went into great detail on how an entrepreneurial capitalist metro economic model would work to restore the American dream of upward social mobility for middle class citizens.

Our logic and intent in spending so much ink on the third section is that the implementation of our formula for success may be delayed by cataclysmic disruptions to the existing American Republic, as the global ruling class invokes violence to maintain their existing privileges and distribution of global income.

Our hope is, that after the era of violence ends, that our suggestions can serve as a template for creating a new entrepreneurial social order, similar in concept to how John Locke's Two Treatises of Government served as a template for George Mason and Thomas Jefferson, in creating the Articles of Confederation and the Declaration of Independence.

We argue that the American Republic is collapsing for the same reasons that the Greek and Roman Republics collapsed.

The stable social order in a republic requires personal moral integrity of the citizens and the leaders in order to perform the duty to protect the public purpose and defend the commonwealth of the republic.

With the collapse of the American family as the essential social organizing unit of society, the American Republic does not have a majority of citizens who possess the moral integrity to defend the voluntary allegiance to obey the rule of law.

The American society is characterized by dishonesty, corruption, absence of honor and personal moral integrity.

No one in America trusts anyone, either in politics or economic exchange, to tell the truth or to honor their promises.

There is widespread lawlessness and criminality at all levels of government and social institutions, as the global ruling class elites attempt to extract plunder from ordinary middle class citizens, in the system of crony predatory capitalism.

A small group of ruling class corporate elites, in collaboration with the vanguard Democrat Marxist party, have seized permanent authoritarian power, and are preying upon a defenseless American middle class.

The business model of the corporate elite depends on manipulating middle class citizens with propaganda about global warming or income inequality in order to keep the status quo arrangement of income distribution in place.

A good example of the manipulation occurs in the American medical business model, where patients are exploited for maximum gain.

ZeroHedge reported on the recent example of how obesity in children was turned into a profit center for the makers of Ozempic. (America's Fat Children Now in Marketers' Crosshairs, ZeroHedge, citing Influence Watch, February 17, 2024.).

The business model for Ozempic is the same for all of the American medical establishment. The doctors and nurses search for some real or imagined illness that can be treated with a drug.

ZeroHedge writes,

"This psychological condition via framing the obesity epidemic as a "disease" with an accompanying "diagnosis" is not to be overlooked, as it provides valuable insight into how the pharmaceutical industry successfully parlays every physical, psychological, and social ailment into a medical diagnosis through a process called "medicalization" which then opens the door for expensive, patented pharmaceutical interventions where they don't naturally belong… The actual disease, whether real or invented, obesity or "gender dysphoria," is rarely resolved, but, given the financial incentives to keep the pill mills churning out product, one has to wonder whether that was ever the point from the industry's perspective to begin with."

No global company is ever held accountable for the damage they do to citizens, such as knowingly, and deliberately, pumping cancer-causing forever chemicals into the nation's water supplies.

No elected representative is ever held accountable for the secret deals they make to undermine United States sovereignty, with open borders, or taking bribes, or unleashing Covid on an unsuspecting American public.

The current American society is being replaced by a two-class one-world-government of global elites, and global serfs.

In the future, the American middle class will be eliminated, unless the middle class wakes up from its slumber to defend individual liberty.

Part of our solution to ending the predatory global corporate war on the American middle class involves restoring the ability of metro regions to create and diffuse technological knowledge by re-creating the metro regional intermediate demand production networks, that were moved to Mexico and China.

The other part of our strategy involves creating a middle class social consciousness, or class awareness, of their common political and economic interests that opposes the social class consciousness of the global ruling class. (Vass, Laurie Thomas, A Civil Dissolution: The Best Solution to America's Irreconcilable Ideological Conflict, Gabby Press, 2024.).

The implementation of our decentralized metro economic strategy depends upon the creation of a middle class consciousness where local elected representatives have regional allegiance and territorial loyalty to the citizens who live in their regions.

We summarize our main arguments below:

Section 1 Chapter 10. What Is Happening to the American Middle Class.

As a result of changes in the global trade relationships among large corporations, in collaboration with the operation of western central banks, the upper 1% of citizens are reaping rewards and a vastly greater share of total income than the rest of the American population.

The middle to lower classes of American citizens are being either squeezed into dead-end gig labor market jobs or else forced into a life-time dependency on government welfare.

This transition to a new world order is a deliberate act by very self-absorbed, selfish global ruling class elites who make decisions that benefit their own social class.

The strategy to hollow out America's middle class with corporate globalism is deliberate, well-thought out, and well-organized.

The point of attack of the globalist strategy is the destruction of United States national economic sovereignty, the destruction of the American middle class family, and the elimination of the American moral value of individualism.

If the global ruling classes are successful in eliminating the philosophy of American individualism, they will eliminate the pre-conditions for entrepreneurial technology innovation.

The ruling class public relations subterfuge of climate change and systemic racism is designed to hide the reality of an unfair political and economic system.

The unrealized perception by the middle class of an unfair economic system would pose a threat to the stability of the privileges of the ruling class because allegiance of the middle class to continue to obey the rule of law is based upon the false reality that the rules of global corporatism are fair.

The glue that held the American society together, prior to the implementation of global corporatism, was the allegiance of the middle and working classes to voluntarily obey the rule of law because they believed that the American society was based upon the principle that every citizen has a fair opportunity to achieve financial success.

The predatory global capitalist is an unfair economic system and the reality of the unfair economy is supported by financial data over the past 50 years that shows the gradual elimination of the American middle class.

A Pew Research report indicates that the number of families in the middle class income range decreased, while the share of income in the upper classes increased.

The Pew report states,

"The middle class, once the economic stratum of a clear majority of American adults, has steadily contracted in the past five decades. The share of adults who live in middle-class households fell from 61% in 1971 to 50% in 2021, according to a new Pew Research Center analysis of government data." (Kochhar, Rakesh, and Sechopoulos, Stella, How the American middle class has changed in the past five decades, Pew Research Center, April 2022.).

The Pew Research found that incomes in the middle class did not increase as rapidly, since 1971, as income growth in the upper income classes.

The report states,

"The median income of middle-class households in 2020 was 50% greater than in 1970 ($90,131 vs. $59,934), as measured in 2020 dollars. These gains were realized slowly, but for the most part steadily, with the exception of the period from 2000 to 2010, the so-called "lost decade," when incomes fell across the board… The rise in income from 1970 to 2020 was steepest for upper-income households. Their median income increased 69% during that timespan, from $130,008 to $219,572."

Diagram 1, below, supports our earlier statement about the unfair income distribution, for the top 1%, caused by the predatory globalist economy.

It is this distribution of income, for the top 1% of the American society. that the ruling class seeks to maintain in the global corporatist economic model.

The average annual income of middle class American citizens is between $57,000 and $107,000.

In comparison, the annual income of top 1% of the American society is about $3 million.

This income obtained by the ruling class is not based upon merit in a competitive free market economy. The income is derived by unfair rules in an unfair global predatory economy.

Chapter 10 Diagam 1. 2020 Average Market Income by Income Percentile.

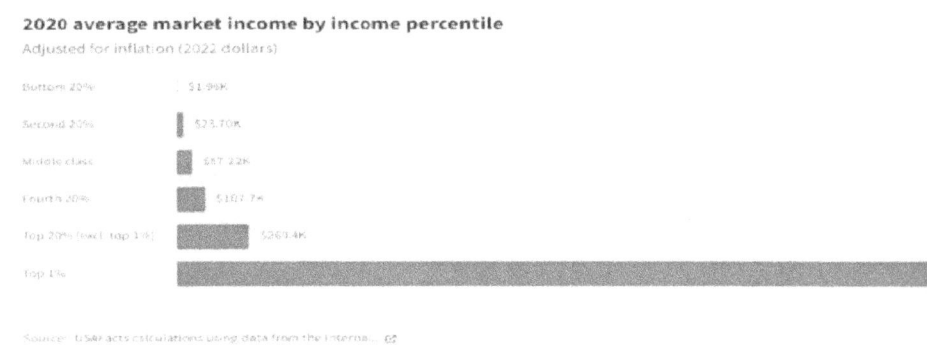

Citation: USAFacts. 2023.

Harvard economist George Borjas estimated that open borders and global trade reduced the wages of American citizens by an estimated $118 billion a year.

At the same time that American workers were losing $118 billion a year, the open borders global economy generated a net increase in profit for global corporations of $128 billion a year. (Immigration and Economic Growth, NBER Working Paper, 2019.).

Almost 80% of all job losses in manufacturing, caused by China trade, were concentrated in just 50 of the nation's 370 metro regions.

The technology innovation in those 50 metro regions were critical to future economic growth because technology innovation in manufacturing plants, in a regional intermediate demand chain, are the cause of future economic growth.

Section 2 Chapter 10. How The Ruling Class Is Destroying the American Middle Class

There are three factors over the past 50 years that created the conditions for starting the predatory global corporate war on the American middle class.

The most often cited factors are the monetary and interest rate manipulations of the Fed, leading up to the economic collapse in 2008, and the Congressional acts, in 1992 and 2001, to allow the transition to a global economy.

Those two factors have eroded the concept of American economic sovereignty, from a prior principle that improving the welfare of American citizens is the first priority of government to a current principle that the financial improvement of the ruling class is the most important mission of the government.

Beginning with the transition to a globalist economy, in 1992, the American ruling class elites traded away the initial American factor endowment of individualism, in favor of a global collectivism, where all citizens of the world were viewed as economically equal.

The ideological logic of the World Economic Forum global ruling class is that American citizens consume too much energy and too much of the world's resources, and that the use of resources must be equalized across the globe to be more fair and more environmentally friendly.

We cite a third factor, that began in the mid-1960s, with the destruction of the American middle class family, as the basic building block of American society.

The policies of the Great Society that destroyed the American middle class families were a deliberate, sinister initiative by President Johnson to wed the Black voting population to the Democrat Party.

As Johnson is quoted at the time, the Great Society programs would have Black citizens voting Democrat for the next 200 years.

By the time 1992 rolled around, the three factors combined to usher in the global predatory capitalist war on the middle class.

Newt Gingrich points out that the destruction of the American family was not inevitable, under the prior allegiance of middle class citizens to obey the rule of law.

But, after the implementation of globalism, that prior principle of shared prosperity for all citizens was replaced by the principle of shared plunder by the ruling class.

As Gingrich writes, the Great Society programs crippled the poor by making them dependent on government welfare. (Gingrich, Newt, The Destruction of the Family Was Not Inevitable, The American Spectator, 2023.).

Gingrich cites research by Daniel Moynihan that showed that children who grow up in disorganized, chaotic, or fatherless homes often do not adapt to structured systems, such as early education. They simply don't have the early experience of structure and behavioral expectations to apply to their new environments.

In other words, those children of broken, fatherless, families do not have the moral integrity to obey the unwritten rule of law in a republic.

Gingrich correctly cites political research which showed, that coincident with the implementation of the Great Society programs, the American ruling class shifted its political ideology from individualism to collectivism.

Gingrich writes,

"For centuries prior to 1964, it was widely agreed that people were responsible for their own lives — and for their own success...But increasingly, those in the policy elite determined that if people were working and still not making ends meet, the entire system was flawed... *People realized they could get roughly the same amount of money not working as they would if they were working a minimum wage job.* Naturally, this perverse incentive led to more people choosing government assistance over working harder and trying to get better jobs."

Gingrich cites the research of Charles Murray, in his landmark study Losing Ground, (1986), of the remarkable rapid shift in ruling class ideology, from individualism to collectivism.

Gingrich, quoting Murray:

"Theodore White (among many others) describes the shift from "equality of opportunity" to "equality of outcome" as a fundamental change…Yet only a year later, (1965) speaking at Howard University commencement exercises, Lyndon Johnson was proclaiming the "next and most profound stage of the battle for civil rights," namely, the battle "not just [for] equality as a right and theory but equality as a fact and equality as a result." A few months later, Executive Order 11246 required "affirmative action." By 1967, people who opposed preferential measures for minorities to overcome the legacy of discrimination were commonly seen as foot-draggers on civil rights if not closet racists."

The premise of equality of outcome was embraced by the World Economic Forum as the primary argument for equality of income for all people, in all nations, of the world.

We argue that the recent crony corporate capitalist endorsements of the use of the term "systemic racism" enables the predatory capitalist class to maintain its privileges by continually pointing out to BLM that their conditions of oppression are caused by White racism, not global crony capitalism.

The unifying principle for the crony corporatist class who offer support to BLM is to maintain their hegemony of globalism by virtue signaling to BLM that BLM can achieve a socially just society, within the framework of crony capitalist globalism.

Predatory Corporate Globalism destroys the families of middle class Blacks and Whites, together, but American predatory capitalism cannot work unless the crony corporations convince Blacks and Whites to hate each other, more than they hate the crony capitalist ruling class.

Chinese communism is the desired end-state goal of the BLM Marxists, and the funding support given by the crony capitalists to BLM is to show BLM that they can achieve Chinese nirvana, if they simply adopt the crony capitalist global economic model.

The global elites use the propaganda of population control and climate change to implement policies that destroy the world supply of food by eliminating the sale and distribution of fertilizer and deliberately contracting food supply chains.

We argue that the New World Order system functions to deliberately lower the rate of economic growth that could be achieved under a fair competitive price system, and limits distribution of the welfare benefits of economic growth to a self-selected social class of elites.

Under global crony corporate monopoly capitalism, the direction and creation of technology is controlled by a small set of corporations, and investment in technology innovation is a politically controlled and manipulated event that displaces the free competitive market environment for private capital investments.

Section 3 Chapter 10. Why the American Middle Class Is Being Destroyed.

In his recent article, "Why the Middle Class Is Being Destroyed?" Edward Ring cites the coherent and unified social class ideology of the global predatory capitalist class. (American Greatness, 2022.).

Ring's term for a unified ideology is "cognitive elite." Cognitive, in his usage, means mentally aware of their social class privileges.

Ring writes,

The emergence of a cognitive elite, and, for the first time in history, the almost total convergence of intellectuals with the financial elite explains the coming extinction of the middle class...Not surprisingly, the interests of [intellectual elite] affluence and the cognitive [corporate] elite have begun to blend."

We extend and modify Ring's analysis to incorporate another reason why the American middle class is being destroyed by the predatory capitalist class.

The American middle class is the most intelligent, most well-educated, most individualistic, and most well-armed social class, in the world.

The ruling class has succeeded in making 50% of the U. S. population subservient to the unchallenged tyranny of the elite.

They cannot implement their desired totalitarian regime until, and unless, they can subjugate the American middle class, and take away their right to own weapons.

Ring predicts the same two-class global society that we also see.

Ring writes,

"The elites in America, joining with their counterparts in most of the rest of the developed world, are engineering a future where there will only be two classes: the elites and a permanent underclass. [serfs] To avoid turning the vast majority of humanity into livestock, which is where we're headed, requires presenting alternative scenarios."

As we noted above, our intent in writing this book is to propose an alternative scenario to the globalist predatory capitalist economic model.

From the perspective of the global elite, the main problem is that the world has too many people.

The best solution, for the predatory elite, is to reduce the world population to a number that can be more easily managed in the vertically integrated global value chains.

As Ring notes,

"There won't be many [job] openings. In most professions and trades, to the extent human involvement is still necessary, competence will be secondary to affirmative action because automated procedures and artificial intelligence prompts will tell workers what to do…By blending and flattening the population of the world's cognitively normal, the cognitive elite will be able to pacify and manage them, distance themselves, and have exclusive access to whatever property and privileges they consider not sustainable or desirable for everyone to enjoy… The consequence, an apparent consensus [social class consciousness] among the two groups [Democrat Marxists and predatory capitalists] to destroy the middle class to protect their own interests while claiming they're saving the planet and promoting "equity," should surprise nobody."

The American crony corporate global capitalist system can best be understood as a rent-seeking economy where elites use the power of government to obtain unearned profits from non-elites.

In BLM Marxism and the Emerging Alliance With Global Corporate Crony Capitalism, we write,

The three main components of both the American global crony national economic structure and the Chinese communist economic structure are:

1. The global firms in the military-industrial complex.
2. The global manufacturing industrial firms with a financial interest in obtaining foreign trade benefits, especially with China.
3. The global banking and investment firms who coordinate global financial transactions in conjunction with global central banks."

The common characteristics of global cronyism, in both the American and Chinese economies, and in all three of the national economic structures, is a preference for collectivist globalism, as opposed to promotion of a sovereign national economic interest.

American middle class families must be destroyed in order for the predatory capitalist class to eradicate the moral foundations of American liberty and individualism.

Section 4 Chapter 10. How To End the Predatory Capitalist War on the American Middle Class.

The only viable economic alternative to the WEF global corporatist fascism is a decentralized economic system called "entrepreneurial capitalism." (Vass, Laurie Thomas, America's Final Revolution: Reconstructing Jefferson's American Dream of An Entrepreneurial Capitalist Society, The Great American Business & Economics Press. 2022.).

Corporate control over the creation and diffusion of technological knowledge in the global macrotechnology is the weak link, and vulnerable point of attack, for updating Schumpeter's gales of creative destruction of the new world order. (Vass, Laurie Thomas, Updating Schumpeter's Gales of Creative Destruction: Exploiting the Vulnerability of New World Order Corporate Globalism With Regional Blockchain Entrepreneurial Economic Growth, Gabby Press, 2022.).

Global corporations require controlled technological innovation, and global crony capitalism, in order to direct the benefits of innovation to themselves, and their crony stakeholders.

If global corporations cannot control the pace of technological innovation, they would lose control over managing and setting prices in the collaborative global economic model.

Following Codevilla, (The Ruling Class, 2010), and William Domhoff, (Who Rules America? Power and Politics in the Year 2006), we argue that the characteristics and attributes of the ruling class constitute a distinct social class awareness of their power and privilege.

The ruling class' foundational proposition is that elites know better than common citizens what is best for society. Not only that the elites know best, but that they are the only force in society that should ever make collective decisions.

That type of moral arrogance could not function unless the elite possessed a well-defined and well-financed class consciousness to manage the distribution of plunder of the political system, from the top.

The common social and cultural value of greed binds the American ruling class together, in a defined social class consciousness.

Ending the predatory capitalist war on the American middle class would require that the American middle class adopt their own social class awareness, based upon the original moral values of the American Revolution.

Codevilla suggests that the American middle class has a budding social class awareness that can vaguely be seen in the "resistance" of their vote against ruling class elites, in favor of Trump, in 2016.

Professor C. Bradley Thompson reminds us, that in a civil war, the two sides share no common or cultural values, but that after the civil war ends, the former national state is re-constitued, with the victors dominating the losers.

In contrast, after a successful revolution, the two sides separate into two distinct nations.

In a historical parallel, the two social classes in America, prior to the Revolution, fought with England to win their independence. (Thompson, C. Bradley, America's Revolutionary Mind: A Moral History of the American Revolution and the Declaration That Defined It, 2022.).

Thompson cites Crevecoeur, and DeTocqueville, 50 years later, that there was a single universal character trait in the new American citizen. The Americans deeply believed in the sovereignty of the individual over the sovereignty of the state.

As Thompson notes,

"The greatest achievement of the American Revolution was to subordinate society and government to this fundamental moral law…The moral philosophy of the American Revolution was closely associated with the idea of self-government—that is, with the idea that individuals must govern their own lives in the fullest sense of the term."

Thompson notes that the new American character of liberty, after the end of the Revolution, demanded three duties from citizens:

- That they not violate each other's rights;
- That they live self-starting, self-reliant, self-governing lives by practicing certain uniquely American virtues and character traits.
- That they deal with each other by means of persuasion and voluntary trade.

Thompson describes this type of social moral value as "ethical individualism."

Unless, and until, the American middle class implements a social class consciousness based upon the ethical individualism of the American Revolution, the predatory capitalist class will win their civil war against the American middle class, and turn them into global serfs.

And, should the American middle class win their revolution for independence from the global tyrants, the new nation will be based upon the principles of George Mason's radical citizen egalitarianism, in a decentralized democratic republic, that replaces the vertically integrated global value chains of the global corporatist regime.

And, restores the American Dream of upward social mobility for all citizens.

Bibliography

Abraham, Katharine G., et al, "Measuring the Gig Economy: Current Knowledge and Open Issues, NBER Working Paper No. w24950, SSRN, 2018.

Akcigit, Ufuk, Ates Sina,, Ten Facts On Declining Business Dynamism And Lessons From Endogenous Growth Theory, Working Paper 25755, NBER, 2019.

Akcigit, Ufuk, Sina, Ates, What Happened to U.S. Business Dynamism? NBER Working Paper No. w25756, SSRN, 2023.

Antràs, Pol and Chor, Davin, Global Value Chains, NBER Working Paper 28549, 2021.

Antràs, Pol and Staiger, Robert W., Offshoring and the Role of Trade Agreements, American Economic Review, 2012.

Autor, David H., Dorn, David, Hanson, Gordon H., The China Syndrome: Local Labor Market Effects of Import Competition in the United States, NBER Working Paper 18054, 2012.

Asian Development Bank, Global Value Chain Development Report 2021: Beyond Production, Asian Development Bank Publication, November 2021.

Backer, Koen de and Miroudot, S., Mapping Global Value Chains ECB Working Paper No. 1677. SSRN, 2014.

Bergman, Edward M., Feser, Edward J., Industrial and Regional Clusters: Concepts and Comparative Applications, 2nd ed., West Virginia University Regional Research Institute, 2020.

Billings, Dwight B., Planters and the Making of a "New South": Class, Politics, and Development in North Carolina, 1865-1900, 1979.

Boehm, Christoph E., et al., Multinationals, Offshoring and the Decline of U. S. Manufacturing, NBER Working Paper 25824, 2019.

Boettke, Peter J. and Coyne, Christopher J., Methodological Individualism, Spontaneous Order and the Research Program of the Workshop in Political Theory and Policy Analysis, George Mason University, Department of Economics, 2004.

Borjas, George, Immigration and Economic Growth, NBER Working Paper, 2019.

Brennan, Geoffrey and Buchanan James M., The Reason of Rules: Constitutional Political Economy, 1985.

Bruhn, Dominique, Global Value Chains and Deep Preferential Trade Agreements: Promoting Trade at the Cost of Domestic Policy Autonomy? SSRN, 2014.

Buchanan, James M., "Rent Seeking and Profit Seeking," In, James M. Buchanan, Robert Tollison, and Gordon Tullock (eds). Toward a Theory of the Rent-Seeking Society, 1980.

Buchanan, James M., and Tullock, Gordon, The Calculus of Consent: Logical Foundations of Constitutional Democracy, Liberty Foundation, 1962.

Buskirk, Chris, Only Bold Proposals Can Displace Globalism, American Greatness, August 13, 2019.

Carllson, Bo, Technological Systems and Economic Development Potential: Four Swedish Case Studies, in Innovations In Technology, Industries and Institutions, 1994.

Carllson, Bo, Technological Systems and Economic Performance: The Case of Factory Automation, Springer-Verlag, 1995.

Cash, W. J., The Mind of the South, 1941.

Christensen, Clayton M., The Innovator's Dilemma: When New Technologies Cause Great Firms to Fail, Harvard Business Review Press, 1997.

Christensen Clayton et al., How Market-Creating Innovation Drives Economic Growth and Development, Innovations /Blockchain for Global Development, 2019.

Christensen, Clayton, et.al., The Third Answer: How Market-Creating Innovation Drives Economic Growth and Development. SSRN, 2018.

Christensen, Clayton M. and Raynor, Michael E., The Innovator's Solution: Creating and Sustaining Successful Growth, 2003.

Codevilla, Angelo M., The Ruling Class: How They Corrupted America and What We Can Do About It, 2010.

Coyne, Christopher J., and Hall, Abigail R., Cronyism: Necessary for the Minimal, Protective State, GMU Working Paper in Economics No. 18-26. SSRN, 2018.

Dahlin, Kristina and Behrens, Dean, When Is An Invention Really Radical? Defining and Operationalizing Technological Radicalness, Research Policy, 2005.

Dallas Federal Reserve Bank, Globalization, No Date.

Decker, Ryan A., et al., Declining Business Dynamism: What We Know and the Way Forward, American Economic Review, May 2016

Díez, Federico J., Leigh, Daniel and Tambunlertchai, Suchanan, Global Market Power and its Macroeconomic Implications, IMF Working Paper, WP/18/137, 2018.

Dollar, David, Global Value Chain Development Report 2021: Beyond Production, Asian Development Bank Publication, November 2021.

Domhoff, William, Who Rules America? Power, Politics, & Social Change, 2006.

Drucker, Joshua M., and Feser, Edward, Regional Industrial Dominance, Agglomeration Economies, and Manufacturing Plant Productivity. US Census Bureau Center for Economic Studies Paper No. CES-07-31. SSRN. 2008.

Eggertsson, Gauti B. et al., Kaldor And Piketty's Facts: The Rise Of Monopoly Power In The United States, NBER Working Paper 24287, 2018.

Escobar, Pepe, How Yemen changed everything: In a single move, Yemen's Ansarallah has checkmated the west and its rules-based order, The Cradle.com, December 28, 2023.

Esser, John P., Institutionalizing Industry: The Changing Forms of Contract, Law & Social Inquiry Vol. 21, No. 3, 1996.

Evangelista, Rinaldo, Knowledge and Investment: The Sources of Innovation In Industry, 1999.

Feser, Edward J., Agglomeration, Enterprise Size, And Productivity, CES Working Paper, U.S. Bureau of the Census, 2004.

Feser, Edward J., A Flexible Test For Agglomeration Economies In Two U.S. Manufacturing Industries, CES Working Paper 04-14, , U. S. Bureau of Census, 2004.

Feser, Edward, and Koo, Jun, Kentucky Clusters: Industrial Interdependence and Economic Competitiveness, Innovation Management and Policy, 2001.

Feser, Edward, National Industry Cluster Templates: A Framework For Applied Regional Analysis, 2000, and A Test For the Coincident Economic and Spatial Clustering of Business Enterprises, 2002.

Feser, Edward J., and Renski, Henry, High-Tech Clusters in North Carolina, North Carolina Board of Science and Technology, 2000.

Fort, Teresa C., The Changing Firm And Country Boundaries Of U. S. Manufacturers In Global Value Chains, NBER Working Paper 31319, 2023.

Gilson, Ronald J. et al., Contracting for Innovation: Vertical Disintegration and Interfirm Collaboration, Columbia Law and Economics Working Paper No. 340, 2009.

Gingrich, Newt, The Destruction of the Family Was Not Inevitable, The American Spectator, 2023.

Grenier, Corinne et al., The Process of Creation and Capitalization of Knowledge Within Distributed Organizations: The Case of Clusters, SSRN, 2008.

Gutterman, Alan S., Product Development for Small Businesses and Startups, SSRN, 2023.

Haber, Stephen, Introduction: The Political Economy of Crony Capitalism, 2015.

Hall, Peter, Innovation, Economics and Evolution: Theoretical Perspectives on Changing Technology, Economic Systems, 1994.

Haltiwanger, John, Job Creation, Job Destruction, and Productivity Growth: The Role of Young Businesses, The Annual Review of Economics, 2015.

Haltiwanger, John, Jarmin, Ron S., Miranda, Javier, Business Dynamics Statistics Briefing: Jobs Created from Business Startups in the United States, Business Dynamics Statistics Briefing, SSRN, 2009.

Hathaway, Ian, et al., Tech Starts: High-Technology Business Formation and Job Creation in the United States, Kauffman Foundation Research Series, 2013.

Holland, John, Hidden Order: How Adaptation Builds Complexity, 1995.

Horrell, Michael and Litan, Robert, After Inception: How Enduring is Job Creation by Startups? Ewing Marion Kauffman Foundation, July 2010.

Hughes, Austin, Adaptive Evolution of Genes and Genomes, 1999.

Inomata, Satoshi, Analytical Frameworks for Global Value Chains: An Overview Global Value Chain Development Report, SSRN. 2017.

Kimura, Motoo, The Neutral Theory of Molecular Evolution, 1983.

Kindleberger, Charles, World Economic Primacy, 1996.

Kochhar, Rakesh, and Sechopoulos, Stella, How the American middle class has changed in the past five decades, Pew Research Center, April 2022.

Konczal, Jared, The Most Entrepreneurial Metropolitan Area? Ewing Marion Kauffman Foundation, SSRN. 2013.

Krause, David, A Primer on Exempt Offerings: Capital Access for Small and Emerging Businesses, SSRN. 2023.

Krugman, Paul, Increasing Returns and Economic Geography, 1991.

Krumm, Brian Kingsley, Fostering Innovation and Entrepreneurship: Shark Tank Shouldn't be the Model Shark Tank Shouldn't be the Model, Arkansas Law Review, SSRN, 2017.

Leontief, Wassily, Input-Output Data Base For Analysis of Technological Change. Economic Systems Research, 1989.

Lerner, Josh, Negotiation, Organizations and Markets, Research Papers, Harvard NOM Research Paper No. 03- 13, 2004.

Levenhagen, M.J., Thomas, H. & Porac, J., The formation of emergent markets: Strategic investigations in the software industry, 1993.

Liu, Amy, The Future of Regional Economic Development and Implications for U.S. Economic Development Administration Programs Testimony submitted to the United States Senate Committee on Environment and Public Works, November 1, 2021.

Locke, John, Two Treatises of Government, 1689.

Loecker, Jan De, and Eeckhout, Jan, Global Market Power, NBER Working Paper 24768, 2018.

Lynn, Leonard and Salzman, Hal, Collaborative Advantage, Issues In Science and Technology, Winter, 2006.

Malloch, Theodore, Exposing the Roots of Globalism, American Greatness February 26, 2020.

Marcus, David, Don't Worry, It's Just Corporate Fascism, The Federalist, January 2021.

McAdams, Robert, Paths of Fire: An Anthropologist's Inquiry into Western Technology, 1996.

Mitchell, Melanie, An Introduction to Genetic Algorithms, 1998.

Muller, H. J., The Relation of Recombination to Mutational Advance, Mutation Research. 1964.

Munger, Michael C., and Villarreal-Diaz, Mario, The Road to Crony Capitalism, The Independent Review, Winter 2019.

OECD, Interconnected economies: benefiting from global value chains, OECD synthesis report, 2013.

OECD, Multinational enterprises in domestic value chains. OECD science, technology and industry policy papers No. 63. March 2019.

Padfield, Stefan J., Crony Stakeholder Capitalism, SSRN, April 23, 2023.

Pew Research Center, Most Americans Say the Current Economy Is Helping the Rich, Hurting the Poor and Middle Class. December 2019.

Prigogine, Ilya, Exploring Complexity: An Introduction, 1989.

Rachman, Gideon, Is there such a thing as a rules-based international order? Financial Times, April 20, 2023.

Reid, Gavin, and Ujjual, Vandanna, Firms in Scottish High Technology Clusters, Semantic Scholar, 2008.

Ridder, Maarten De, Market Power and Innovation in the Intangible Economy, Working Paper, University of Cambridge, 2019.

Ring, Edward, Why the Middle Class Is Being Destroyed, American Greatness, 2022.

Rostow, W. W., The Stages of Economic Growth: A Non-Communist Manifesto, 1960.

Rousseau, Stephan, Internet-Based Securities Offerings By Small and Medium-Sized Enterprises: Attractions and Challenges, Canadian Business Law Journal, 2001.

Saviotti, Pier, Technological Evolution, Variety and The Economy, 1996.

Schumpeter, Joseph, Capitalism, Socialism, and Democracy, 1942.

Schumpeter, Joseph, The Theory of Economic Development, 1961.

Schwienbacher, Armin, Innovation and Venture Capital Exits, Economic Journal, 2007.
Sobel-Read, Kevin, Global Value Chains: A Framework for Analysis, SSRN. 2014.

Solow, Robert M., A Contribution to the Theory of Economic Growth, The Quarterly Journal of Economics, 1956.

Solow, Robert M., Technical Change and the Aggregate Production Function, The Review of Economics and Statistics, 1957.

Stankiewicz, Rikard, Technological Systems and Economic Performance: The Case of Factory Automation, 1995),

Talbott, Strobe, The Birth of the Global Nation, Time Magazine, 1992.

Temin, Peter, "Entrepreneurs and Managers," in Higonnet, P., Landes, D. Rosovsky, H., (Eds.), Favorites of Fortune, 1991.

Thompson, C. Bradley, America's Revolutionary Mind: A Moral History of the American Revolution and the Declaration That Defined It, 2022.

Un, C. Annique, et al., R&D Collaborations and Product Innovation, Journal of Product Innovation Management, May 2008.

Vass, Laurie Thomas, A Critical Analysis of the Recent Georgia Initiatives to Promote Intrastate Crowdfunding, SSRN, 2013.

Vass, Laurie Thomas, Adding a Geographical Component to an Equity Crowdfunding Project, SSRN, 2013.

Vass, Laurie Thomas, America's Final Revolution: Reconstructing Jefferson's American Dream of An Entrepreneurial Capitalist Society, Gabby Press, 2022.

Vass, Laurie Thomas, BLM Marxism and the Emerging Alliance With Global Corporate Crony Capitalism, SSRN, 2022.

Vass, Laurie Thomas, Buchanan's Fair Constitutional Rules as the Foundation of the Entrepreneurial Economy, SSRN, 2009.

Vass, Laurie Thomas, A Civil Dissolution: The Best Solution to America's Irreconcilable Ideological Conflict, Gabby Press, 2023.

Vass, Laurie Thomas, Creating the Private Capital Market Infrastructure for Sustainable Innovation Economics, SSRN, 2013.

Vass, Laurie Thomas, Do Cities Still Matter? The Economic Strength of Cities and the Economic Failure of Globalism in Promoting Regional Technological Innovation and Economic Prosperity, SSRN, 2013.

Vass, Laurie Thomas, Doing More Deals: Re-Envisioning the Use of Industrial Clusters to Target Regional Innovation Investments, SSRN, 2008.

Vass, Laurie Thomas, Establishing The Capital Market Transition From Private Capital To Public Capital, SSRN, 2008.

Vass, Laurie Thomas, Exploiting Knowledge: The Importance of Regional Allegiance and Territorial Loyalty in Implementing a Regional Small Business Innovation System, SSRN, 2009.

Vass, Laurie Thomas, Exploring the Idea of the Atlanta Capital Growth Fund: Equity Crowdfunding as One Component of the New Atlanta Private Securities Exchange, SSRN, 2015.

Vass, Laurie Thomas, Favorable Terms and Conditions for a Small Business Private Offering: Taking Full Advantage of the Direct Corporate Private Offering, SSRN, 2012.

Vass, Laurie Thomas, George Mason's America: The State Sovereignty Alternative to Madison's Centralized Ruling Class Aristocracy, Gabby Press, 2023.

Vass, Laurie Thomas, How Economic Developers Can Manage the Regional Deal Flow Pipeline, SSRN, 2013.

Vass, Laurie Thomas, How a New Market Emerges from a New Radical Product, SSRN, 2008.

Vass, Laurie Thomas, Income Distribution and Technological Evolution. SSRN, 2019.

Vass, Laurie Thomas, Industrial Recruitment and the Path of North Carolina's Economic Development to the Year 2000: A Public Discussion Paper for North Carolina's Project 2000 - Advocating the Creation of the NC Council for Entrepreneurial Development (CED), North Carolina Department of Labor, Raleigh, NC, 1982. SSRN.

Vass, Laurie Thomas, Justice and the Rule of Law, SSRN, 2019.

Vass, Laurie Thomas, North Carolina's New Nexus of Innovation: Where Local Capital in N. C. Cities Funds Local Investment Opportunities in Technology Commercialization, SSRN, 2012.

Vass, Laurie Thomas, Placing the Concept of the RTP Startup Ecosystem into a Regional Innovation Policy Framework, SSRN. 2015.

Vass, Laurie Thomas, Searching for Signs of Technological Innovation in the Ruins of the American Economy, SSRN, 2008.

Vass, Laurie Thomas, Searching for Investments in the Nine High Technology Clusters, SSRN, 2008.

Vass, Laurie Thomas, The American Left's Emerging Social Class Consciousness of Envy In Collusion With the Existing American Ruling Class Consciousness of Greed, SSRN. 2020.

Vass, Laurie Thomas, The American Rule of Law and the Collapse of the American Economy, SSRN, 2008.

Vass, Laurie Thomas, The Case for Increasing the Supply of Private Placement Securities Lawyers in North Carolina: The Law of Supply and Demand for Securities Lawyers, SSRN, 2015.

Vass, Laurie Thomas, The Contribution of Schumpeter to the Theory of Technology Evolution, SSRN, 2019.

Vass, Laurie Thomas, The Crowd Funding Business Bonanza for Lawyers, Accountants and Consultants: Professional Business Advisors about to Surf a Financial Tsunami of New Crowd Funding Business, SSRN, 2013.

Vass, Laurie Thomas, The Importance of Regional Allegiance and Territorial Loyalty For Elected Representatives In Implementing Economic Development and Job Creation Policies: Economic Policy Advice For Local and State Elected Representatives Who Oppose the New World Order Crony Corporate Fascism. SSRN, 2023.

Vass, Laurie Thomas, The New Financial Factory for Innovation Economic Development, The Journal of Financial Transformation, August 2009.

Vass, Laurie Thomas, The Nexus of Financial and Political Interests between Crowd Funders and Regional Economic Development Professionals: The New-New Innovation Economics, SSRN, 2013.

Vass, Laurie Thomas, The Origins of Southern Equity Crowdfunding: The Rise of the Textile, Tobacco, and Furniture Industries in North Carolina after the Civil War, SSRN, 2013.

Vass, Laurie Thomas, The Theory of Technology Evolution, Gabby Press, 2019.

Vass, Laurie Thomas, The Three Year Time Lag Between Innovation Collaboration and New Product Introduction, SSRN, 2008.

Vass, Laurie Thomas, Updating Schumpeter's Entrepreneurial Economic Growth Model as the Economic Alternative to the Corporate New World Order. SSRN, 2022.

Vass, Laurie Thomas, Updating Schumpeter's Gales of Creative Destruction: Exploiting the Vulnerability of New World Order Corporate Globalism With Regional Blockchain Entrepreneurial Economic Growth, Gabby Press, 2022.

Vass, Laurie Thomas, Using Feser's Input-Output Model of Technological Affinities to Target Innovation Investments to Regional Industrial Value Chains, SSRN, 2008.

Vass, Laurie Thomas, Where Were They and What Were They Doing Before They Became Entrepreneurs? SSRN, 2008.

Vass. Laurie Thomas, Why Exits Matter For Future Innovation Investments, SSRN, 2008.

Vass, Laurie Thomas, Will More Venture Capital Spur Regional Innovation? SSRN, 2008.

Van Graaff, Jan de, Theoretical Welfare Economics, 1957.

Von Feigenblatt, Otto, Corporatism and Benevolent Authoritarianism: Viable Antidotes to Populism, SSRN, 2021.

Wolff, Richard D., How racism became the essential tool for maintaining a capitalist order, Salon, June 26, 2020.

World Economic Forum, A Brief History of Globalization, WEF, Jan 17, 2019.

ZeroHedge, America's Fat Children Now in Marketers' Crosshairs, ZeroHedge, citing Influence Watch, February 17, 2024.

Zhang, Hao, Commerce, Coalitions, and Global Value Chains: Coordinated and Collective Lobbying on Trade, SSRN, 2023.

Zywicki, Todd, Rent Seeking Crony Capitalism, and the Crony Constitution, SSRN, 2015.

Zywicki, Todd J., The Rule of Law, Freedom, and Prosperity. SSRN, 2002.